Democracy Challenged

Democracy Challenged

The Rise of Semi-Authoritarianism

Marina Ottaway

Carnegie Endowment for International Peace
WASHINGTON, D.C.

Carnegie Endowment for International Peace   Tel 202-483-7600
1779 Massachusetts Avenue   Fax 202-483-1840
Washington, D.C. 20036 USA   www.ceip.org

The Carnegie Endowment for International Peace normally does not take institutional positions on public policy issues; the views and recommendations presented in this publication do not necessarily represent the views of the Carnegie Endowment, its officers, staff, or trustees.

To order, contact Carnegie's distributor:
The Brookings Institution Press   Tel 800-275-1447 or 202-797-6258
Department 029   Fax 202-797-2960
Washington, D.C. 20042-0029 USA   Email bibooks@brook.edu

Printed in the United States of America on acid-free, 20% recycled content paper with vegetable-oil based inks by Jarboe Printing.

Interior design by Jenna Dixon.
Text set in Wessex, designed by Matthew Butterick, Font Bureau.

Library of Congress Cataloging-in-Publication Data

Ottaway, Marina.
Democracy challenged : the rise of semi-authoritarianism / Marina Ottaway.
       p.   cm.
   Includes bibliographical references (p.   ) and index.
   ISBN 0-87003-196-1 (cloth) — ISBN 0-87003-195-3 (paper)
   1. Authoritarianism. 2. Democracy. 3. Democratization—International cooperation. I. Title.
JC480.O88 2002
320.53 – dc21   2002013712

14   13   12   11   10   09   08   5   4   3   2   1st Printing 2003

Contents

Foreword

DEMOCRACY PROMOTION, a new activity on which aid agencies and NGOs embarked with some trepidation and misgivings in the early 1990s, has come of age. It is a well-established and accepted part of the assistance that the United States and other industrial democracies provide to countries around the world. No longer a pioneering endeavor, it has settled down into a set of standardized approaches and programs. Unfortunately, the learning process by the government agencies and NGOs that promote democracy has been accompanied by a parallel learning process on the part of regimes that feel threatened by democracy. Many of these regimes have learned to defuse the impact of the programs devised by foreign experts to introduce democratic reform. They go through the motions of holding elections and building institutions, they allow some political space for civil society organizations and the independent media, but they have learned to stubbornly resist real change that might threaten their power. Increasingly, democracy promotion efforts lead to the rise not of fledgling democracies but of semi-authoritarian regimes adept at respecting the forms of democracy while adamantly rejecting its content.

The rise of semi-authoritarianism is becoming the major challenge to democracy around the world. The democracy promotion tools used by the United States and other countries are effective in forcing some opening in closed, authoritarian regimes, but there the process gets stuck. These countries do not move to real democracy, and the number of those that only pretend to be democratic is multiplying rapidly. New approaches are clearly needed.

Democracy Challenged: The Rise of Semi-Authoritarianism suggests such new approaches to democracy promotion in countries mired in semi-authoritarianism. Case studies of Egypt, Azerbaijan, Venezuela, Senegal, and Croatia, as well as insights gleaned from Ottaway's previous studies of numerous other countries, provide the raw material used to build a comprehensive view of the political games used by semi-authoritarian leaders to stay in power, of the structural conditions that allow them to be successful, and of more effective policies to thwart semi-authoritarianism.

This book is the latest in a series of studies produced by the Democracy and Rule of Law Project at the Carnegie Endowment for International Peace. It builds on Thomas Carothers' field-defining text *Aiding Democracy Abroad: The Learning Curve*, Carothers' and Ottaway's edited volume *Funding Virtue: Civil Society Aid and Democracy Promotion*, and on the numerous articles the project has generated to address the major challenges in the field of democracy promotion. With *Democracy Challenged: The Rise of Semi-Authoritarianism*, the Democracy and Rule of Law Project once again proves its ability to define the learning curve in this important field.

JESSICA T. MATHEWS
President, Carnegie Endowment
for International Peace

Acknowledgments

THE DAUNTING TASK of researching and writing a book is only made possible by the assistance and support of many people. I am indebted to all those who helped me in different guises along the way.

Some of these people must remain anonymous, above all the large number of individuals in political parties, government offices, international organizations, nongovernmental organizations, the media, universities and research institutes who generously gave me their time and shared their insights in each of the countries I visited while researching this book.

Others can be mentioned. Four Carnegie Endowment junior fellows—Will Barndt, Gideon Maltz, Jeff Krutz, and Bethany Lacina—helped me in the entire process, from the initial documentary research to the editing of the manuscript, sharing in the excitement of the research and the tedium of fact checking. Jennifer Little, Kathleen Higgs, Chris Henley, and the entire staff of the Carnegie Endowment library cheerfully supplied with great speed even the more obscure articles I requested. Trish Reynolds and Sherry Pettie of the Endowment's publication department handled the production of the book competently and kept me firmly on schedule.

The idea for the book was generated in the course of the discussions of a study group on semi-authoritarian regimes that met at the Carnegie Endowment for a series of spirited discussions during 1998–1999. I am indebted to the participants in that group for stimulating my thinking on the topic, although many of them probably do not share my conclusions. As the project unfolded, I benefited from frequent discussions with Tom Carothers, then vice-president for studies at the Carnegie Endowment. Together with Catharine Dalpino, Tom also read and provided extensive comments on the entire manuscript.

Financial support for the research, as well as for many other activities of the Democracy and Rule of Law Project, was made possible by a generous grant from the William and Flora Hewlett Foundation.

Finally, the Carnegie Endowment, under the leadership of Jessica Mathews and Paul Balaran, provided a perfect environment for writing a book—with plenty of support, stimulating events when I needed stimulation, and the possibility of closing my office door and disappearing when this became necessary to complete the study.

Democracy Challenged

The Challenge of Semi-Authoritarianism: An Introduction

THE LAST DECADE of the twentieth century saw the rise of a great number of regimes that cannot be easily classified as either authoritarian or democratic but display some characteristics of both—in short, they are *semi-authoritarian regimes*. They are ambiguous systems that combine rhetorical acceptance of liberal democracy, the existence of some formal democratic institutions, and respect for a limited sphere of civil and political liberties with essentially illiberal or even authoritarian traits. This ambiguous character, furthermore, is deliberate. Semi-authoritarian systems are not imperfect democracies struggling toward improvement and consolidation but regimes determined to maintain the appearance of democracy without exposing themselves to the political risks that free competition entails.

Semi-authoritarian regimes are political hybrids. They allow little real competition for power, thus reducing government accountability. However, they leave enough political space for political parties and organizations of civil society to form, for an independent press to function to some extent, and for some political debate to take place. Such regimes abound in the Soviet successor states: In countries like Kazakhstan and Azerbaijan, for example, former Communist Party bosses have transformed themselves into elected presidents, but in reality remain strongmen whose power is barely checked by weak democratic institutions. Semi-authoritarian regimes are also numerous in sub-Saharan Africa, where most of the multiparty elections of the 1990s failed to produce working parliaments or other institutions capable of holding the executive even remotely accountable. In the Arab world,

3

tentative political openings in Algeria, Morocco, and Yemen appear to be leading to the modernization of semi-authoritarianism rather than to democracy, in keeping with a pattern first established by Egypt. In the Balkans, the communist regimes have disappeared, but despite much international support most governments are semi-authoritarian, with only Slovenia and—more recently and tentatively—Croatia moving toward democracy. Even more worrisome is the case of Latin America, where economic crises and sharply unequal distribution of income create the risk of popular disenchantment with incumbent democratic governments, and even with democratic institutions. Already in two countries, first Peru and then Venezuela, steady progress toward democracy has been interrupted by the emergence of semi-authoritarian regimes. In Asia, formal democratic processes are accompanied by strong authoritarian features in countries such as Pakistan, Singapore, and Malaysia, putting them in the realm of semi-authoritarianism.

Semi-authoritarianism is not a new phenomenon—many past regimes have paid lip service to democracy while frequently violating its basic tenets. But the number of such regimes was limited because until the end of the Cold War many governments, often supported by their countries' leading intellectuals, rejected liberal democracy outright. They did so in the name of people's democracy (that is, socialism), or in the name of communal cultural traditions that precluded the egoistic individualism on which, they claimed, liberal democracy is based. Since the end of the Cold War, few governments and even fewer intellectuals are willing to mount an ideological defense of nondemocratic systems of government; most feel they have to at least pretend adherence to the concept of democracy. Even the argument about the cultural bias of democracy is heard less frequently. On the other hand, the number of governments willing to accept the strict limitations on the extent and duration of their power imposed by democratic rule remains small. As a result, semi-authoritarian regimes have become more numerous.

The number of such regimes is likely to increase even further. In many countries that have experienced a political transition since the early 1990s, unfavorable conditions—including weak democratic institutions and political organizations, persistent authoritarian traditions, major socioeconomic problems, and ethnic and religious conflicts—create formidable obstacles to the establishment and, above all, the consolidation of democracy. Nevertheless, citizens everywhere have shown their disillusionment with authoritarian regimes, and a widespread return to the unabashedly top-down forms of government so common in the past is improbable. These conditions, unfavorable to both genuine democracy and overt authoritarianism, further enhance the prospects for the spread of semi-authoritarianism.

With their combination of positive and negative traits, semi-authoritarian regimes pose a considerable challenge to U.S. policy makers. Such regimes often represent a significant improvement over their predecessors or appear to provide a measure of stability that is welcome in troubled regions. But the superficial stability of many semi-authoritarian regimes usually masks a host of severe problems and unsatisfied demands that need to be dealt with lest they lead to crises in the future. Despite their growing importance, however, semi-authoritarian regimes have not received systematic attention. In the present study, I propose to start filling the lacuna in the understanding of semi-authoritarian regimes and to put forth some suggestions about how to address the policy challenges they pose.

It is tempting to dismiss the problems created by the proliferation of semi-authoritarian regimes with the argument that, all things considered, they are not that bad and should be accepted as yet-imperfect democracies that will eventually mature into the real thing. For instance, compared to the old communist Yugoslavia, or to a deeply divided Bosnia suffering from the aftermath of civil war and ethnic cleansing, or to a Serbia in state of economic collapse but still defiant, Croatia under Franjo Tudjman did not appear too badly off; nor did it create insurmountable problems for the international community. Similarly, the semi-authoritarianism of President Heydar Aliyev in oil-rich Azerbaijan poses fewer immediate problems for policy makers and for oil companies than would a protracted power struggle with uncertain outcome. The widespread discontent in at least some semi-authoritarian states, however, suggests that further change is inevitable and that it is not in the interest of the United States to ignore the problem until crises erupt.

Promoting the democratization of semi-authoritarian regimes is a frustrating undertaking, since they are resistant to the arsenal of reform programs on which the United States and other donor countries usually rely. Semi-authoritarian regimes already do much of what the most widely used democratization projects encourage: They hold regular multiparty elections, allow parliaments to function, and recognize, within limits, the rights of citizens to form associations and of an independent press to operate. Indeed, many countries with semi-authoritarian regimes are beehives of civil society activity, with hundreds of nongovernmental organizations (NGOs) operating with foreign support. Many have a very outspoken, even outrageously libelous, independent press. Nevertheless, incumbent governments and parties are in no danger of losing their hold on power, not because they are popular but because they know how to play the democracy game and still retain control. Imposing sanctions on these regimes does not appear to be an answer. Such measures are usually ineffective, and the political and economic costs they entail, both for those who impose them and for the citizens of the targeted country, do not appear justified under the circumstances.

In general, sticks are in short supply for donors seeking to address the problem of semi-authoritarian regimes. Carrots are even scarcer: There is little the international community can offer to a stable regime to entice it to risk losing power. The deepening of democracy is in the long-run interest of these countries, but it is definitely not in the short-term interest of the leaders who stand to lose power if their country becomes more democratic. Going down in history as an enlightened leader appears to be less attractive to most politicians than maintaining their power intact.

Analytical Challenges

In addition to creating a policy dilemma about how to deal with specific countries, the growth of semi-authoritarianism poses analytical challenges. The first of these is differentiating semi-authoritarian regimes from others that are neither fully authoritarian nor fully democratic. There is a vast gray zone that occupies the space between authoritarianism at one end and consolidated democracy at the other. The existence of this gray zone is well recognized by analysts, but there is little consensus on the types of regimes residing in it.[1] In general, analysts discuss two broad categories of countries occupying this gray zone, depending on whether they look at the process of change or at the character of the regimes: countries still in transition and imperfect democracies.

Analysts who focus on the unfolding process of political transformation but assume that the process will eventually lead to democracy talk variously of unconsolidated or consolidating democracies or countries experiencing protracted transitions. Essentially, nonconsolidated democracies are countries that are democratic, at least to a certain extent, but where there is as yet no guarantee that democracy will last.[2] Countries experiencing protracted transitions are not democratic, but they are on their way to becoming democratic in a particularly slow, gradual way.[3] The problem with both concepts is that they cannot be applied with any rigor except in retrospect—Mexico can now be classified as a country that experienced a protracted transition, but one could not have classified it that way ten years ago without indulging in wishful thinking or making unwarranted assumptions about the inevitability of a democratic outcome. Similarly, democracies that eventually consolidate may not look very different from those that will suffer reversals until the process has unfolded.

Analysts who focus on regime characteristics usually try to capture the ambiguity of gray zone countries by adding a qualifier to the word *democracy*: semi-, formal, electoral, partial, weak, illiberal, virtual, and many others—the differences seem to be based more on the preference and imagination of the analyst than on the characteristics of different regimes.[4] Attempts to classify hybrid regimes on a continuum, ranging from those that are closest to authoritarianism to those that are closest to democracy, have greater rigor and are more satisfactory in theory, but they tend to break down in the application, given the uncertainty and the inherent instability of most hybrid regimes.[5]

I have chosen the term *semi-authoritarian* to denote these hybrid regimes because labels including the word *democracy* are not adequate to capture their defining feature, namely, their deliberate nature. Semi-authoritarian regimes are not failed democracies or democracies in transition; rather, they are carefully constructed and maintained alternative systems. If semi-authoritarian governments had their way, the system would never change. One of the countries included in this study, Egypt, has developed a particularly resilient, almost institutionalized, semi-authoritarianism that has already lasted more than twenty years and even survived the transition from the presidency of Anwar Sadat to that of Hosni Mubarak. While the Egyptian system is highly unlikely to last forever, there is little explanatory value in defining a system that maintains its stability over a long period as transitional.

Different semi-authoritarian regimes present different mixtures of democratic and authoritarian features. For instance, Egypt is a semi-authoritarian state because it has a formally democratic political system and some open political space, but that space is rather narrow, and it would not take much more narrowing for Egypt to cross the boundary into the realm of authoritarian countries. Conversely, Croatia has a large, open political space and is changing rapidly. Reviewing the entire process of change in the country, beginning with the fall of socialism, analysts may conclude in the future that this was really a case of protracted transition, but such a conclusion could be premature now. But even if specific countries will have to be reclassified, the concept of semi-authoritarianism provides a useful tool for assessing the outcome of many recent political transitions and the challenges the United States and other countries face in dealing with them.

A second analytical challenge posed by semi-authoritarian regimes concerns the validity of some widespread ideas about democratic transitions that underpin the democracy promotion strategies of the United States and other industrialized democracies. First, such regimes challenge the assumption, dominant since the end of the Cold War, that the failure of the socialist regimes means the triumph of democracy. This "end of history" argument puts too much emphasis on the importance of ideologies.[6] It accurately notes that socialism, viewed for the best part of the twentieth century as the ideological alternative to democracy, lost its appeal with the collapse of the communist regimes of the Soviet Union and Eastern Europe. As a result, the particular type of naked, institutionalized authoritarianism associated with socialism, with its massive single party and complex ideological apparatus, has become exceedingly rare. But relatively few governments, propelled by the genuine pluralism of their society and by an economic system capable of supporting such pluralism, have embraced democracy. Many have devised less heavy-handed, more nimble, and in a sense more imaginative systems that combine authoritarian and liberal traits: This is semi-authoritarianism in its various forms.

The deliberate character of semi-authoritarian regimes also forces a reconsideration of the visually appealing image of countries that fail to democratize because they are caught in a "reverse wave." This idea, set forth and popularized by Samuel Huntington, is that in a particular period many countries embrace democracy—figuratively, a wave propels them forward.[7] Some of these countries safely ride the wave to dry land and prosper as democracies. Others are sucked back into the nondemocratic sea as the wave recedes, hopefully to be pushed back toward land by the next wave some decades in the future. It is an enticing idea, but it is not entirely accurate. It assumes that the leaders of all the countries supposedly being caught in a reverse wave intended to reach the shore, but in many cases they did not, and probably neither did many of these countries' citizens.[8] Most countries that fail to reach the shore are not failed democracies caught in the wave's reflux; on the contrary, many are successful semi-authoritarian states that rode the wave as far as they wanted and managed to stop.[9] The countries discussed in the present study belong to this group. They are semi-authoritarian by design, not by default: They are successful semi-authoritarian regimes rather than failed democracies.

Another widespread idea challenged by the proliferation of semi-authoritarian regimes is that liberalization is a step toward democracy because it unleashes the democratic forces of a country. Liberalization, which can be defined as the opening up of an authoritarian system so that debate and at least limited challenges to the old system become possible, undoubtedly allows all types of previously repressed ideas and political forces to bubble up. What actually surfaces depends on what was there. If a strong substratum of democratic ideas and above all of democratic organizations existed in the country, then liberalization indeed leads to greater democracy. But it can also lead to an outburst of ethnic nationalism, as in Yugoslavia, or of religious fundamentalism, as in Egypt—it just depends on the existing conditions, widely diffused ideas, and the emerging leadership. In developing countries where life is difficult for most, liberalization always releases a vague demand for something better, for change, which can be manipulated by able leaders in almost any direction. It is true that in countries that become democratic the process starts with liberalization.

Semi-authoritarian regimes demonstrate, however, that liberalization can also free ideas and trigger political processes that make democratization difficult, if not impossible.

Policy Challenges

From the point of view of policy makers in the United States and other democratic countries, the most immediate challenge posed by semi-authoritarian regimes is a policy one: How should such regimes be dealt with? Should the United States try to force democratization programs on Egypt, an important U.S. ally in the Middle East, although the Egyptian government would resist and the programs might even prove destabilizing? How should the international community react to Heydar Aliyev's plan to anoint his son as his successor as president of Azerbaijan, as if the country were a monarchy rather than a republic? What action is warranted when Venezuela starts slipping back from democracy to a semi-authoritarian populism? How can donors facilitate Croatia's second transition, the one from semi-authoritarianism? But there is another layer of issues raised by semi-authoritarian regimes, which may appear abstract when first formulated but are actually very important to the outcome of democracy promotion policies. Generally, these issues can be organized under the question, Why do semi-authoritarian regimes come into existence? Is it because of bad leaders (support efforts to vote them out of office), weak institutions (set up a capacity-building program), or a disorganized civil society incapable of holding the government accountable (fund and train nongovernmental organizations)? Or is it because there are underlying conditions that seriously undermine the prospects for democracy (and what can be done about underlying conditions)? Even more fundamentally, does the proliferation of semi-authoritarian regimes indicate that the assumptions about democratic transitions that undergird assistance programs need rethinking?

As long as the United States and other industrial democracies continue funding democracy assistance programs, questions about the nature of semi-authoritarian regimes and the mechanisms of democratic transitions are not abstract, but have a direct bearing on policy options. Democracy assistance programs are based on a concept of how democratic transitions take place that owes a lot to theory and relatively little to concrete evidence. This is not strange. Democratization is a complicated and little-understood process. In part, this is because the number of well-established democracies is relatively small, making it difficult to detect regular patterns. In part, it is because studies of democratization vary widely in their approaches and methodologies, yielding noncomparable conclusions. As a result, we understand much better how democratic systems function than why and how they emerged in the first place.

In the course of more than a decade of democracy promotion efforts, policy makers in the United States and other countries have developed their own model of democratic transitions. This model is based in part on a highly selective reading of the literature on democratization and in part on the operational requirements of agencies that need to show results within a fairly short time frame—in the world of democracy promotion, ten years already qualifies as long-term, although many studies of democratization highlight processes unfolding over many decades and even centuries. Inevitably, historical studies of democratization that point to the long process of socioeconomic transformation underlying the emergence of democracy have been ignored. There is little policy guidance to be derived from learning that the social capital that made democratic development possible in Northern Italy after World War II started to be built up in the fifteenth century, or that the rise of the gentry in the seventeenth century contributed to the democratic evolution of Britain.[10] As a result, the studies with the greatest impact on democracy promotion have been those that looked narrowly at the final phase of democratic transitions, without asking too many questions about what had happened earlier or what kind of conditions had made the democratic outcome possible.

Furthermore, sophisticated studies are often given simplistic interpretations when they become a tool to justify policy choices. For example, among the most influential works often cited by democracy promoters are the studies of transitions from authoritarian rule in Latin America and Southern Europe carried out in the 1980s by a team of investigators, with Philippe Schmitter and Guillermo O'Donnell drawing the overall conclusions.[11] These conclusions were highly preliminary, as Schmitter and O'Donnell made clear with the final volume's subtitle: *Tentative Conclusions about Uncertain Democracies.* As is often the case with successful works, these highly qualified conclusions took on a life of their own, losing their nuances and turning into outright policy prescriptions. In the midst of the transition from apartheid in South Africa in the early 1990s, I heard many political commentators invoke O'Donnell and Schmitter in support of their favorite policies, ignoring the two authors' careful qualifications of their conclusions. A similar fate has befallen Robert Putnam, whose concept of social capital has been transformed to denote not a culture of trust and cooperation developed over centuries, but something that could be quickly created by funding NGOs and training them in the techniques of lobbying the government, administering funds, and reporting to donors.[12]

The Donors' Model

The model of democratization that donors have developed through this process of distilling the complex lessons of history into policy prescriptions capable of implementation is simple. Democratization is interpreted as a three-phase process: liberalization, lasting at most a few years, but preferably much less; the transition proper, accomplished through the holding of a multiparty election; and consolidation, a protracted process of strengthening institutions and deepening a democratic culture. The tools used to facilitate this project are also fairly simple: in the liberalization phase, support for civil society and the independent press; during the transition, support for elections, including voter education, training of NGOs for election observing, and, more rarely, training for all political parties in the techniques of organizing and campaigning; and in the consolidation phase, new programs to build democratic institutions and the rule of law, as well as the continuation of activities to further strengthen civil society and the media, educate citizens, or train parties.[13]

The model is considered applicable to any country, although different conditions require some adjustment in the programs implemented. This is because the real obstacles to democracy are authoritarian leaders' resistance to change, which can be softened with carrots and sticks, and the weakness of civil society, political parties, and democratic institutions, which can be lessened through democracy assistance programs. Indeed, the idea that there are virtually no conditions that preclude the possibility of democratization has become an article of faith among democracy promoters.

In the present study I argue that semi-authoritarian regimes call into question the validity of the donors' model. First, these regimes show that liberalization and transitional elections can constitute the end of the process rather than its initial phases, creating semi-authoritarian regimes determined to prevent further change rather than imperfect but still-evolving democracies. Furthermore, this outcome is not necessarily a failure of democratization, but the result of a deliberate decision to prevent democratization on the part of the elites controlling the process.

Second, an analysis of the workings of semi-authoritarian regimes shows that all sorts of conditions—for example, stagnant economies or ethnic polarization—matter, and matter a great deal at that. The semi-authoritarian outcome is not always something imposed by autocratic leaders on a population that wanted something quite different, but it is often something accepted and even desired by the population. In many countries—Venezuela for example—people willingly, even enthusiastically, reject democracy at least for a time. The problem cannot be explained away by arguing that what people reject in such cases was not true democracy to begin with. The reality is more complicated, as the present study will show. Conditions really do affect citizens' priorities and the way they perceive democracy.

Third, semi-authoritarian regimes also challenge the view that democracy can be promoted by an elite of true believers. Democracy promoters extol in theory the virtue and necessity of broad citizen participation beyond the vote, and innumerable projects target the strengthening of civil society. But civil society as defined by donors is much more part of the elite than of the society at large. Donors favor professional advocacy NGOs, which speak the language of democracy and easily relate to the international community.[14] For understandable reasons donors are leery of mass movements, which can easily slip into radical postures and can get out of hand politically. But a problem strikingly common to all countries with semi-authoritarian regimes is that the political elite, whether in the government, opposition parties, or even civil society organizations, has great difficulty reaching the rest of the society. In the end, this situation plays into the hands of semi-authoritarian regimes.

Dealing with semi-authoritarian regimes thus requires going beyond blaming leaders for nondemocratic outcomes of once-promising democratization processes, no matter how tempting this is. To be sure, leaders with authoritarian tendencies are a real obstacle to democratic transformation. It was pointless to hope for real democratization in Serbia as long as Slobodan Milošević was in power, and Azerbaijan will likely never be a democratic country under the leadership of Heydar Aliyev. Hugo Chávez is not the man who will restore and revitalize Venezuela's now shaky democracy. But the problem goes well beyond personalities. Countries do not necessarily deserve the leaders they get, but they do get the leaders whose rise conditions facilitate. If the leader is removed, the conditions remain. For democracy promoters this is an unpleasant thought, because it is easier to demonize individuals and even to oust them from power than to alter the conditions that propel those leaders to the fore.

Semi-authoritarian regimes usually feature in discussions of democratization as transitional regimes or as imperfect democracies. They would be more properly studied as a distinct regime type that calls assumptions about democratization into question and challenges policy makers to devise more effective policies to stimulate further change.

Understanding Semi-Authoritarianism

It is useful at this point to set forth some preliminary ideas about the nature and major characteristics of semi-authoritarian regimes to back up the claim that they represent a special type of regime, and are not simply imperfect democracies. In particular, I call attention here to four issues, all of which are discussed at greater length in subsequent chapters of the present study: the way in which power is generated and transferred, the low degree of institutionalization, the weak link between political and economic reform, and the nature of civil society.

Limits on the Transfer of Power. The most important characteristic of semi-authoritarian regimes is the existence and persistence of mechanisms that effectively prevent the transfer of power through elections from the hands of the incumbent leaders or party to a new political elite or organization. It is the existence of such mechanisms that makes the term *semi-authoritarian* more appropriate than any that contains the word *democracy*—if power cannot be transferred by elections, there is little point in describing a country as democratic, even with qualifiers. These mechanisms for blocking power transfers function despite the existence of formally democratic institutions and the degree of political freedom granted to the citizens of the country. Semi-authoritarian states may have a reasonably free press. The regime may leave space for autonomous organizations of civil society to operate, for private businesses to grow and thus for new economic elites to arise. The regime may hold fairly open elections for local or regional governments or even allow backbenchers from the government party to be defeated in elections. But there is little room for debate over the nature of political power in society, where that power resides, and who should hold it. Most important, there is no way to challenge the power of the incumbents. At the center, competition is a fiction; even if elections are held, outsiders are not allowed to truly challenge the power of the incumbents. Elections are not the source of the government's power, and thus voters cannot transfer power to a new leadership.

The issue of the source of the regime's power is central to any discussion of semi-authoritarian states. There are conceptual difficulties in confronting this issue, but the problem cannot be avoided. A definition of democracy, and of semi-authoritarianism, that hinges on determining the source of the government's power is admittedly inconvenient, because the source of power is never easy to ascertain in practice. Despite common expressions such as "seizing power" or "assuming power," power is not something concrete, which can easily be detected or seized, as Samuel Huntington pointed out long ago.[15] Power is something that is generated and regenerated through protracted engagement of the governors and the governed in society. In democratic systems, it is relatively easy to see how power is generated and how it is exercised. Access to positions of power is consistently determined by election results, although many factors ultimately enhance or decrease the elected leaders' ability to shape policies. Decisions are made by elected leaders operating within institutions, and while many pressures are brought to bear on those institutions, the process is relatively transparent and the outcome clearly visible. Nondemocratic systems are more opaque. Power is the result of relationships established among individuals. Because these relationships are not institutionalized, they are difficult to map and to explain. And while even in authoritarian countries decisions are influenced by a multiplicity of actors and factors, the process through which influence is exercised is much more opaque than in democratic countries.

Weak Institutionalization. Because of the discrepancy between the way in which power is generated and allocated in practice and the way in which it ought to be generated and allocated according to the formal institutional framework, semi-authoritarian regimes are never fully institutionalized, although some, above all Egypt, come close. Democratic countries build strong institutions—they are organized through the rule of law and institutions, rather than by individuals. Authoritarian regimes also can and do build institutions to generate and allocate power in an orderly, predictable way—see, for example, the powerful single parties developed by communist regimes. But semi-authoritarian regimes cannot develop the institutions they would need to perpetuate the allocation of power without causing the democratic facade to crumble. Nor can they allow the democratic institutions to function without hindrance without putting the continuation of their control in jeopardy. Semi-authoritarian regimes thus constantly undermine their own institutions, usually by generating and exercising much power outside their realm, or more rarely by manipulating them endlessly, as the government of Senegal does. Semi-authoritarian regimes have institutions, but the semi-authoritarianism itself is not institutionalized.

Nevertheless, many semi-authoritarian regimes are remarkably stable over time. Since their stability is based on the leadership of an individual or small elite, rather than on institutions, semi-authoritarian regimes invariably face difficult successions. In single-party authoritarian systems, the problem of succession is solved by the party machinery; in democratic countries, it is routinely solved by the occurrence of elections every few years. Semi-authoritarian regimes, however, have neither the party machine nor an open election system.

Another factor that can shake the delicate balance of these regimes is the level of popular participation—there has to be enough to maintain the facade of democracy and provide a safety valve for social discontent, but not so much as to permit challenges to the incumbent regime. Semi-authoritarian regimes have trouble developing channels for popular participation that are neither threatening to the government nor destructive of the democratic facade.[16]

The dynamics that keep most semi-authoritarian regimes in power are based on a mixture of two factors: deliberate manipulation of formal democratic institutions by incumbents and acceptance of the regime by citizens. Manipulation can take many forms. Semi-authoritarian regimes are adept at avoiding defeat in multiparty elections, often through fairly subtle methods, without resorting to open repression or crude stuffing of ballot boxes; indeed, some go to great lengths to give their elections an aura of legitimacy. Prior to its country's October 1999 parliamentary elections, judged by observers to be neither free nor fair, the embassy of Kazakhstan in Washington, D.C., was publishing a weekly bulletin spelling out in great detail all the measures supposedly being taken to ensure the integrity of the process. Semi-authoritarian governments are good at pressuring the independent press into self-censorship and at delegitimizing democratic institutions by accusing them of being insufficiently democratic. For example, in Venezuela in 1999, Hugo Chávez, a democratically elected president who had no intention of accepting the limits on his power imposed by the constitution, embarked on a campaign to discredit the parliament as unrepresentative and unresponsive to the will of the people. He soon succeeded in replacing the parliament with a pliant constituent assembly.

But semi-authoritarian regimes do not stay in power through manipulation and repression alone. They often also enjoy a degree of popular support because many citizens believe that they offer some public goods that democratic governments are incapable of delivering. In countries where formal democracy is accompanied by high levels of poverty, or where ethnic or religious conflict divides and mobilizes the population, for example, semi-authoritarian governments play on the public's grievances and fears and get support by promising solutions.

Reform Disconnect. Another trait common to countries with semi-authoritarian regimes is the lack of positive synergy between political and economic reform. In these countries, political openings have not led to economic reform, nor has economic reform led to a more democratic process. On the contrary, both economic and political change have been controlled and manipulated by the regime. The result is that semi-authoritarian regimes have a facade of democracy and a facade of market economy. Semi-authoritarian regimes do undertake economic reform in response to international pressure to free up markets and reduce the sphere of government control. But in most cases, hurried and corrupt privatization programs transfer control over major economic assets from government officials as state representatives to the same government officials as private entrepreneurs.[17] Thus, semi-authoritarian regimes can undergo market liberalization with little political liberalization or separation of economic elites from political elites. The linkage between economic liberalization and democratization is complex, and it is dangerous to assume that the former always encourages the latter.

Limits on Civil Society. Most countries with semi-authoritarian regimes appear to have fairly active civil societies. While their governments usually impose restrictions on openly political organizations, they allow space within which a variety of civil society organizations can operate. Egypt, for example, has an array of organizations independent of the state, ranging from Islamic charities to modern professional associations. Azerbaijan first experienced a flourishing of civic organizations in the period of political liberalization under former Soviet leader Mikhail Gorbachev, but new organizations have continued to spring up even in the less free period of independence.

Yet, in countries with semi-authoritarian regimes the contribution of civil society to democracy and openness is more limited than it appears.[18] First, semi-authoritarian governments do impose limitations on civil society organizations, including restrictive registration laws and overt and covert pressures to limit activities to politically safe areas. In 1999, for example, Egypt enacted a restrictive law on voluntary organizations that makes registration difficult and limits the range of activities they can undertake.[19] But even more fundamentally, organizations of civil society in many countries are a manifestation of a social pluralism that is not democratic in character; or they contribute to organizational pluralism but not to political pluralism.[20]

In some countries, organizations of civil society reflect the social pluralism of religion and ethnicity—there may be Muslim or Christian charities, or ethnic associations of all types. It is often difficult even for democratically minded organizations to overcome the social barriers that make it difficult to operate across ethnic or religious barriers, or even across gender lines. Thus, civil society easily ends up simply reflecting old social divisions. All countries provide examples of this, but Egypt, with its proliferation of Islamist groups, offers a particularly stark reminder of the extent to which the organizational life of a country is inevitably rooted in its social structures. The paradox here is that the same organizations that reflect ethnic or religious divisions may be working for goals that are associated with democracy—religious freedom, for example—while creating barriers to it by perpetuating these divisions.

In all countries with semi-authoritarian regimes, there are some organizations that try to overcome the legacies of social division. Most of the donor-supported NGOs formed since the early 1990s to promote human rights, carry out civic education, or advocate a variety of policy reforms considered to be associated with democracy fall into this category, at least in theory. These are referred to by donors as civil society organizations, although they constitute only a small part of the civil society that exists in a country. The problem is that these groups often have shallower social roots than less democratic ones—for example, human rights organizations in Egypt are small elite groups, while Islamic charities are part of the social fabric. The so-called civil society in semi-authoritarian states, in conclusion, is often shallower and makes a lesser contribution to democracy than it would first appear from looking at the number of organizations and the government's willingness to let them operate.

Types of Semi-Authoritarian Regimes

While semi-authoritarian regimes share some common characteristics, they also exhibit many differences. They do not represent a single regime type but rather a range of types. Some countries fall close to the authoritarian end of the political spectrum—for example, Egypt and Azerbaijan. Other are closer to the democratic end—in Senegal, for instance, the dominant party managed to block a transfer of power for forty years, including a decade when it enjoyed little popularity, but it also managed to maintain a fairly positive, and gradually improving, human rights record. All semi-authoritarian regimes take steps to preserve their core, namely the power of the central government, even if it means resorting to nondemocratic methods. They differ, however, in their assessment of what constitutes a dangerous challenge to that power. As a result, such regimes show a great deal of variation concerning issues such as freedom of the press and individual liberties. These differences can be quite visible, as the case studies in the present study show.

Semi-authoritarian regimes also differ in terms of their internal dynamics and possibilities for further change. In this regard, it is possible to differentiate among three types of semi-authoritarian regimes: regimes in equilibrium, which have established a balance among competing forces and are thus quite stable; regimes in decay, where the authoritarian tendencies appear increasingly strong and the counterbalancing factors weak, suggesting the possibility that the government will revert to full authoritarianism; and regimes that are experiencing dynamic change that may undermine the government's ability to maintain the status quo, forcing it into opening up new political space and thus providing the possibility of incremental progress toward democracy.

All three types of semi-authoritarian regimes have the potential to become democratic at some point. I am not assuming that democratic transformation is impossible anywhere. However, while semi-authoritarian regimes experiencing dynamic change can become democratic through incremental change, regimes that are in equilibrium would have to undergo too stormy an upheaval before such change could take place. Decaying regimes are probably those least likely to democratize, because they are caught in a downward spiral that may lead back to authoritarianism.

The semi-authoritarianism of equilibrium is the purest form, a stable condition that has already persisted over a long period and is likely to continue in the absence of upheaval. Semi-authoritarian regimes in equilibrium have proven that they can handle ordinary challenges—such as the activities of opposition parties or structural change brought about by a steady period of economic growth—without a major modification in the structure of power. Egypt (discussed in a later chapter) and Indonesia before the fall of President Suharto are good examples of semi-authoritarianism in equilibrium—some of their citizens would say stagnation.

An interesting feature of such countries is that political equilibrium, or stagnation, can persist even while the countries experience rapid economic growth. Until 1998, Indonesia was one of the most dynamic emergent Asian economies; Egypt's growth has been more modest, but the country has undergone far-reaching economic restructuring since the 1970s and steady economic growth for sustained periods. The two cases suggest that economic growth per se does not necessarily break the equilibrium of a semi-authoritarian regime. Indeed, what made political transformation possible in Indonesia was not economic growth. Rather, it was a sudden economic crisis in the late 1990s that caused widespread hardship and eroded the legitimacy of a regime whose major accomplishment had been economic growth.

The semi-authoritarianism of decay is found in countries that are stagnating or declining economically and socially. This is the most discouraging form of semi-authoritarianism, because it is likely to regress toward full-fledged authoritarianism. Azerbaijan (discussed in a later chapter), Kazakhstan, Malawi, and Zambia, among many others, are examples of this semi-authoritarianism of decay. In many of these countries, the democratic stimulus was relatively weak from the beginning. It came from the outside, from the general post–Cold War political climate and from direct pressure by the international community, but there was a dearth of domestic forces to ensure continued government responsiveness and accountability. In other countries, such as Zimbabwe, there was real internal demand for political change, but also a government determined to stay in power at all costs. Such a situation leads to violence and further political decay rather than democracy.

In all countries experiencing the semi-authoritarianism of decay, there are residual areas of openness. There has been no formal return to the single-party system, and opposition political parties as well as civil society organizations are still allowed. Some independent media organizations still operate despite the many restrictions, the frequent arrests of journalists, and, above all, the ever present possibility that the government will shut them down. But the political space is under constant threat. In some cases, such as Zimbabwe, it has clearly been shrinking in recent years.

Despite their superficial similarity to stable semi-authoritarian regimes, regimes in decay are in reality quite different, because the balance of power is slowly shifting in favor of the incumbent government. In a country like Egypt, there is an established political culture that makes it difficult for the government to close the existing areas of openness. There is real political pluralism, with political parties, NGOs, and think tanks with a proven capacity to get the necessary political and financial support to continue operating. There are independent media and a rich intellectual life, although there is also a regime that has been able to prevent real competition for about two decades. But in the case of semi-authoritarian regimes in a state of decay, the future is less predictable. There is no established culture that precludes the complete closure of the political space. Pluralism is fragile, with parties forming and folding all the time, and civil society organizations remaining insecurely rooted domestically and heavily dependent on outside donors. Economic conditions likewise do not facilitate political change in countries with decaying semi-authoritarian regimes such as those I have mentioned. The private sector is weak and likely to remain so for the foreseeable future. The natural resources sector does not lend itself to privatization and even less to the development of small and medium-size businesses. For example, monopolies or oligopolies dominate the oil industries of Azerbaijan and Kazakhstan and the copper mines of Zambia. In many countries a privatization program is in place, but it does more to enhance the wealth and power of the ruling elite than to create a new stratum of independent entrepreneurs. Corruption becomes the defining factor in these systems, further reducing the development of small and medium-size enterprises. This greatly diminishes the pluralism of the political system by reducing the autonomy of economic interest groups vis-à-vis the government.

Under decaying regimes, in conclusion, semi-authoritarianism is probably as good as it gets. In the absence of some major new factor affecting the balance of power, the semi-authoritarianism of decay is more likely to regress to authoritarianism than to evolve toward democracy.

The third category of semi-authoritarian states—those undergoing dynamic change—is also characterized by a lack of equilibrium. However, these countries are experiencing a process that leaves open the possibility, and indeed the likelihood, of further, positive political change and even of democratization. Croatia, discussed in a later chapter, provides an example of a country that appears to be pushed toward democracy by the general ferment the country is experiencing. Taiwan offers an example of a country that outgrew its political system and democratized. In such countries, pressure for change comes from both the political leadership and from autonomous forces operating outside the government and independent of it, although the government's role is probably the most important. Such countries are governed by reformist elites rather than democratic ones. They have leaders who want to promote economic growth, free trade, and fuller integration into the international community—a set of goals they view as critical to the modernization of their respective countries. Such governments usually want to retain control of the process of change, and thus are wary of popular participation, but they also recognize that the modernization they envisage is bound to lead to political change as well. Rapid economic growth is often key to this dynamic process that leads such countries to move beyond semi-authoritarianism, as illustrated by the case of Senegal, which is also the subject of a chapter in the present study. Ruled by a particularly benevolent semi-authoritarian regime, Senegal has been poised for a breakthrough to real democracy for about fifteen years, and yet it continues to be stymied by the lack of dynamism in its economy and society. The semi-authoritarianism of dynamic change very starkly poses the question about the relationship between political and socioeconomic change.

The Present Study

The present study is organized into three sections. The first, consisting of succinct case studies of five countries, highlights the distinctive features of semi-authoritarianism in each and thus the special challenge each poses to policy makers. In the second section, I extrapolate from the case studies and other material the salient characteristics of semi-authoritarian regimes and seek to explain the mechanisms that make semi-authoritarianism possible. In the third section, I discuss the weak impact on these countries of the democracy promotion strategies usually implemented by the international community, and explore possible alternatives.

The process of choosing five case-study countries from numerous candidates was driven by several criteria: First, I wanted multiple regions to be represented, to support my contention that semi-authoritarianism is not a phenomenon tied exclusively to specific areas, cultures or civilizations; second, I wanted countries that represented different types of semi-authoritarianism, to stress that there is a great deal of diversity among these regimes and thus that in the end no single democracy promotion strategy is likely to be effective everywhere. Finally, I chose countries that are not considered crucial to U.S. security or economic interests, because issues concerning democracy tend to be relegated to the background in such countries' policy-making. However, I made an exception for Egypt, because it is such a perfect example of the semi-authoritarianism of equilibrium. Based on these criteria, I chose Egypt, Azerbaijan, Venezuela, Senegal, and Croatia.

Egypt represents the model of a stable semi-authoritarian regime; the system has long been in equilibrium and comes as close to being consolidated and institutionalized as a semi-authoritarian regime can possibly be—it even weathered a succession (from Anwar Sadat to Hosni Mubarak in 1981) without changing its character. Egypt has also widely oscillated over time between the authoritarian and democratic ends of the semi-authoritarian continuum.

Azerbaijan is a much more recent example of semi-authoritarianism. The country did not become independent until 1991, and the Aliyev regime only established its hold on power in 1993. Although this regime is relatively young it is also quite consolidated, to the point where President Aliyev is seeking to develop a succession strategy that will put his own son in power. Azerbaijan represents a case of the semi-authoritarianism of decay—the overall situation in the country, the fragmentation and disarray of other political parties and of civil society, and the stagnation of the economy in all sectors except oil suggest that for the time being semi-authoritarianism may be as good as it gets in the country. As a relatively new state, Azerbaijan also provides an avenue for exploring the relationship between the process of state building and the development of a political regime.

Venezuela is also an example of the semi-authoritarianism of decay, but quite a different one: It did not move from authoritarianism to semi-authoritarianism; rather, it regressed to semi-authoritarianism from democracy. Venezuela had a well-functioning democratic system for decades, and until the late 1980s was considered by all analysts to be a consolidated democracy, indeed, an oasis of democratic stability in the ever problematic politics of Latin America. Some democratic processes and institutions still function quite well even now, in particular the election process. President Chávez was elected and reelected in free and fair elections. Political space remains open. But the signs of democratic decay are unmistakable. The president refused to accept the power of the old legislature even for an interim period while a new constitution was being prepared. He was then slow to implement the new constitution and allow the new legislature to play its full role. He politicized the military by appointing large number of officers to government positions—the consequence of this politicization was an unsuccessful coup d'état in early 2002 and continuing divisions between pro- and anti-Chávez officers. Furthermore, the confrontation between supporters and opponents of the regime has moved out of the realm of democratic politics and into the streets. The facade of democracy is wearing perilously thin. It seems increasingly possible that the next transfer of power in the country will take place not through elections but by unconstitutional means.

The semi-authoritarianism of the Chávez regime is extremely unstable. There is no political equilibrium, and even the president claims that the country is in a transitional stage. Furthermore, the past experience with democracy is already leading to demands for a revitalization of that system. There is no doubt, however, that Venezuela is experiencing a period of deep and threatening political decay, and that a regime with strong semi-authoritarian features has emerged in that country with the initial support of a large majority of the population. This decay of an established democratic system raises important issues about the conditions that make democratization possible and democracy sustainable.

Senegal is a relatively open semi-authoritarian state—rather prematurely, some analysts consider it to be democratic. Furthermore, there is a new political dynamic in Senegal. After forty years under the rule of the same political party and of only two presidents, in 2000 the country experienced the long-awaited *alternance*, with the opposition candidate winning the presidential election. A year later, the new president's party also won the parliamentary elections, by a very large majority. The elections, a milestone in the history of the country, nevertheless did not signal a real transformation of the Senegalese political system. The period since the *alternance* shows the difficulty of changing the politics of a country that is stagnant, even decaying, in other respects. The new regime shares the political culture of the old and operates under the same socioeconomic conditions. The country will likely settle down under a regime that is very similar to the old one, reducing the impact of elections to nothing more than the rotation of personnel within the same elite. Senegal's government was, and will likely remain, a benevolent semi-authoritarian regime, but nonetheless will continue to fall short of being democratic.

Croatia is a country in a period of dynamic transformation. It is struggling to move away from the semi-authoritarianism of the 1990s, and its experience highlights many of the problems that even a country with a willing leadership experiences in going beyond semi-authoritarianism and building a democratic system. The political will of the government that was formed in 2000 is not in doubt; furthermore, most Croatians believe that the country must join the European Union, and expect democracy to be part of the process. However, this new political will and political aspirations are developing in a context of slow economic growth and strong ethnic tensions. In essence, the transition from semi-authoritarianism is being complicated by socioeconomic conditions.

In the second section of this book I draw upon the five case studies to raise crucial issues about semi-authoritarian regimes. First, I discuss the functioning of semi-authoritarian regimes and the mechanisms they use to maintain the balances between openness and closure and between liberalization and repression that are necessary to prevent a transfer of power while maintaining a democratic facade. These issues have direct policy implications, because democracy promotion in these countries has to eliminate, or at least circumvent, the political devices that prevent power transfer. Second, in this section I also discuss the more complicated underlying issues concerning the conditions that facilitate the emergence of semi-authoritarian regimes. These are the most difficult issues for donors to address, but are also the most important.

Finally, in the third part of the study, I consider how the United States and other aid-giving nations have sought to promote democracy in the five case-study states, outline the scant efficacy and sometimes even counterproductive impact of these programs, and offer suggestions about means of addressing the challenge of semi-authoritarianism.

PART I

Varieties of Semi-Authoritarianism

I

Egypt:
Institutionalized Semi-Authoritarianism

EGYPT IS THE PERFECT MODEL of semi-authoritarianism. It has formal democratic institutions, a lively press, political parties, and a multitude of civil society organizations of all types. But it also has a well-honed political system that protects the government from real competition, limits the freedom of all organizations sufficiently to make them harmless to the incumbent leaders, makes it impossible to transfer power through elections, and maintains stability.

This semi-authoritarian system started developing in the mid-1970s, when Egyptian president Anwar Sadat cautiously moved to dismantle the single-party state inherited from his predecessor, Gamal Abdel Nasser, and to reintroduce a minimal degree of political pluralism. He opened the ruling party to internal competition, then allowed the formation of two opposition parties, preparing the way for the eventual holding of formally democratic and competitive parliamentary elections. Under the conditions of the time, when single-party regimes still dominated the developing world, Sadat appeared to be a daring reformer, despite the fact that he never put his own position on the line (under the Egyptian constitution, the president is chosen by the National Assembly, and his nomination is then ratified by a referendum in which he is the only candidate). By the end of the decade, the process of democratization had come to a halt. Sadat had succeeded in giving his government a more liberal look, but he was not willing to risk his position by allowing real competition.

Since the late 1970s, the process of political transformation has re-mained stalled and a regime of semi-authoritarianism has become firmly consolidated. It weathered the assassination of President Sadat at the hand of Islamic extremists in 1981 and has fended off the contin-uing challenge of radical Islam ever since. It has done so with a heavy hand at times—more than 10,000 political prisoners were being held in 2002—but without abandoning the facade of constitutional democ-racy. By combining a formally democratic political system with a state of emergency continuously in force since Sadat's death, the Egyptian regime has come close to doing what semi-authoritarian regimes usu-ally find difficult to accomplish: It has become virtually institutional-ized.

Even economic transformation has not created pressure for politi-cal reform. Since the mid-1970s, the Egyptian economy has under-gone significant liberalization, although it has not completely dis-mantled the statist industrial sector developed by the Nasser regime. There is a new business class in the country, but it is more interested in working closely with the government than in challenging it.

To understand the remarkable stability and resilience of Egypt's semi-authoritarian system and the challenges involved in promoting further political transformation, it is helpful to consider events that unfolded long before Sadat launched his cautious experiment with po-litical liberalization. The roots of semi-authoritarianism extend back to the early part of the twentieth century, when Egypt broke away from British control and started developing a modern political system under a constitutional monarchy. It is in that period that the central dilemma of Egyptian politics became apparent: how to bring together, in a society that is sharply divided economically and socially, an elite that aspires to modernize the country and a large, impoverished, and poorly educated population whose enormous material needs make it susceptible to radical appeals, whether they be those of socialism or of political Islam. The semi-authoritarian system that started develop-ing under Sadat and was perfected by his successor, Hosni Mubarak, is the latest of three attempts to find a solution to this dilemma. The first was the shaky democracy of the constitutional monarchy period (1922–1952), the second was Nasser's socialist experiment (1952–1970), and the third is the semi-authoritarian system in place today.

Egypt's Early Attempt at Democratization

Between the end of the British protectorate in 1922 and the Free Officers' coup that brought Nasser to power in 1952, Egypt experienced a democratic opening highly unusual outside the industrial world at the time, with a constitutional monarchy, a multiparty system, and universal male suffrage. To be sure, some aspects of the political system would be considered highly questionable today. Women could not vote, and under both the 1923 and 1930 constitutions, elections were organized on the basis of a two-tier system, in which electors in groups of thirty chose a single delegate who would actually cast a vote. By the standards of the time, and in view of the prevailing conditions in the country, the system was remarkable.[1]

This democratic experiment of sorts was built on unsure social foundations. Egyptian society was high unequal. It had a small but very wealthy landed class and an even smaller but quite dynamic urban entrepreneurial class, self-consciously playing a modernizing role. It also had a vast, poor, largely illiterate, largely peasant population, tied to the landed class in an essentially feudal relationship. Creating and sustaining democracy under such conditions was a tall order. Although it was an appealing ideal to the modernizing elite, it was a threat to the conservative elements of the landed class and did not offer much to the rest of the population. What created common ground among these disparate groups, at least temporarily, was the common resentment of the British presence and the nationalism that ensued. The convergence of nationalism and democratic ideals was represented by the Wafd, the dominant political party of the time.[2]

Despite its shaky foundations, this rough democratic system lasted a remarkably long time—like the present semi-authoritarianism, it persisted through a period of profound political turmoil in both the world and the region. In this period, Egypt even started developing what in today's parlance would be called a strong civil society, particularly strong, one might add, because it developed on its own, without the need for external prompting and support. This civil society was small, but its members were highly educated and capable of sustaining a rich political and intellectual life. It published newspapers and books, it organized political parties and civic society organizations, it advocated all sorts of reforms—it did everything, in other words, that today's donors would like civil society to do.

The most remarkable, and most durable and influential, among the civil society organizations that sprang up in this period were the professional syndicates, organized first by lawyers and doctors but extending over the following decades to every possible group of professionals in the country. Partly guilds protecting their members' interests, partly advocates for reform in their respective fields, professional syndicates have been a thorn in the side of all Egyptian governments, with their constant striving toward freedom from government interference and their penchant for becoming centers of political activity.

The modernizing elite that dominated political institutions and civil society organizations during the period of the democratic opening proved ultimately incapable of governing effectively and bringing about change. The main problem was not, as it is not now, the rebelliousness or volatility of the Egyptian population. On the contrary, Egyptians always tended to be surprisingly accommodating and patient despite the tremendous difficulties of life in their overcrowded country. Rather, the elite of the period did not effectively deal with the problems directly affecting the majority of the population, and thereby failed to give the population a vested interest in the continuation of democratic government.

One of the results was that the same elite that promoted democracy also remained leery of popular participation, and probably for good reason, because political and civic organizations did not penetrate the society. The choice of a two-tier election system, in which voters chose delegates who then participated in the elections, briefly abrogated by the Wafd but then reinstated, is symbolic in this respect—it was a means of filtering and limiting participation, of making democracy a more controllable process. The failure of the modern political and economic organizations to penetrate beyond the elite had another consequence: It left the field wide open to the activities of the Muslim Brothers. Founded in 1928, the Muslim Brotherhood was an organization calling for religious and moral renewal, not just of individuals but of the whole society.[3] The political implications of such a call for renewal were obvious. The Brotherhood, like Islamist organizations today, was at least in part a religion-clad manifestation of the resentment against foreign influence and the precarious economic condition of much of the population.

Eventually, the tenuous ties between the small political elite and the rest of the population broke. With the end of the British protectorate, nationalism ceased to be a unifying factor—and to make matters worse, the British and the French still occupied the Suez Canal area. After World War II, with the wind of independence blowing across the world and resentment against the establishment of the state of Israel rife throughout the Arab world, the government found itself pressured by nationalists of more radical bent and by a population generally dissatisfied with economic conditions. The political model favored by the political elite—that of moderate reform pursued from the top under a constitutional monarchy—could no longer contain dissatisfaction. The 1952 coup d'état put an end to a system that was already under stress.

Democratization Interrupted under Nasser

In July 1952, Egypt's attempt at democratization from the top came to a sudden halt with the Free Officers' coup and the rise to power of Gamal Abdel Nasser. Nasser's policies differed radically from those of the Wafd. That party had opted for formal but limited democracy and political participation, but had neglected the problems affecting the daily life of most Egyptians. Nasser essentially eliminated political participation, except through the limited channel of the ever-troubled Arab Socialist Union, but he focused the government's efforts on satisfying some of the most pressing needs of the population.

Both political and economic liberalization came to an end during the Nasser period, replaced by a single-party system and the imposition of state ownership of, or at least control over, the most important sectors of the economy. While a small-scale private sector continued to function, and a program of land reform extended and democratized ownership of land, economic control passed to the state. As a result, the emerging bourgeoisie that had guided the process of liberalization during the preceding decades was sidelined and rendered quiescent.

Nasser's policies had a clear popular bias: land reform, job creation through state investment in industrial development, the organization of a health care system, the exponential growth of the educational system, and the expansion of the civil service to accommodate the ballooning population of university graduates. Whether the major beneficiaries of Nasser's policies were the peasants and workers in whose names policies were decided, or the lower middle class from which many of the Free Officers came, it is certain that the changes were introduced at the expense of the elite.[4]

Politics, however, remained the domain of a small elite, with no input from the rest of the population. The people who benefited from Nasser's reforms had no role in bringing them about. Change was introduced from the top and any form of political organization independent of the state and ruling party was quickly repressed. The old political parties that had competed for power before the coup were outlawed, and movements of all political colorations that sought to appeal to the mass of the population, from the Muslim Brothers to the Communists, incurred Nasser's wrath and were banished from the political scene. In other words, the adoption of policies with a popular appeal was accompanied by the imposition of rules that restricted political participation even more than previously.

In this attempt to control and limit participation by any independent organization, Nasser initiated a policy of playing the religious elements against the Left. Facing the opposition of the Communist Party, he encouraged the Muslim Brothers, hoping their religious ideas would act as an antidote to those of the radical Left. But the Muslim Brothers challenged him in turn, and, after an assassination attempt in 1954, Nasser outlawed the organization. This was the same policy Sadat followed later, when he encouraged the growth of religious organizations in an attempt to lessen the influence of the Nasserites, particularly among the students. Like Nasser, Sadat eventually had to face the much more threatening challenge of religious groups.

In his two decades of rule, Nasser had to contend with the same problems that had confronted his predecessors: a society that, despite reforms, remained deeply divided socially and economically; a population susceptible to the call of radical socialist and Islamist ideas; and a liberal political elite that felt entitled to govern but provided no answers to major societal problems. He responded by addressing the socioeconomic problems, while barring from participation both the liberal political elite and the rest of the population, and concentrating power in the hands of an even smaller political elite of Free Officers and their allies. At his death of a heart attack in 1970, he left behind a country that was much changed economically and socially but was farther than ever from having a system that could accommodate Egypt's disparate political constituencies.

Rethinking Democratization under Sadat

Anwar Sadat, the vice president who succeeded Nasser as prescribed by the constitution, was an unlikely democratizer. One of the Free Officers, he had been a faithful member of the regime throughout the Nasser period, rewarded for his faithfulness with an appointment to the vice presidency. After years in Nasser's shadow, Sadat faced a difficult task in establishing his own credibility and power once he assumed the presidency. Nasser's memory, though tarnished by domestic economic difficulties and defeat in the 1967 Six-Day War, in which Israel captured the Sinai Peninsula, was still much venerated not only in Egypt but throughout the Arab world. Yet once in power, Sadat proved to be a much more self-assertive and daring leader than anybody had imagined, both in his foreign policy, which will not be discussed at length here, and in his domestic policies.[5]

As a first step toward consolidating his position, Sadat undertook a purge and reorganization of the Arab Socialist Union, the party set up by Nasser, to eliminate individuals who could challenge his leadership. In the following years, however, he went much further, giving a new direction to Egypt's politics and economy, as well as to its foreign policy.

In 1974, Sadat decided to open up the Arab Socialist Union, at the time still the only legal party, by encouraging the formation of three "platforms" within it. Instead of trying to be an ideologically monolithic organization, the party would in the future recognize and even welcome the existence of discrete rightist, centrist, and leftist tendencies within itself. This modest first step toward political liberalization was followed two years later by the disbanding of the Arab Socialist Union and the transformation of the three platforms into full-fledged

—though tame—political parties. The centrist party, renamed the Arab Socialist Misr Party, was organized by the then-prime minister with Sadat's support. Two years later, Sadat launched his own National Democratic Party, and the Arab Socialist Misr Party disappeared.

Sadat also sought other ways to dismantle Nasser's political legacy and to head the country in a new direction. In particular, he encouraged Islamic groups to organize, in the hope that their ideas would curb the still-popular socialism of the Nasser period—ironically, this was a repeat of Nasser's earlier attempt to play the Muslim Brothers against the Communists.[6] And like Nasser, Sadat got more than he had bargained for from this maneuver: Organizations that promoted Islam as a religion thrived, but so did those that promoted Islam as a political ideology, filling the vacuum left by the demise of the Arab Socialist Union. Islamist groups quickly gained a following among lower-class students in Egypt's overcrowded universities, particularly those from small towns and rural areas.[7] To them, Islamist organizations offered both a spiritual home and material support. What Sadat had seen as an antidote to Nasserism soon became a force in its own right, threatening his control.

The final piece of Sadat's domestic reforms was the launching of the so-called Open Door Policy, which entailed the reopening of the economy to free enterprise. It was a cautious opening in that Sadat did nothing to dismantle the public sector that had mushroomed during the 1960s. Nevertheless, he allowed the private sector to revive alongside public enterprises. The impact was considerable. Old money that had remained well hidden in Nasser's day found its way to new projects; a new wealthy class arose alongside the old one, thriving at least in part on government contracts. And a small-enterprise sector emerged, informal in large part and financed by the remittances of the two million Egyptians who had found jobs in the Persian Gulf states, Libya, and Iraq when those countries' economies boomed following the oil price increases of 1974. The new Egyptian economy was more vibrant than the old and provided real opportunities for many. But the transformation also entailed the fraying of the broad security net that had been cast by the Nasserite state, under the dual impact of a growing population and a lack of funding. In rural areas, land expropriated by Nasser started being returned to its former owners. The old socioeconomic cleavages of Egyptian society reappeared in full force.

It was a lot of domestic change for a country to absorb and for a president who wanted reform but not revolution to manage. Adding to the difficulty, Egyptians also had to adjust to a sea change in foreign policy that was taking place at the same time. Sadat had inherited a country deeply humiliated by its defeat in the 1967 war, especially by the loss of the Sinai. The country also remained tense because of the continuation of the endless, low-intensity confrontation with Israel in the Suez Canal area. But Sadat took action to reverse the situation. In 1973 he launched a surprise attack on Israel, which brought Egyptian troops across the Suez and back into the Sinai.[8] Although the attack was not the resounding military victory Egyptians claimed—the Israelis launched a counterattack across the canal—it was enough to break the stalemate in the war of attrition and relaunch negotiations, which would lead to the signing in 1979 of the peace treaty between Egypt and Israel brokered by President Jimmy Carter at Camp David.

The country did not absorb so much change in so short a time without strife. In early 1977, street riots broke out in Cairo and other cities in reaction to the dislocation created by the economic reform under the Open Door Policy and in particular against the elimination of subsidies on the price of basic commodities such as rice, sugar, and cooking oil. The violence caught the government by surprise, forcing it to reinstate the subsidies. Later in the year, Egyptians were stunned by Sadat's surprise decision to accept Israel's invitation to visit Jerusalem in order to restart the peace process. The historic trip was well received by many segments of the Egyptian population, but it turned others toward the Islamist organizations and was rejected by the overwhelming majority of Arab countries.

By the end of the 1970s, Egypt was a freer country than it had been in a long time, but it was also more deeply divided and essentially unstable. Sadat had set in motion many different processes that he could no longer control. The Open Door Policy had injected life into the Egyptian economy and created opportunities, but it had also caused deep discontent. Egyptians welcomed the end of the war of attrition with Israel and were proud of their success in the 1973 conflict, but many had reservations about the new relationship with the Jewish state. The influence of the Nasser-era socialist ideology had largely waned, but a politicized, militant brand of Islamism was on the rise.

Political liberalization initially strengthened Sadat's position. It allowed him to dismantle the Arab Socialist Union, which he could not totally control, build his own party, and decrease the influence of Nasserite ideas. But liberalization also made it easier for other, less tractable forces to emerge. Not only Islamist organizations but all kinds of opposition groups took advantage of the more liberal climate to express their criticism. The press was becoming more outspoken. New political parties were trying to organize. Sadat had envisaged a three-party system, with a strong centrist party he would control and two tame opposition groups to his right and left. What he got instead was democracy at its rawest, a process that was becoming truly competitive and whose outcome could not be ensured. Faced with this apparently unforeseen situation, Sadat backtracked into repression and censorship. He also started calling for popular referenda to give legitimacy to his decisions and manipulated the results to ensure that the rate of approval would always be higher than 99 percent.

The crisis came to a head in September 1981, when Sadat ordered the arrest of more than 1,500 political figures and then called for yet another referendum to bless the move. It showed, to nobody's surprise, that 99.5 percent of the population approved of the purge. Among those arrested were people who, in light of what transpired after Sadat's assassination, were undoubtedly extremists ready to use violence to pursue their goals. But many well-known political figures were also arrested, many of whom were guilty of nothing more than trying to organize political parties or expressing critical opinions in newspapers. Such detainees included Fuad Seraggeddine, a very elderly Wafd leader who was trying to revive the historical party, and Muhammed Hasanein Haikal, a newspaper editor who had been close to Nasser but who could in no way be thought to constitute a security threat.[9] Sadat's flirtation with liberalization and democracy was quickly coming to an end, and it was brought to an abrupt halt by his assassination on October 6 at the hands of Islamic extremists. Ironically, he was killed by Islamists in the army during a military parade commemorating one of his greatest triumphs, the crossing of the Suez in 1973.

The Sadat period provides the second instance of attempted democratization from the top in Egypt. Sadat did not put the process into motion in response to pressure that could not be resisted but because it suited his need to establish his own political identity and emerge from Nasser's shadow. There were groups in Egyptian society ready for liberalization after the Nasser years, and they started reorganizing into political parties and pressure groups once the climate became somewhat more favorable to political activity. But there is no evidence that Sadat was forced to open up political space by the strong pressure of organized groups.

There is plenty of evidence, however, that Sadat was extremely intolerant of any challenge to his authority—several analysts have concluded that he sought to establish more complete personal control over his government than even Nasser ever did. Democracy was fine as long as it remained a gift he bestowed on the country, but it was unacceptable when people started treating it as a right.

But even under a leader more willing to accept challenges to his authority, top-down democratization would inevitably have come up against the old dilemma of how to broaden political participation in a country where the distance between the mass of the population and the elite was as wide as it was in Egypt. Sadat had unified the country during the 1973 war, when he became the "hero of the crossing" and a symbol of a resurgent Egypt. But his economic policies helped broaden the divide between the elite and the rest of the population. Coupled with the decision to sign the peace treaty with Israel, these policies contributed to the rise of radical Islam and the further polarization of Egyptian society. This was the situation Hosni Mubarak inherited.

Mubarak and the Consolidation
of the Semi-Authoritarian State

At Sadat's death, Egypt could still be considered a country in transition from authoritarianism to democracy. Sadat had taken some very important steps. Despite the dramatic backsliding of the last year of his presidency, he had left behind a country that was much more open, politically as well as economically, than the one he had taken over at Nasser's death in 1970.

The view that Egypt might be a country in transition to democracy gained credence in the early period of Hosni Mubarak's presidency. Mubarak, Sadat's vice president, succeeded him in an orderly, constitutional process blessed by the military. He started his presidency on a conciliatory note that was remarkable under the circumstances.[10]

Sadat's assassination made it clear that Islamist groups had infiltrated the military, and that they were ready to turn to violence and willing to accept the consequences—the perpetrators of October 6 knew in advance that they could not possibly get away, shooting as they did in full view of a large audience, in an enclosed space, and surrounded by other soldiers. Inevitably, the assassination was followed by a wave of arrests of members of Islamist organizations, particularly the group to which Sadat's assassins belonged, al-Gama'a al-Islamiyya. But the rhetorical salvos fired indiscriminately against anybody daring to express reservations about government decisions, which had become a hallmark of Sadat's presidency, stopped, and most victims of Sadat's last purges were promptly released, as long as they had no ties to Islamist organizations.

In the following years more political parties were allowed to form, and independent newspapers were given more leeway. The parliamentary elections of 1984 were contested by six parties. The Muslim Brotherhood was not allowed to constitute itself as a political party, but candidates with known affiliation with the Brotherhood were allowed to compete through other parties. In general, Mubarak appeared determined to move toward greater political openness, although with less fanfare than his predecessor, in keeping with his cautious personality.

Two decades later, the reality is quite different. Egypt cannot possibly be considered a democratizing country any longer. Without reverting to the complete authoritarianism of the Nasser period, Mubarak has halted further transformation. Egypt has become a prime example of consolidated semi-authoritarianism. This does not mean that it is bound to remain politically static forever, but for the time being there is no indication that the present system cannot meet the challenges it faces and that it is thus unable to perpetuate itself. The consolidation of semi-authoritarianism can be traced through many processes, including the history of elections, the seemingly endless state of emergency, and the way the government has dealt with the challenge of political Islam.

The history of elections in post-Sadat Egypt tells a lot about the closing of the democratic space in the country, showing not only the regime's determination to hang on to power, but, equally important, the incapacity of the democratic opposition to become a meaningful force. After a positive start in 1984, elections under Mubarak showed a negative trend in the quality of the process and in the outcome, with the National Assembly becoming less pluralistic over time.

The 1984 and 1987 elections were, in retrospect, a high point, fostering the illusion that Mubarak intended to revive the democratization process. The 1984 election marked the return of the Wafd to the political scene. Surviving members of the old Wafd had tried to register the party anew as early as 1978, but were prevented from doing so by Sadat, who feared that the party might become a real contender because of its deep roots and historical legitimacy. Denied permission to register the party, the Wafd leaders took the matter to the courts, which in 1983 finally decided in the Wafd's favor. The reappearance of the Wafd caused a considerable stir in Egypt, particularly when the party entered into an informal electoral alliance with the Muslim Brotherhood, which had not, and has not to this day, been allowed to register. The fact that the government tolerated this alliance also seemed at the time to be a sign of democratic progress, perhaps a first step toward recognizing the Muslim Brotherhood as a legitimate political force. But election results were disappointing. The Wafd took 57 out of the 448 seats in the National Assembly, with 8 of the 57 going to Brotherhood candidates. No other opposition party won seats.

The 1987 elections saw a realignment of political parties. The Wafd ran on its own, winning only thirty-six seats. The Muslim Brotherhood, still outlawed, joined forces with the Socialist Labor Party and the Socialist Liberal Party; the alliance won fifty-seven seats, with more than half going to Muslim Brothers. This was the best performance ever for the opposition parties—and yet they took less than one-fourth of the seats.

By 1990, the situation was worsening. Convinced that the government was manipulating the elections, most opposition parties boycotted the vote. The Tagammu (National Progressive Unionist Party) broke ranks with the rest and participated, but it won only six seats. Eighty-three supposedly independent candidates also won seats, only to promptly join Mubarak's National Democratic Party (NDP), which thus gained almost complete control over the Assembly.

Having discovered that the election boycott only increased the National Democratic Party's control over the National Assembly, the opposition parties took part in the 1995 elections, but they won only fourteen seats, with an additional thirteen going to independents. Claiming electoral fraud, the opposition lodged some 900 appeals, and the courts invalidated the election of more than 200 deputies. Furthermore, in a remarkable show of independence that amounted to a declaration that the government was manipulating the elections, the courts decreed that in 2000 the polling places would be put under judicial supervision to ensure fairness.

In keeping with Egyptian procedural legalism (which is not matched by respect for the spirit of the law), the court order was faithfully implemented. To make it possible for judges to monitor the vote effectively, the 2000 elections were held on three separate days, with different regions voting each time. By the end of the process, the National Democratic Party controlled 388 of the 454 seats in the National Assembly. One of the most interesting aspects of the elections was the fact that the National Democratic Party had initially won only 175 seats, while independent candidates had secured some 250. Immediately, however, 213 of these independents joined the National Democratic Party, once again giving that party overwhelming control of the National Assembly. These so-called independents were simply National Democratic Party members who had been denied nominations by the party leadership, ran as independents against the official candidates and defeated them, and then rejoined the ranks of the party. It is a reflection of the National Democratic Party's grip on Egyptian politics that even these individuals, who had successfully defied the party leadership and got elected in their own right, could not envisage a political future for themselves outside the ranks of the ruling party.

A second important process in the consolidation of semi-authoritarianism in Egypt is the government's perpetuation of the state of emergency. Imposed in the days of uncertainty following the assassination of President Sadat, the state of emergency has never been lifted, neither in the quiet period of the 1980s, when the problem of Islamist extremism appeared under control and Mubarak was trying to project a reasonably liberal, open attitude, nor in the late 1990s, after a second wave of Islamist violence was well under control and many analysts were beginning to think that the radical groups were a spent force.

The state of emergency was a crucial tool in the consolidation of semi-authoritarianism because it allowed the government to contend that Egypt was a state of laws and democratic institutions while at the same time maintaining a free hand in the repression of the groups it deemed dangerous to the security of the state and in the end to its own political security. In particular, the state of emergency allowed the government to sideline the judiciary, transferring politically sensitive cases from civilian to military courts.

The Egyptian judiciary, despite its administrative obsolescence and glacial pace, traditionally has maintained a large measure of independence.[11] For example, as already noted in the present chapter, it reversed the government's decision not to allow the Wafd to register as a political party, found against the government in hundreds of lawsuits over election fraud, and went so far as to put the 2000 elections under judicial supervision. Significantly, the government felt it had to abide by these decisions, because not doing so would have destroyed the democratic facade. But in cases the government was not willing to lose, it could turn instead to the politically more compliant military courts set up under the state of emergency. Such courts have been called upon to try not only people accused of subversive acts or terrorism, but individuals who at most present nothing more than a political challenge to the regime. For example, the government turned to military courts to try Saad Eddine Ibrahim and his colleagues at the Ibn Khaldoun Center—an independent research and democracy promotion organization. The lack of fit between the charges brought against the defendants—such as illegally accepting foreign funds and making false statements in their research reports about Egypt's internal situation—and the decision to try the defendants in a military court was a clear example of the way in which military courts have been used by the government to silence political opposition and not just to curb dangerous subversive groups.

Another significant process in the consolidation of semi-authoritarianism in Egypt has been the way in which the government has dealt with the Islamist opposition—indiscriminately banning political organizations as well as violent subversive groups. There are three major components to political Islam in Egypt. The first, headline-grabbing one, consists of violent radical movements whose goal, at least in theory, is the replacement of a corrupt government with one faithful to the precepts of Islam. The best known of these groups is al-Gama'a al-Islamiyya, which gained prominence with the assassination of Sadat. These groups embrace an ideology that would make it impossible for them to become part of a democratic process, since the give-and-take and compromises of a democratic system are irreconcilable with the view of a state based on absolute principles. After gaining strength in the late 1970s, these groups suffered an initial setback at the hands of the government after Sadat's assassination, but revived and became very active and violent, particularly in Upper Egypt, in the 1990s. This particularly violent phase, which left hundreds of people dead, culminated in the gunning down of fifty-eight foreign tourists in Luxor in 1997. Since then, the influence of the more extremist groups has been declining, according to all analysts. The Egyptian public turned against the militants, in a combination of moral revulsion toward what most considered an act of mass murder and anger at the sharp decline in tourism—and, consequently, in domestic economic conditions—that followed the attack.[12]

The second component in the Egyptian configuration of political Islam is the Muslim Brotherhood, which is the best-established Islamist organization and also the most difficult to understand. The Muslim Brotherhood has been a political force in Egypt for more than 70 years and under all the different regime types the country has known. Today, its leaders claim to be committed to nonviolent methods, and undoubtedly they have shown their willingness to gain a political role through the democratic process. But there is no way of knowing whether the Brotherhood also pursues its goals in other ways, such as through ties to radical groups—there is no obvious line separating the Muslim Brotherhood and extremist organizations. The government has made sure the line remains blurred by refusing to allow the Brotherhood to become a political party; following the 1987 elections, it even forbade the Brothers to stand for election on the slate of another party. As a result, all of the Brotherhood's activities are illegal, and its members can be arrested for nonviolent political acts as well as violent ones.

Barred from electoral competition, the Muslim Brothers have tried to use other avenues to gain influence. In one move, they attempted to gain control over the professional syndicates, presenting their candidates in the internal elections for the leadership of each syndicate and winning. It is impossible to determine to what extent the vote for the Brotherhood candidates indicated widespread support for the organization and to what extent it was simply a statement of dissatisfaction with the government and its attempts to impose its control over all organizations. According to some estimates, Muslim Brothers never constituted more than 15 percent of the syndicates' membership, which suggests a protest vote.[13] The Brotherhood's success led the government to freeze elections within the professional syndicates to prevent more such victories.

But the government can do little to stop the influence the Muslim Brothers and other Islamist organizations exercise through the mosques and charitable organizations. Closing down mosques, except the occasional small, private mosque, is not a step a regime anxious to prove its Islamic credentials can undertake lightly. The paradoxical result is that Islamist organizations, of which the government is particularly afraid, have found it easier to continue to organize and prose-lytize than the secular political parties. The latter find they cannot hold meetings; the former always have the Friday gatherings. In this process of organizing and proselytizing through the mosques, the line separating moderate and more radical groups gets even more blurred. Islamic charities, particularly those providing health care and after-school programs for children, have also become channels through which moderate Islamist groups gain support.[14]

The third component of political Islam in Egypt is the official, state-aligned Islamic establishment, centered at Al-Azhar University. This element represents the government's efforts to combat the inroads of independent Islamist groups by becoming more Islamist itself.[15] Sadat started the trend by making public display of his religiosity, casting himself as the "pious president" in the public eye. Mubarak continued it not by underlining his personal piety but by allowing the Islamic establishment to gain more influence.

Political Islam in Egypt is thus far from a monolithic entity, but ranges all the way from radical, violent groups to those closely allied with the state. Mubarak has turned to the latter for support, but has indiscriminately repressed all independent groups, radical and moderate alike. This random repression is explained by the nature of the regime, not by the threat these groups pose, because many only challenge Mubarak's political hegemony, not the security of the state.

Egypt's Semi-Authoritarianism and the Nature of Politics

In this discussion of the consolidation of Egypt's semi-authoritarianism, I have cast President Mubarak and the Egyptian government in the role of villains. This is correct in the sense that the closure of democratization and the consolidation of semi-authoritarianism have been the result of deliberate government policies over which Mubarak has had great influence. But there is another component to this story, namely the fact that the consolidation of semi-authoritarianism has been greatly facilitated by the elitist character of political organizations in Egypt and their incapacity to forge links with the Egyptian population.[16] The exceptions here are probably some of the Islamist groups, although their banned status makes reliable information difficult to come by.

The fact that the Wafd and other political parties have gained so few seats in the National Assembly cannot be attributed solely to government manipulation. That certainly has played a role, but the government's task has been made much easier by the weakness of these parties and their incapacity to craft a platform with popular appeal. First, most Egyptian political parties are gerontocracies. In the opposition parties as in the government, leaders occupy their position for life. For instance, when the new Wafd was launched, it chose as its leader Fuad Seraggeddine, who had started his political career in the old Wafd before Nasser rose to power. Seraggeddine remained the party's leader until his death in 2000, when he was replaced by a man almost as old. Other parties have the same problem of aging leaders and even aging members.

Out of touch because of the age of their leaders, the parties are also out of touch because of their platforms. The Wafd again provides an example. Its main message is that Egypt needs constitutional reform, which is what its leaders tell any visitor willing to listen, and, more important, what they tell the Egyptian public. Whether or not the Egyptian constitution needs amending, this is not a message likely to attract many voters, least of all the mass of impoverished people whose immediate problems are a lack of jobs, poor housing in overcrowded cities and towns with crumbling infrastructure, and the collapse of the health and education systems. Constitutional reform is not a top priority for many. The lack of a relevant message is not just the Wafd's problem. Other parties are facing the same difficulty.

The weakness of the legal opposition leaves the way open for the National Democratic Party, which does not have a strong popular message either, but can get support through patronage and voter intimidation. The weaknesses of the legal opposition also provide more political space for the outlawed Islamist organizations, which have both a moral message appealing to many in a conservative society and a demonstrated ability to deliver sorely needed tangible goods, such as education and health care.

Looking Ahead

For foreign governments and organizations interested in promoting democracy, the Egyptian regime presents a dismal picture because it is so consolidated. Furthermore, the weakness of the legal opposition and the ambiguous nature of even the moderate Islamist organizations such as the Muslim Brotherhood suggest that, if change takes place, it may not lead to democracy. One of the most troubling questions about Egypt is how much support there really is in the country for organizations promoting political Islam—lack of democracy makes this impossible to fathom. Another is how to determine where the radical, violent Islamist organizations end and moderate forces amenable to participation in a democratic system begin. The government, which could find answers to both questions, is not interested in knowing.

Egyptians who support neither the present regime nor Islamist organizations believe that change must come from the top and envision two alternative versions of how it could happen, neither necessarily leading to democracy. The first version assumes that at some point the president may decide it is time for liberalization, as Sadat did in the 1970s, when he took the initiative to open up the political system in the absence of strong pressure from below. It is unclear what, in the present situation, could convince the president to promote change from the top after two decades in power, and even less clear what could convince him to introduce more than cosmetic changes and allow himself to be challenged. The second version also envisages change coming from the top, but as the result of the emergence of a new generation. This version is based on an assessment that neither Mubarak nor other members of his generation have shown interest in political reform and that Mubarak is far too cautious to do anything that might disrupt his control. This scenario is based on hope, rather than on evidence that there is a cohort of Young Turks waiting in the wings. Curiously, the most frequently expounded version of this democracy-through-the-next-generation scenario casts Gamal Mubarak, one of the president's two sons, in the role of main protagonist. The idea that democratization in Egypt could be revived by a dynastic succession in a republican setting is oxymoronic at best.

For their part, the United States and other members of the international community have not been anxious to put real pressure for democratic change on the Mubarak regime, choosing stability over political reform. For the United States in particular, Egypt has proven a reliable ally. Even after September 2001, Washington remains uncertain whether terrorism in Egypt is best combated by helping Mubarak repress Islamist organizations or by embarking on a long-term and potentially destabilizing project of democracy promotion. As a result, the democracy promotion activities the United States funds in Egypt are somewhat pro forma, while those of European countries are only slightly more assertive. Furthermore, it has proven very difficult to design and implement meaningful democratization programs in Egypt. Activities to reform Egyptian institutions have met with a lot of resistance (for example, a U.S. initiative to strengthen the Egyptian parliament) or have simply failed to have an impact on the functioning of the notorious Egyptian bureaucracy (as was the case of a U.S. decentralization program). Civil-society assistance also falters because truly independent organizations are increasingly fearful of taking foreign money—this was one of the accusations against Ibrahim's Ibn Khaldoun Center—while those that accept foreign grants with the blessing of the government become part of the patronage system rather than independent representatives of civil society.

Prospects for political renewal thus appear extremely limited in Egypt at present. It is impossible at this point to predict what will trigger change. It is possible to predict, however, that a new process of change will lead to democracy only if it solves the old dilemma of how to bring together, in a society that is sharply divided economically and socially, an elite that aspires to modernize and democratize the country and a large, impoverished, and poorly educated population that aspires above all to survive and is open to radical appeals.

2

Azerbaijan:
The Semi-Authoritarianism of Decay

IT IS A TESTIMONY to the enthusiasm for political reform of the 1990s, particularly in the former communist world, that the issue of democracy should even be under discussion in Azerbaijan. A decaying republic of the Soviet Union, with an ailing oil industry and not much to replace it, Azerbaijan did not gain its independence on a wave of nation-building fervor but, rather, drifted into it because of the disintegration of the Soviet Union. Nothing in the short history of the country favors democratic development. Azerbaijan was at war with neighboring Armenia when it gained its independence, and to this day the conflict is unresolved, with about 15 percent of the territory of former Soviet Azerbaijan now in Armenian hands and tens of thousands of refugees living in precarious conditions. War and the state-building imperative continue to dominate the country, but the effects of the former undermine the objectives—such as well-defined borders—of the latter. A former Communist Party boss is back in power, perceived by many as the savior in a period of chaos. Democratic political organizations, by contrast, are weak and dependent on outside aid.

The economy is in shambles, and experience elsewhere shows that this augurs poorly for democracy. The population has experienced a precipitous decline in living standards and income security. Furthermore, the best hope for economic revival is provided by the oil industry, which has benefited already from billions in foreign investment, with the possibility of much more to come if the Caspian Sea deposits prove as rich as some projections suggest. While increased oil revenue could reduce immediate pressure on the government, it would also perpetuate the already serious problem of corruption and encourage the consolidation of an already highly centralized political system. Historically, oil-producing countries find it very difficult to escape the political and economic imbalances typical of the "petro-state."[1]

On the surface, independent Azerbaijan appears to have accepted the new international expectation that any country can become democratic no matter what the initial conditions are, as long as its political elite chooses that path. Under the leadership of a former communist boss, Heydar Aliyev, Azerbaijan portrays itself as a Europe-oriented country that has embraced democracy wholeheartedly and is ready to join the North Atlantic Treaty Organization and other European institutions.

The reality is quite different. Azerbaijan has a formally democratic system, with a constitution proclaiming respect for civil and political freedoms. But its leaders—including those in the opposition—are products of the Soviet system, with little familiarity with the give-and-take of democratic politics and little apparent desire to learn. Aliyev has mastered the language of democracy with great ease—his performances before Western audiences are impeccable—but he does not practice what he preaches. The regime organizes regular multi-party elections, but it successfully limits competition. It allows the operation of a so-called independent press—in reality a party-aligned press—but it still dominates the flow of information. The state no longer controls all economic assets, but it controls oil and gas, the major sources of revenue, while the political elite surrounding Aliyev, including his own family, has succeeded in establishing its hold on other important enterprises. But for Aliyev's age and poor health, there would be no reason to doubt his capacity to maintain power for a long time to come. Aliyev's goal appears to be an institutionalized semi-authoritarian regime such as Egypt's, perpetuated through the succession to the presidency of his son Ilham.

Aliyev may not have the time to follow through with his plan and consolidate semi-authoritarian rule, but this failure would probably not be a victory for democracy. Pulled between internal forces that make democracy an unlikely outcome and external ones that prescribe and promote it, Azerbaijan today fits the profile of a semi-authoritarian state. It is also possible that this is the best outcome that can be expected in the country for the foreseeable future, given the weakness of the factors that might promote a real democratic transformation.

A Sketch of Independent Azerbaijan

Soviet Republic Status

Azerbaijan's history as an independent country is short but complicated. Azeri nationalism, which flourished at the end of the nineteenth century and came to fruition during a two-year period of independence following the Bolshevik Révolution, revived in the 1980s in the new climate created by President Mikhail Gorbachev's glasnost policy. But for the disintegration of the Soviet Union, however, it is highly doubtful that Azerbaijan would have gained its independence in 1991 solely on the strength of strong nationalist sentiments.[2]

The country has little on which to build a common identity.[3] The memory of the first Azerbaijani republic has been a rallying point for some, but for others it is a source of division, since the short-lived republic was torn asunder by strife between nationalists and socialists. The population is not ethnically homogeneous, with 20 percent consisting of non-Azeris.[4] The predominant religion is Shi'i Islam, but seventy years of communism reduced the importance of religion.[5] This may be a good thing, because Shi'ism creates a tie between the Azeris and Iranians, strengthened by the fact that the population of northern Iran is ethnically Azeri.[6] Such links to Iran, however, are not welcome by the majority of Azeri nationalists, who favor strong ties with Turkey instead. Azerbaijanis speak a Turkic dialect, and Azeri nationalists have historically identified with Turkey, and through it with Europe, rather than with Iran. Turks, however, are Sunni rather than Shi'i Muslims.

Azeri nationalism was initially directed against the Soviet Union and took the form of demands for greater autonomy. With the Azerbaijan Communist Party still in power in the capital, Baku, and the Soviet

Union intact, nationalists could not organize formal political parties, but had to rely instead on so-called informal organizations. The most important and elaborate of these groups was the Azerbaijan Popular Front, which was officially launched in March 1989; by this time, it had some 200 cells in Baku alone. Soon, the organization was agitating for complete independence, rather than simply greater autonomy. The conflict with Armenia that erupted in 1988, however, made independence a secondary issue again, particularly since the Azeris hoped that Moscow would help curb Armenian expansionism.[7]

The Azeri-Armenian conflict stems from the mixture of ethnic and religious groups in a relatively small geographic area of the Caucasus. The territory of the Soviet Republic of Azerbaijan included two autonomous republics: Nagorno-Karabagh, an Armenian enclave within Azerbaijan; and Nakhichevan, an Azeri enclave caught between Armenia and Iran and separated from the rest of Azerbaijan by a strip of Armenian territory. In February 1988, Armenian representatives in the National Council of Nagorno-Karabagh voted to unify their region with Armenia. Immediately, the Armenians became Azerbaijan's main enemies, while the Soviet government, which was still trying to maintain its vast empire, came to be perceived as the best guarantor against the annexation of Nagorno-Karabagh by Armenia. The perception that Azerbaijan needed Soviet help against Armenia helped bolster the previously fading influence of the Azerbaijani Communists.

The February 1988 decision by Nagorno-Karabagh to seek annexation to Armenia led to anti-Armenian violence in Azerbaijan and to the expulsion of Azeris from most of Nagorno-Karabagh and from some districts bordering on Armenia. Consequently, a large Azeri refugee population was created that still has not been able to return home. The annexation decision also led to fighting in Nagorno-Karabagh and along the Armenia–Azerbaijan border; a blockade by Azerbaijan of highway, railroad, and electrical power links to Armenia; and a blockade by Armenia of links to Nakhichevan.

The Azerbaijan Communist Party and its first secretary, Ayaz Mutalibov, initially reacted to the growing nationalism of the Azerbaijan Popular Front and to the war in Nagorno-Karabagh by pulling closer to Moscow, counting on it for protection against both Azeri nationalists and Armenian separatists. But the failed coup against Mikhail

Gorbachev in August 1991 made it clear to the Azerbaijani Communists that they could no longer count on Moscow's protection. Faced with large nationalist demonstrations in Baku, in November 1991 First Secretary Mutalibov disbanded the Azerbaijan Supreme Soviet, replacing it with an appointed National Council in which posts were equally divided between Communists and nationalists. Events in Moscow again trumped the domestic process of change, however. In December the Soviet Union dissolved, and Azerbaijan suddenly became independent. Mutalibov, still reluctant to give up whatever protection Moscow might still be able to offer, immediately enrolled Azerbaijan in the Russian-dominated Commonwealth of Independent States, an action that generated resentment among Azeri nationalists.

Independence

The first six months of independence were chaotic. Mutalibov was forced to resign in March 1992, after Armenians took over an important town in Karabagh, with more than a thousand Azeris dying in the fighting.[8] Yacub Mamedov, president of the supposedly disbanded Supreme Soviet, became acting president, as prescribed by the Soviet-era constitution still in force. But Mamedov did not have sufficient support to stay in power. He was part of the old Communist establishment and was considered particularly corrupt. In an effort to recast himself as a reformer, Mamedov included some opposition members in his cabinet, but this did not decrease the hostility of the nationalists. Most important, the situation in Karabagh continued to deteriorate. The final blow came on May 9, 1992, when the Armenians captured the last town the Azeris controlled in the region. In the tumultuous weeks that followed, the Azerbaijan Popular Front launched campaigns of protest, Mutalibov tried to stage a comeback, and Mamedov was forced to resign. Once again citizens took to the streets, Mutalibov fled, and a leader of the Popular Front became speaker of the parliament and acting president for the three weeks remaining before the elections scheduled for June 7.

The presidential elections of June 1992 were the high point for democracy in Azerbaijan's transition: Foreign diplomats and observers from the Organization for Security and Cooperation in Europe concluded that the elections, though marred by irregularities, were not controlled or manipulated by any party. Abulfaz Elchibey, leader of the Azerbaijan Popular Front, emerged as the clear winner, with 60 percent of the vote; his closest competitor received only 30 percent.

Events of the following year unfortunately demonstrated that the nationalist leadership was not even remotely prepared to govern the country, particularly under the difficult circumstances it faced. It also showed that a strong popular mandate, which Elchibey had initially possessed, is not a sufficient basis on which to build a democratic state —at least not during a war and not when the fledgling democratic government is in competition against a well-established, formerly communist party machine. Elchibey had no political experience and no control over the administrative apparatus. The Azerbaijan Popular Front had many supporters but was a weak organization. It had come to power because the disintegration of the Soviet Union and the defeats in the war in Nagorno-Karabagh had weakened the Communist leadership, not because of its own capacity to organize. Making things worse, Elchibey did not have time to focus on consolidating his government and putting into place a program of reform, because war consumed his attention. He had been elected on an ambitious platform, promising full civil liberties, full cultural rights for all national groups, the freeing of state and legal systems from the ideological influence of the Communist Party, the creation of a market economy, and environmental protection.[9] But once in office, he was consumed by the problem of consolidating his power and fighting a war.

Despite the support it enjoyed as a nationalist movement, Elchibey's Azerbaijan Popular Front did not control the administrative apparatus, much less the military forces engaged in the war in Nagorno-Karabagh. The administration was controlled by former Communists, who still constituted a powerful network of experienced politicians even though their party was discredited. The military forces engaged in Nagorno-Karabagh were also outside Elchibey's control. Azerbaijan had been plunged into war without a real army. The war was being fought instead by inexperienced troops, loosely organized into units that looked more like the private militias of improvised commanders than the units of a disciplined national army. Most important among these groups were those under the command of Surat Huseinov, a self-styled colonel who proved more adept at forging alliances with political figures and officers of the Russian garrison still present in Azerbaijan than at fighting the Armenians.

Trying to reassert his power against a commander with manifest political ambitions, Elchibey dismissed Huseinov in February 1993. The latter refused to comply and instead withdrew his troops from the front, sought refuge with the Russian garrison, and, in late May, marched on Baku armed with equipment the departing Russian garrison had turned over to him instead of the government. Unable to control the situation, Elchibey resigned and withdrew to Nakhichevan, his home area.

The Return of Aliyev

The beneficiary of the confrontation between Elchibey and Huseinov was Heydar Aliyev, a man whose long career in the Soviet Union included leadership of the Azerbaijan Committee for State Security, or KGB, and service as first secretary of the Communist Party of Azerbaijan. He eventually rose to membership in the Soviet Politburo before being sidelined by Gorbachev. During the Elchibey presidency Aliyev made a political comeback, maneuvering his way into the speakership of the National Council. When Elchibey was forced to flee Baku as Huseinov advanced, Aliyev became acting president under the succession rules established by the Soviet-era constitution still in effect. Aliyev immediately named Huseinov prime minister, not because the two were allies but because he wanted to avoid an armed confrontation.

Azerbaijanis appeared relieved that the country was spared more fighting. People did not take to the streets to protest Elchibey's demise because they had lost confidence in his abilities. When Aliyev, trying to give his regime a veneer of legitimacy, organized a public referendum of confidence on the Elchibey government in August 1993, Azerbaijanis overwhelmingly voted against the former president, whom they had come to associate with military defeat and chaos. Still, Aliyev took no chances. When he decided to complete his legitimization by organizing presidential elections in October, he controlled the process tightly and then announced Soviet-style results: a 98.8 percent majority in his favor, with 96 percent of the voters participating. Understandably, international monitors, including those from the Organization for Security and Cooperation in Europe, dismissed the election as neither free nor fair.

Despite his considerable political experience, contacts, and organizational skills, even Aliyev had trouble consolidating his power in the chaos of Azerbaijan. He faced several coup attempts, one as late as 1996, before he finally gained full control of the domestic political situation. He then proceeded to consolidate a semi-authoritarian regime.

The Consolidation of Semi-Authoritarianism

Nothing in the events that followed Aliyev's return to power indicates that the momentous events of the period, above all the collapse of the Soviet Union and the demise of communist ideology, caused him to rethink his approach to politics. Aliyev did not become a democrat, not even a social democrat. Nor did he apparently come to see and accept the potential for growth and development deriving from a market economy. Judging by his actions, he continued to believe that the way to govern the country was through a strong political machine that allowed no real competition and that economic assets should also remain under the control of the political elite.

Yet the regime Aliyev built cannot be defined as completely authoritarian. He was too pragmatic to push for the reinstatement of such a system. Furthermore, he did not need to do so. Faced with only a weak, fragmented, and rather inept opposition, the new government could afford to maintain a democratic facade, albeit a flimsy one. There was no crude attempt to reinstate the single-party state. Opposition political parties continued to function, although they were subject to some degree of harassment. The so-called independent press, in reality an array of publications controlled by the political parties, continued to publish. Nongovernmental organizations (NGOs) were allowed to proliferate and to receive funds from international donors. As a result, the country quickly developed the array of human rights groups, women's organizations, professional associations, and civic education groups of the kind favored by international democracy-promotion organizations in the 1990s. Indeed, the government even tolerated the fact that the overwhelming majority of these groups were affiliated with one or another opposition political party. Rather than openly repress them, the government tried to play the game, and set up its own organizations.

Establishing Political Control

Under a relatively benevolent facade, the control of Aliyev and his New Azerbaijan Party became increasingly strong. The new government perfected the art of conducting elections without allowing any real competition. It was greatly helped in this effort by the loss of support suffered by the Azerbaijan Popular Front during its one year in power, a situation exacerbated in 2000 by the death of Elchibey and the ensuing factional struggle for control of the party.

The pattern of electoral manipulation was established early. After having himself elected president in a rough-and-ready fashion in 1993, Aliyev proceeded to regularize the process. Enactment of a new electoral law in August 1995 was followed by the first multiparty parliamentary elections in November. At the same time, a new constitution was submitted to a referendum. However, the draft document was published only a few days before the vote, leaving no time for discussion and certainly none for comments and amendments. The elections, according to a report by the Organization for Security and Cooperation in Europe, were "multiparty and multi-candidate," but "the election campaign, the voting and the counting of ballots did not correspond to internationally accepted norms in many respects." This, the report concluded, deprived "the electorate of the possibility to exercise fully its right to choose freely its representatives."[10] Dexterous manipulation of the electoral law by a government-controlled electoral commission led to the disqualification of one-third of the opposition political parties and 60 percent of their candidates before the election, but a certain amount of ballot stuffing was added for good measure. Predictably, the constitution won overwhelming approval, and opposition parties gained only a few seats. Trying to preserve the facade, the government allowed so-called independent candidates to win more seats than Aliyev's New Azerbaijan Party. Given the election commission's careful vetting of all candidates and its rejection of more than half of them, the label "independent" should not be taken at face value; most of these legislators were consistently loyal to Aliyev.

The pattern of election manipulation established in the 1995 balloting has been repeated in every subsequent election. In the 1998 presidential election, international observers noted some improvements, including a revised election law and the formal abolition of media censorship, but concluded that "in significant respects, the conditions for democratic elections do not exist yet in Azerbaijan."[11] They also claimed that "there was no clear dividing line between state affairs and the incumbent's campaign."[12]

Municipal elections in December 1999 were also seriously flawed. As for the November 2000 parliamentary elections, they represented "a continuation of a pattern of seriously flawed elections in Azerbaijan that fail to meet even minimum international standards." Indeed, they even failed to comply with Azerbaijani election laws.[13]

After coming to power in the midst of chaos, Aliyev and his New Azerbaijan Party thus succeeded in establishing a firm grip on the country. Aliyev's own political acumen and organizational experience, coupled with his ruthless disregard for the spirit of democracy and the letter of electoral law, are major reasons for this success. But he was also aided by the weakness of the opposition parties and the almost complete absence of a mobilized civil society conscious of its rights.[14]

The Azerbaijan Popular Front, which had genuine support in the 1980s and at the time of independence, was greatly weakened by the failure of the Elchibey government to handle the admittedly difficult situation of 1992 and 1993. After Elchibey's death in 2000, the party was further undermined by a succession fight. Ali Karimov (who later changed his name to Ali Kerimli) eventually established control, but the party only won six seats (with an additional seat going to a dissident faction) in the 2000 parliamentary elections. It was a dismal showing that cannot be attributed entirely to Aliyev's machinations. Other parties were even weaker. All told, the opposition only controlled 17 of the 125 parliamentary seats, and remained fragmented.

Efforts to strengthen the opposition by creating a united front have been only partly successful. The Democratic Congress, a coalition formed in the late 1990s, has led an uncertain existence. In January 2002, a broader group, the Movement of the United Opposition, was launched, with twenty-five parties joining. The basic problem remains unchanged, however—the major parties are all dominated by strong personalities unwilling to yield to others. Most parties, furthermore, are divided into factions and are prone to splitting. Indeed, old age and poor health remained more serious threats to Aliyev than the opposition parties.

Civil society organizations are also small, without deep roots or popular followings. Most are closely allied with political parties, with even the government party having set up its own groups. Despite support from international donors, who have provided both funding and training, NGOs have not become a significant force in Azerbaijan. They certainly have not become sources of political change and democratic renewal.

Establishing Economic Control

Behind a free-market facade, the pattern of unchallenged control that had shaped the political sphere was replicated in the domestic economy. Two factors allowed the new government to do this: oil and corruption. Together, they gave the ruling elite unchallenged control, relegating the free market to inconsequential, marginal activities. They also condemned the economy to stagnation, lack of foreign investment, and increasing dependency on oil.

After 1991, the economy of Azerbaijan experienced the double shock that sooner or later affected every Soviet successor state: First, it had to convert from being a component of the integrated Soviet economy to functioning as a freestanding entity in competition with other countries for access to its former markets. Second, it faced the difficult problem of making the transition to a market economy. Aliyev addressed the first problem by turning to oil for salvation, and the second by maintaining control over most assets in the hands of the political elite, including Aliyev's own family.

Oil is Azerbaijan's main and most immediately exploitable asset. It was oil that built up the country in the late nineteenth century, fueling the nationalist movement that led to the brief period of independence following the collapse of imperial Russia. An important resource in the early part of the Soviet period, the Azerbaijani deposits were later neglected, as Moscow's strategy shifted to developing deposits in Siberia and leaving Caspian Sea oil as a long-term reserve. When it again became independent in 1991, Azerbaijan rekindled the interest of the Western oil companies. In September 1994, President Aliyev signed a thirty-year, $8 billion agreement with the Azerbaijan International Operating Company, a consortium of companies from Azerbaijan, Western countries, Russia, Japan, and Turkey, to develop the Chirag oil fields and the related infrastructure. New contracts followed in rapid succession. For the government, oil and gas became the keys to economic survival, the means to build a new economic system, and the avenue leading the country out of the Russian sphere of influence and toward the West.

Oil revenue has often proven a mixed blessing at best—some have called it a curse—for many oil-rich countries where large-scale oil exploitation started when other economic sectors were still weak, and before strong administrative institutions and a democratic system of government were in place. On the basis of the experience of Venezuela, which is discussed in a later chapter of the present study, Terry Lynn Karl concluded that problematic outcomes are especially likely

> if petroleum exploitation coincides with modern state-building, as has so often been the case. Where this historical coincidence occurs, petro-states become marked by especially skewed institutional capacities. The initial bargaining between foreign companies anxious to secure new sources of crude and local rulers eager to cement their own base of support—whatever their mutual benefits—leaves a legacy of overly-centralized political power, strong networks of complicity between public and private sector actors, highly uneven mineral-based development subsidized by oil rents and the replacement of domestic tax revenues and other sources of earned income by petrodollars. In effect, this alters the framework for decision-making in a manner that further encourages and reinforces these initial patterns, producing a vicious cycle of negative development outcomes.[15]

Azerbaijan fits this profile perfectly. The large-scale growth in oil exploitation coincided with the process of state building and also with the collapse of the old, Soviet-based economy. Gross domestic product (GDP) declined precipitously, from $9.8 billion in 1987 to $3.4 billion in 1997, as a result of the economic dislocation caused by the structural problems of the economy, the fighting in Nagorno-Karabagh, and the dissolution of the Soviet Union. All areas of production were affected. Despite the favorable prospects, even oil suffered from the deterioration of the old infrastructure and the depletion of the fields under exploitation. By 1998 per capita income was only $490, with 68 percent of the population living below the poverty line. It would have been a rare government not to turn to oil for salvation under the circumstances.

This was the second time in the history of Azerbaijan that the development of the oil industry coincided with an attempt at state building. The first Azerbaijani oil boom, which began in 1872, brought about both economic growth and political change. It created a wealthy elite and led to the formation of a political movement embracing the nineteenth-century European ideal of liberal nationalism, which found a ready audience among better educated people and the members of the new entrepreneurial class. Oil, nationalism, state–building, and democracy went hand in hand for a brief period. It will never be known whether this promising beginning could have led to the consolidation of a democratic state, because history took a dramatically different turn. An independent republic, declared in 1918, was swallowed up within two years by the turmoil of the Bolshevik Revolution and incorporated into the Soviet Union.

This convergence of oil development, nationalism, and democratization is unlikely to be repeated. Contemporary nationalism is more narrowly ethnic and distinctly less liberal than its nineteenth-century counterpart everywhere, but particularly in the region affected by the Soviet system, with its heavy emphasis on ethnic identities. Today, Azeri nationalism also has to contend with the revival of political Islam, which offers Azerbaijanis another, and likewise illiberal, identity. The character of the oil industry had also changed drastically in a century. The early Azerbaijani oil industry was a pioneering concern. Although it soon attracted relatively large investments from Moscow, as well as from outside Russia, it also left room initially for small-scale operators, both in the production of oil and in its refining into kerosene. Oil and related industries thus encouraged the development of a small, indigenous entrepreneurial class. Today's multibillion-dollar contracts and capital-intensive oil industry do not foster domestic entrepreneurship, however. Finally, state building is also a different undertaking at present. While the Azerbaijani state is new and fragile as an independent entity, it is also the heir to a Soviet tradition of strong, centralized administration, state intervention in economic management, and state control in all areas. Building the new Azerbaijani state is thus an altogether different process. It is difficult to envisage that these factors could somehow combine to generate a democratic outcome.

Nor is there much evidence that the oil sector is fueling the overall process of economic growth that might in the long run provide the support for a less centralized political system.

After a few years of precipitous decline, the economy is beginning to make some progress toward stability. An economic reform program supported by the International Monetary Fund (IMF) and the World Bank was only put in place in 1995; by 1998 inflation seemed under control and economic growth had finally resumed, although GDP remained only one-third of what it had been in the mid-1980s. But within the framework of stabilization, little economic reform had actually taken place, something that even the bland and ever-optimistic language of IMF and World Bank reports could not hide.[16]

The scope of the reforms international financial institutions consider essential to stimulate broad-based growth in Azerbaijan is daunting. An IMF document outlining economic objectives for the period 1999–2001 sums up the problem eloquently: In addition to continuing macroeconomic policies that ensure a stable financial environment, in that three-year period Azerbaijan was expected to carry out deep reform of the public sector; reform tax administration and tax policy; restructure the banking system; develop a market for government and private securities; deepen and broaden the privatization process; reform public enterprises, including the state oil company SOCAR; and complete the privatization of agricultural land and the distribution of land titles, as well as put in place essential infrastructure.[17] This is the typical list of painful reforms countries emerging from communism face today. With the prospect of substantial and growing oil revenue, the Azerbaijani government had little incentive to embark down this difficult path, and indeed it did little. The state could become rich even if its citizens were poor. An interim "Poverty

Reduction Strategy Paper" prepared by the Azerbaijani government in May 2001 with the help of the World Bank and the IMF confirmed this picture of continuing devastating poverty.[18]

In addition to decreasing the incentive for reform, the expected rapid increase in oil revenue poses other obstacles to broad-based economic growth and political democracy. First, it perpetuates centralization. Political decentralization, as opposed to administrative deconcentration of services, is impossible to implement unless the lower levels of government are able to raise and manage a significant part of their own revenues independently. In a country that has lost much of its productive capacity and where only the oil industry is thriving, it is going to be very difficult for these local governments to establish such financial autonomy. Tax reform can help by carving out certain sources of revenue for local governments. However, tax reform does not create revenue. Thus, so long as privatization only affects small businesses, land redistribution and registration are incomplete, and per capita income remains as low as it is, no source of revenue can compete with the oil sector, and the weight of the central government will remain overwhelming.

To the typical problems caused by the "paradox of plenty," Azerbaijan adds another problem, in that it is still unclear how large the oil deposits in the country really are, and thus how much revenue the government can expect. After signing the much-heralded initial contract, the Azerbaijan International Operating Company consortium struck a number of dry wells, a development that raised questions about the accuracy of earlier estimates. The precipitous decline in oil prices in the late 1990s and their volatility in subsequent years has added to the uncertainty.

Compounding the oil-induced problems is the fact that Azerbaijan still lacks a genuine private sector. As in many other formerly communist countries, privatization was a corrupt process, closely controlled by the president and his associates. The most valuable economic assets moved from the control of members of the political elite in their capacity as officials of the state to the control of members of the political elite as entrepreneurs in their own names. Transparency International rates Azerbaijan one of the most corrupt countries in the world.[19] The effects are seen not only in the growing income inequality—again a typical phenomenon in postcommunist societies—

but also in the flight of foreign investors, who find conditions extremely difficult. A significant number of Turkish investors, for example, pulled out in 2000, claiming that corruption and government interference made it impossible for them to do business profitably. Corruption may stanch healthy economic development, but it helps the political and business elites maintain their hold on power.

War

Azerbaijan's political and economic transitions took place against the backdrop of war, further reducing the possibility of a democratic outcome and rapid economic recovery. From the beginning, the war in Nagorno-Karabagh inflamed ethnic and religious intolerance on all sides. There were violent incidents targeting the Armenian minority in many Azerbaijani cities, convincing many Armenians to seek refuge across the border. Azeris were expelled from Nagorno-Karabagh and adjoining districts, as well as from Armenia. The possibility that Azeri nationalism would take an all-embracing civic or liberal democratic character, rather than a particularistic ethnic one, was thus obliterated.

There were other lasting consequences as well. Fighting a losing war, the Azerbaijan Popular Front saw its support and legitimacy vanish. This opened the way for Aliyev's return to power and left him without a strong and credible opposition. Finally, the war aggravated the economic problems caused by the dismantling of the integrated Soviet economy and by the typical initial difficulties created by market reform. War, in other words, was a major obstacle to a democratic transition, although by no means the only one.

By 1993 Armenia had occupied the territory it wanted, and the following year Azerbaijan, where Aliyev was still trying to consolidate his rule, accepted a Russian-mediated cease-fire that recognized the facts on the ground and left Armenians in control of the conquered territory. Peace talks were subsequently held under the auspices of the Minsk group of the Organization for Security and Cooperation in Europe. After some initial progress, those talks stalled. Even in the absence of fighting, the unresolved conflict prevented Azerbaijan from settling into a normal situation. The presence of large numbers of refugees and the loss of 16 percent of the country's territory are constant reminders of the effects of war. The memory of 1993, when Armenia was winning the war and Azerbaijani militias were marching on Baku rather than the enemy, makes the population more reluctant to turn decisively against a government that has brought stability, even if it is undemocratic and corrupt.

As Good as It Gets?

Nothing in the situation in Azerbaijan encourages an observer to feel optimistic about the country's political prospects. Azerbaijan is not a new and thus imperfect democracy, still trying to put institutions in place, reform its laws, and in general learn to play by the rules. It is a country governed by a political elite that wants all power and knows how to get it. The opposition political parties are organizationally weak and do not have messages and programs likely to garner enthusiastic support. Civil society, regarded by donors as the best hope for democratic change under adverse political conditions, is weak, and furthermore has little independence from the political parties. Although the possibility of civil society groups playing a more important role in the future cannot be dismissed out of hand, it is unlikely that existing organizations, deeply enmeshed in the unhappy politics of the Azerbaijani parties, will be the ones to do so.

It is tempting to blame the emergence of the semi-authoritarian Azerbaijani state on the incompetence of Elchibey, the nationalists' lack of political experience, and above all Aliyev's authoritarian bent, which is well rooted in the KGB and the Communist Party. Undoubtedly these are important factors. So are the war and the consequences of oil and corruption. But the most serious problem is that democracy was not a major concern or demand of the major politically active groups in the country before independence, and it is not to this day. The issues that determined the political dynamics of Azerbaijan in the 1990s were relations with Russia and Armenia, the conflict in Nagorno-Karabagh, and the struggle to establish control over the new country and its resources. In a few instances, large numbers of Azerbaijanis tried to weigh in on these issues by taking to the streets. However, most of the time they stood by as members of the elite fought among themselves. Furthermore, the frightening events of mid-1993, with the country appearing close to civil war, territory being lost to Armenia, thousands of Azerbaijanis becoming war refugees, and income levels dropping dramatically because of the collapse of the economy, all inclined the population to value stability more than political freedom and civic participation. In other words, there is no reason to believe that democracy was the default outcome of Azerbaijan's transition to independence, thwarted by the political machinations of an elite. Democracy was simply never in the cards.

What made democracy an issue in Azerbaijan were external rather than internal factors: Azerbaijan became independent in the 1990s, in the midst of a wave of democratization, not in the 1960s, when the orthodoxy for newly independent countries was to build single parties. Successive governments could not totally ignore the pressure to take formal steps to enter the processes and build the institutions that characterize a democratic system. Azerbaijan dutifully amended its constitution, held multiparty elections, and even slightly broadened the civil and political liberties of its citizens. All these steps, however, were slow in coming, incomplete, and in reality little more than a facade behind which a different political game unfolded.

The pull and the transforming power of the international community are limited, however, in Azerbaijan more so than in some other countries. First of all, Azerbaijan does not need to be a good, democratic, international citizen to attract foreign investment. Like all extractive industries, the oil industry has to follow the deposits, and Azerbaijan would either have to sink into complete chaos or commit acts sufficiently egregious to trigger international sanctions before investment in oil exploration and production would stop. Second, the pull of the international community—actually of Europe, in the case of Azerbaijan—is limited by the country's conflicting identification with Europe, Turkey, and Islam.

President Aliyev provides one version of Azerbaijan's claim to a European identity. He argues that the country is Europe's door to Asia and a crucial link in the overland trade between Asia and Europe that he would like to see develop along the ancient Silk Road. Many Azerbaijanis would like to share this identification with Europe, which has obvious economic and political advantages. But Azeri nationalists identify first and foremost with Turkey, with which they share language roots, and they identify with Europe through Turkey. Few Azerbaijanis are aware that Turkey, while technically a European country, is far removed from Europe's cultural and political mainstream, and thus cannot help Azerbaijan establish a European identity.

Azerbaijan's Islamic identity has the greatest potential for limiting the role and impact of the international community. Potentially, the Shi'i Islam of Azerbaijan could pull the country toward Iran, as could the fact that 12 million ethnic Azeris live in Iran, about twice as many as in Azerbaijan. At present, the impact of Islam remains limited, even though the call to prayer is now heard in Baku, an Islamic university has opened, and the president takes his oath of office on the Koran.[20] The Azeri communities of Iran and Azerbaijan are separated not just by a border but by centuries of divergent experience. But the situation could change, and even now it is clear that there are other identities at play in Azerbaijan that can further attenuate the pull of Europe and democratic values.

Given this overall picture, why classify Azerbaijan as a semi-authoritarian society rather than an authoritarian one? One reason, as I have already mentioned, is that there are still areas of relative openness in the country, with opposition parties holding meetings, publishing newspapers, and presenting candidates in elections; NGOs forming everywhere; and private universities opening.

Another, even more important reason is that the present regime is not institutionalized. It lacks both the strong institutions of democracy the donors would like to promote and the strong single party on which the Soviets relied. Aliyev is powerful, but his power does not come from the fact that he was elected, and he does not exercise it through the institutions. Above all, he controls the formal institutions to such an extent that they cannot check his power. Aliyev has consolidated his power; he has not necessarily consolidated a political machine capable of outlasting him and reproducing itself. He has not, so far, created a political *system* that can last.

The problem is already becoming manifest in the looming crisis of succession. Aliyev cannot count on the political apparatus to maintain control and choose a successor after his death, because he is the center of that political apparatus, and it would probably disintegrate without him. He has been trying as a result to push forward his own son,

Ilham, as the successor, hoping that the coalition that keeps him in power will continue to cohere around his son. However, Ilham is apparently a reluctant candidate and certainly not the seasoned, experienced politician his father is.

It is thus likely that by default, if not by design, the political competition in Azerbaijan will be reopened in a few years, particularly if Aliyev's effort to ensure that his son replaces him does not succeed. But even if that happens, the obstacles to democracy discussed in the present chapter will continue to exist. In Azerbaijan, semi-authoritarianism may be as good as it gets, no matter how much pressure donors exert.

3

Venezuela:
Democratic Decay

IN FEBRUARY 1992 a Venezuelan army officer, Colonel Hugo Chávez, organized an unsuccessful coup d'état against the elected government of President Carlos Andrés Pérez. In November of the same year, with Chávez behind bars, a new, more violent coup attempt was led by some of his associates, which also ended in failure. But Venezuela did not settle back into its old political tracks. It entered instead a long period of turmoil that has persisted into the present, posing a serious threat to the country's once-solid democratic tradition.

Six months after the November coup, President Pérez, accused of corruption, was forced to step down. His successor pardoned and released Chávez and his co-conspirators. In 1998, Chávez, heading a loosely organized political movement, ascended to the presidency with large popular support in free and fair elections. That was not the end of the story, however.

Chávez's rise was precipitated by the sudden introduction in 1989 of neoliberal economic reforms similar to those adopted by innumerable countries during the 1980s and 1990s. The reforms were part of an attempt by younger members of the Venezuelan elite to unblock an economic situation that had stagnated for years, with the country dependent on ever-volatile oil prices and unable to transform its substantial oil revenues into a tool to promote balanced growth. The need for reform was obvious to everyone familiar with Venezuela, but the measures battered an already reeling population, which had experienced a phenomenal 40 percent drop in per capita income over the previous decade.[1] Furthermore, the painful economic reforms did not address the issues to which the population attributed the crisis, namely the corruption and ineptitude of the political elite and above all of the two parties that had taken turns in governing the country since 1958—*Acción Democrática* (AD) and the *Comité de Organización Politica Electoral Independiente* (COPEI).

Chávez's announcement that his first priority would be to revamp the political system thus received widespread approval. However, his actions pushed the limits of legality to an extreme. Relying on his popularity and on widespread discontent with the old system, he introduced a series of measures that brought Venezuela into the realm of the semi-authoritarian states, where much power is exercised not by or through democratic institutions but on their margins, or even outside their boundaries altogether.

As a result, in the following years Chávez became an increasingly controversial figure, losing some of his popular support and turning the business community and even the labor unions into sworn enemies. This enmity culminated in April 2002 in an unsuccessful military coup against him, fully backed by the business community and clearly dividing popular opinion. The attempted coup laid bare the full extent of democratic decay in Venezuela. Democracy was under attack not only by an idiosyncratic president with strong populist and authoritarian leanings but by his adversaries as well. Democratic institutions could no longer provide a framework capable of containing and regulating the competition for power in the country.

Venezuela's semi-authoritarianism is highly unstable. There is a sufficiently strong democratic tradition in the country to make many citizens uneasy about Chávez's tampering with the democratic process. Furthermore, the president has not been able to deliver what his supporters expected from him, namely jobs and a reprieve from grinding poverty. The business community and the labor unions, always suspicious of his policies, became even more adamant that he must be replaced after he issued a series of decrees in late 2001 aimed at increasing his control over the economy and especially over the state oil company. Chávez's public approval ratings, which once hovered around 85 percent, plummeted to about 33 percent by late 2001. But when the president was threatened in the April 2002 coup attempt, his supporters rallied behind him, as did most military officers.

Underlying Chávez's semi-authoritarianism and Venezuela's continuing political instability are the deep polarization of the society and the unresolved tension between the demand for democratic government and that for socioeconomic change.

Democratic Consolidation and Democratic Decay

Until 1992, when Chávez brought the military back into Venezuelan politics for the first time in three decades and was greeted with jubilation rather than consternation by the majority of the population, Venezuela was considered to be a consolidated democracy. But the rise of a semi-authoritarian regime and the even deeper democratic decay suggested by the 2002 coup attempt call into question the idea of democratic consolidation. Consolidation, the case of Venezuela suggests, should not be looked at as a condition that is achieved once and for all, but as a process that needs to be constantly renovated.

To some extent, the view of Venezuela as a consolidated democracy was rooted in Cold War politics. Since the return to civilian rule in 1958, Venezuela had been a trouble-free country and an oasis of political stability from the point of view of the United States. It was blessedly free of armed leftist movements and even of strong radical political parties. It was a reliable supplier of oil to the United States, free of the political problems and the volatility affecting the Middle East. The once-threatening AD, which had frightened foreign investors and Venezuelan elites when it first controlled the government, from 1945 to 1948, had turned into a tame social-democratic party after 1958. Venezuela could be counted upon to hold orderly free elections and to handle the transition of power from one of the two major political parties to the other easily and routinely. These turnovers were facilitated by the decreasing ideological difference between the two parties, their commitment to similar policies, and a long-standing agreement that the electoral loser would not be completely cut off from the spoils of power. Until the late 1970s, furthermore, the country appeared prosperous, with oil revenue allowing the government to maintain social peace through an extensive system of services and patronage. This happy situation lulled observers into concluding that Venezuelan democracy was no longer likely to be challenged. [2]

But there was more than Cold War politics behind the positive appraisal: Venezuela's political system truly satisfied the basic tests of democratic consolidation.[3] It had experienced many multiparty elections leading to an alternation of parties in power. Until 1992 it also appeared to satisfy another, more demanding expectation, namely, the belief on the part of both the elites and the general public that democracy was, in Juan Linz and Alfred Stepan's expression, "the only game in town."[4] The political elite had made a conscious choice for democracy in 1958 and had abided by its rules ever since, accepting that power relations had to be filtered through democratic mechanisms. The public, according to numerous surveys, expressed support for democracy, although it considered most politicians to be corrupt and was highly critical of government policy.[5]

But support for democracy was beginning to erode. Surveys done shortly after the attempted coup d'état of 1992 showed a much greater ambivalence among the population. Only 60 percent of respondents supported the existing political system. Most of the rest opted for reform, with only a small percentage of respondents expressing preference for a nondemocratic system.[6] Yet many believed that a military coup d'état could be justified under some circumstances.[7]

Studies of democracy and democratization have focused primarily on the transition and consolidation periods. These are considered to be delicate phases when much can go wrong. The international community worries about democratic reversals in countries that appear to have entered a transition and seeks ways to support the process of consolidation. Consolidated democracies, however, receive little attention, because they are considered to have moved beyond the danger zone. But Venezuela suggests that even consolidated democracies are subject to reversals.

The Beginning of Democracy in Venezuela

The history of modern Venezuelan democracy started in 1958, when two political parties—the socialist-leaning *Acción Democrática* (AD) and the Christian-democratic *Comité de Organización Política Electoral Independiente* (COPEI)—entered into an agreement on a basic program of governance and power sharing prior to elections. The Pacto de Punto Fijo, as the agreement is known, was a response to an earlier bitter experience with unchecked majority rule, and it proved to be a turning point for Venezuela. It was supplemented by other agreements that together constituted the basis for Venezuela's "pacted democracy," or "*pactismo.*"[8]

In 1945, Venezuelans had voted in democratic elections for the first time, and had given a large majority to the socialist-leaning AD. Bolstered by this popular support, the party proceeded to enact a series of reforms unacceptable to conservative groups and the military. The result was a coup d'état in 1948, followed by ten years of harsh military rule under President Marcos Pérez Jiménez. Pérez Jiménez was eventually brought down by a broad-based protest movement, which was spearheaded by the banned political parties but had support in the military, the economic elite, and the Catholic Church, as well as, seemingly, most of the population of Caracas.[9] The memory of the strife-torn *trienio* (as the three years of AD rule became known) and of the ten years of dictatorship that followed it pushed the country's political elite onto a course of compromise and moderation that allowed democracy to take hold. The benefits of the pacts were immediately evident. Their costs would not become clear until much later.

The military junta that ousted Pérez Jiménez and supervised the transition committed itself to elections and democracy. This could easily have been the beginning of a new vicious cycle: elections leading to the overwhelming victory of AD, the adoption of policies unacceptable to the business elite and conservative elements, a new coup, and so on—a familiar scenario elsewhere. Instead, Venezuela embarked on the course of pacted democracy. The Pacto de Punto Fijo aimed at reassuring all interest groups that AD would not dominate the country and impose radical policies, as it had during the *trienio*, but would instead forge a consensus with other groups and thus follow a more moderate course. AD also negotiated agreements with business elites, unions, and the Catholic Church to reassure them that their interests would be respected. The pacts helped Venezuela go through the electoral process and the initial difficult period without plunging into chaos, but it was not an easy transition, and the possibility of renewed military intervention hung over the country for years. In the longer run, though, the country settled into a comfortable pattern in which

AD and COPEI could alternate in power on the basis of election re-sults without major interest groups feeling threatened.[10]

The Petro-State

Under the reasonably democratic political arrangement devised in 1958, Venezuela developed a lopsided economy; in the end, the eco-nomic problems affected the political system as well. A large oil pro-ducer, Venezuela fell victim to the common ailments that afflict coun-tries where the large-scale exploitation of oil starts before the establishment of a strong and diversified industrial economy. "Petro-states"—a term not coincidentally coined in a study of Venezuela—are characterized by the underdevelopment of all economic sectors other than oil and thus by the dependence of the state on oil royalties rather than on taxes paid by its citizens.[11] This can make the government rich even when the country is still poor. Oil revenue in petro-states is rarely used to transform the economy, reduce oil dependence, or cre-ate jobs. Instead, it tends to be used to subsidize goods and provide services to the population, thus shoring up the position of the govern-ing party. Worse yet, oil revenue is often embezzled by the governing elite and salted away in overseas banks. The larger the oil revenue and the more rapid its increase, the less likely it is to be used productively. Furthermore, dependence on oil, a commodity with volatile prices, leaves petro-states vulnerable to cycles of boom and bust.

Venezuela is the prototype of the petro-state. Oil created an urban-ized society in which new political organizations and interest groups soon gained much greater importance than the old rural elites. Oil fi-nanced government programs. Venezuela's first democratic govern-ment, the AD regime of the *trienio*, financed an increase in public spending by forcing oil companies to pay a larger share of their rev-enues to the government. The Pérez Jiménez administration bene-fited from a major increase in the demand for Venezuelan oil follow-ing the 1954 political crisis in Iran that led to the deposition of Prime Minister Mohammad Mossadeg and the closing of the Suez Canal by Egyptian president Gamal Abdel Nasser in 1956. Burgeoning oil rev-enues led to high investment rates and a tripling of industrial production. Characteristically, this rapid increase in oil revenue also brought in its wake overspending, corruption, and increasing frustration on the part of labor unions and other urban groups incensed at the increased inequality in income distribution.[12]

The democratic governments after 1958 continued to rely on oil revenue. Terry Lynn Karl argues that it was this revenue that sustained Venezuela's pacted democracy, making it possible for the government to provide benefits to all major groups, thus perpetuating the agreements.[13] Oil revenue subsidized a policy of import-substitution industrialization and financed increases in social spending. Job creation and increased services helped maintain social peace.

Although the pattern of economic development fueled by oil revenue was unbalanced and eventually unsustainable, in the 1950s and 1960s it promoted steady economic growth of about 6 percent a year.[14] This was not a spectacular rate, but it was enough to make a real difference in the standard of living of the majority of the population and to change the character of the economy. It also convinced Venezuelans that they were citizens of a rich country and entitled to share in that wealth, although at least a third of them continued to live below the poverty line.[15] The view that Venezuela is a rich country and that its citizens would be comfortably off but for corrupt politicians is prevalent to this day.

As long as oil revenue continued to increase at a moderate pace, the Venezuelan system remained in equilibrium, with steady growth and a low rate of inflation. But the sudden oil price increase in the wake of the 1973 war in the Middle East upset the balance. Oil revenue, expenditure on major capital projects, and inflation all skyrocketed. As oil prices started to decrease later in the decade, the government resorted to borrowing. By 1976, the real growth rate of gross domestic product (GDP) was slowing down, and by 1980 GDP was shrinking.[16] By 1985, GDP had decreased by 25 percent.[17] In 1989, more than half the population lived below the poverty line,[18] and by 2000 the proportion of Venezuelans in poverty had grown to nearly 70 percent.[19]

The need for reform was obvious. "Every administration since the early 1980s," writes Javier Corrales, "has come to office hoping to introduce economic correctives."[20] But no administration was willing to pay the political costs of painful and thus unpopular reforms, or to shake the political boat sufficiently to build a political coalition capable of supporting such reforms. Instead, AD and COPEI continued to rely on their well-entrenched machines to get out the vote and get their candidates elected, and avoided making difficult decisions, introducing piecemeal reforms and then abandoning them. The problem with Venezuela, one analyst has concluded, was not complete avoidance of neoliberal reform, but one of "reform non-consolidation."[21]

The Venezuelan economy never really recovered from the reversals that started with the oil boom of 1974. Government attempts to stabilize the economy during the 1980s were unsuccessful, and the standard of living for most citizens continued to deteriorate rapidly. This economic decline had considerable political repercussions, undermining the pacts that had sustained democracy since 1958. Without the revenue, the two dominant parties continued to share power and the spoils of office between each other, but they were unable to finance social spending. It is not surprising that Venezuelans lost faith in the system.

The Degeneration of Venezuela's Pacted Democracy

Punto Fijo and the other pacts that facilitated the historic transition to democracy in 1958 were powerful tools. However, the pacts kept the system from evolving over the following decades, even as domestic conditions underwent great change. As a result, the political system became rigid and unresponsive.

By forcing the political parties to agree on a basic, common platform, the Pacto de Punto Fijo narrowed the political spectrum, excluding radical ideas and demands. This narrowing of the spectrum was indispensable to the establishment of democracy, because no country can long tolerate the alternation in power of political parties with radically different ideologies and platforms. The parties agreed on a minimum program of government, committing themselves to increased social spending and enactment of strong labor laws, but they also provided assurances to employers and conservative elites that their properties would be respected and their businesses allowed to operate. AD toned down its socialist rhetoric.

Some groups were excluded from the pacts. Radical elements were purged from peasant and labor organizations, and the Communist Party was kept out of all agreements. When the AD youth branch left the party in protest and tried to launch a guerrilla movement, the response was repression.[22] The more conservative forces that had supported Pérez Jiménez were also left out. Despite the exclusion of the extremes, the legal political spectrum remained fairly broad and gave representation to the most important political forces. Underpinned by the growing oil revenue, the pacts provided a solution to the problems of the time.

After 1958, AD and COPEI established a virtual monopoly of power in Venezuela, initially because of the genuine support they commanded, but later because of the strength of their political machines. All other parties further to the left or right together only controlled about 20 percent of the vote during the 1970s and 1980s. AD and COPEI became highly centralized, bureaucratic organizations with the capacity to reach out in both urban and rural areas through their various mass organizations.[23] Thanks to these organizations, voters developed a strong allegiance to one or the other of the major parties, which were thus assured of a constant base of support.

The system worked fairly well for the citizens, as long as the economy prospered and oil revenue allowed the government to support education and health services, create jobs, and subsidize utilities and staple foods. When oil prices started decreasing while the population continued to grow rapidly, the weakness of the system became apparent: The party bureaucracies had become distant and unresponsive, incapable of listening to new demands and making the changes a population buffeted by economic crisis expected. The parties had become, in the words of one analyst, "citizen-detached."[24]

It is worth noting that such sclerosis is typical of political systems based on a founding pact. In Lebanon, for example, a political pact forged in 1943 reserved specific political posts for representatives of specific religious groups on the basis of their numerical importance at the time. In subsequent decades the composition of the population changed, but the pact remained rigidly in place. This created serious strife and was one of the causes of civil war in the 1970s and 1980s.

In a 1987 analysis of pacted democracies, Karl argued that "pact making promulgates regime norms, substantive policies, and state structures that channel the possibilities for economic as well as political change in an enduring manner."[25] In Venezuela, they did all this too well. The regime norms created by the original pact left the parties incapable of adapting to a changing situation. "Channels for activist pressure were restricted as the *cogollo* [the parties' core leadership] freed themselves from the constraints of lower level opinion. The cost of maintaining moderate centrism was the gradual disincorporation of activists from the parties."[26]

The Unraveling of the System

The literature on Venezuela in the late 1990s traces the beginning of the democratic decay to the financial disruption brought about by the oil boom of 1974 and the economic crisis that developed by the end of the 1970s. But this is merely hindsight. Analyses of Venezuela published during the 1980s gave no hint that a political crisis was in the making. On the contrary, they expressed continued confidence in the strength and resilience of democracy in the country. Analysts recognized that the worsening performance of the economy was undermining the government's capacity to play the redistributive role that had bolstered it in the past; as a result, the state would come under pressure to introduce reforms, and perhaps the balance of power among the major parties would once again swing in favor of AD, as it had in the first period of Venezuelan democracy. The conventional wisdom was that Venezuelan democracy would muddle through the crisis. "The most likely shape of Venezuela's political system over the coming decade," wrote two analysts in the late 1980s, "will be an austerity-modified version of the existing limited pluralist arrangement."[27]

In reality, Venezuela did not muddle through the crisis, and the political system eventually degenerated from a pacted democracy with its limited pluralism into a semi-authoritarian system where power was increasingly exercised outside the institutions. The ossified leadership of the two major political parties allowed the economic situation to continue deteriorating without taking strong, corrective measures. The result was the collapse of the currency in February 1983, followed by both inflation and stagnation. Again, the government was slow to respond, not taking strong measures until after the presidential elections of 1988.[28]

That year, Carlos Andrés Pérez was reelected president on the AD ticket. He had been president during the boom years after 1974 oil price increases, when the government was flush with revenue, Venezuelans felt rich, and the long-term impact of the spending spree was not yet evident. In 1988, many Venezuelans expected that the reelection of Pérez would usher in a new period of prosperity. What they got instead was a structural adjustment program, which was all the more radical for having been postponed for so long. Making things worse, the program was launched without a serious attempt to prepare the population for the shock or even to explain why it was being introduced.

The government had little choice but to implement tough economic measures. With a budget deficit of 9 percent of GDP, rapidly declining oil revenues resulting from low prices, and high levels of inflation and indebtedness, the government had to move, and it did so decisively.[29] Confident that it enjoyed widespread support, as shown by its decisive electoral victory, the government launched a typical neoliberal reform program to reduce the budget deficit, eliminate subsidies, introduce new taxes to reduce dependence on oil revenue, allow the currency and interest rates to float, and liberalize trade.

At the macroeconomic level, the reforms started bearing fruit after a few months, as Moisés Naím shows.[30] At the microeconomic level, where people live, the reforms translated into sharply increased inflation, a loss of jobs, a fall in real wages, and higher prices for goods and services. Coming after the steady deterioration of the 1980s, which had already impoverished the population, the reforms were the final blow. Popular response was swift. In February 1989 riots broke out in Caracas, leading the government to call out the army and put down the protest by force—the number of casualties remains a matter of controversy. Despite the strong steps taken by the government, social peace was not restored. In the following months job actions became more common, and included a twenty-four-hour general strike in protest of government policies. This was all the more remarkable because the labor unions that called the strike traditionally had been aligned with AD, the party that had introduced the reforms. Anger against Pérez continued to mount, and legal proceedings were initiated against him on the basis of corruption.

In 1992 there were the first signs of unrest in the military, an alarming development in a country where military interference in politics had ceased by the early 1960s. The coup attempt led by Hugo Chávez in February 1992 was stopped immediately, but this did not prevent a new coup from being launched in November of the same year. It was led by officers in the high command, particularly the air force, with the support of small groups of leftist civilians. This effort was also suppressed, but only after heavier fighting, because the insurgents succeeded in taking over the television station in Caracas.

There were no mass demonstrations of support for the coup plotters, but neither did citizens take to the streets to reaffirm their support for the democratically elected government and above all for democracy. The country subsequently entered a downward political spiral. Pérez responded to the coup attempts by declaring a state of emergency, suspending constitutional guarantees, and ruling by decree. His popularity continued to plummet, but he kept pushing forward with implementation of the economic reforms. By May 1993, he was forced to resign to stand trial on corruption charges.[31]

The 1993 elections spelled the demise of the parties that had dominated Venezuela for forty years. In the parliamentary vote, AD and COPEI received 23.6 percent and 22.7 percent of the vote, respectively —together, they had received 93 percent in 1988. On the other hand, La Causa Radical (La Causa-R), a leftist party that in twenty years of existence had never risen above splinter-group status, won 20.7 percent of the vote.[32] Despite his historical association with the now unpopular COPEI, former president Rafael Caldera managed to hammer together enough support to win the presidential election running as an independent. Betraying the uncertainty and unease gripping the country, the abstention rate, normally quite low in Venezuela, reached almost 40 percent in these elections.

For the next five years Caldera waffled, taking no decisive steps as social unrest mounted. The 1998 elections showed that the voters had had enough with the old politicians and wanted radical change. Chávez, who had been arrested, tried, and then amnestied by Caldera, was elected president with 56 percent of the vote; his closest opponent received 39.9 percent. In the parliamentary elections the decline of the two dominant parties of old continued, with COPEI in particular slipping to only about 12 percent of the vote. The winners of 1993 did not fare well, either: La Causa-R slipped from 20 percent of the vote back down to an insignificant 3 percent, while two newly formed parties, Movimiento V República (associated with Chávez) and Proyecto Venezuela, received 21 percent and 12 percent of the vote, respectively. Venezuelans were casting about for new faces and new solutions.

The Making of Semi-Authoritarianism

The years following Chávez's election were tumultuous. The events of this period can be summarized as an unsuccessful attempt to put in place a new political and economic pact for Venezuela to replace the clearly defunct Pacto de Punto Fijo. But at least until the crisis of April 2002, Chávez did not try to negotiate such pacts with other parties and politicians, or with the major economic interest groups. Rather, he turned directly to the Venezuelan population, promising a new approach more responsive to their needs in exchange for their political support. From the point of view of democracy, it was an extremely dangerous move. His appeal to the population was highly personal and populist, based on vague promises rather than policy proposals. Essentially, he asked people to trust him to clean up the country's economic and political problems.[33] And in trying to solve these problems he weakened the country's institutions, brought the military back into politics, and decreased the prospects for economic recovery by destroying business confidence. His support declined over the years. And yet when an attempt was made to depose him, a majority of Venezuelans rallied around him, as did foreign governments. Despite all his faults, Chávez was the democratically elected leader of the country, and his overthrow would be even more threatening to democracy than his populist and erratic semi-authoritarianism.[34]

The process that has so threatened Venezuela's long-standing democracy began with democratic elections. Chávez won the 1998 elections campaigning on a platform of political rather than economic reform, even announcing that he would devote the entire first year of his presidency to political reform before turning his attention to economic problems. In the midst of an economic crisis, Chávez promised not jobs and subsidies but constitutional reform—and the population responded positively.

The idea that the Venezuelan political system needed to be reshaped did not start with Chávez, but had become widely accepted by the mid-1980s. In 1984, the Presidential Commission for the Reform of the State (Comisión Presidencial para la Reforma del Estado) was set up to study the changes needed to make the Venezuelan state more efficient and democratic. It addressed four issues: strengthening checks and balances at the national level, decentralizing the government, reducing the role of the parties in the elections, and making the parties themselves more democratic. The main outcome of this effort was legislation that provided for direct election of state governors and mayors, who heretofore had been political appointees. In 1989, the government also set up a committee to review the constitution.

Chávez went much further. Upon taking office in February 1999, he issued a decree calling for a referendum to approve the election of a constituent assembly to be held in April, and opened a confrontation with the Supreme Court by taking the position that this constituent assembly could dissolve the Congress and thus act as an interim legislature. The referendum produced a 92 percent majority in favor of a constituent assembly, although fewer than 40 percent of the voters participated. The Asamblea Nacional Constituyénte (Constituent Assembly), elected in July, was dominated by pro-Chávez delegates.[35] In August, this body declared a "legislative emergency" and named itself the supreme power of the nation, thus curtailing the power of Congress and also claiming the power to fire judges and reform the judiciary. Eventually, an appointed *congresillo* replaced the elected Congress in the transition period.

The constitution, ratified in December 1999 by 71 percent of voters, expanded presidential powers, which had been nominally weak under the old constitution although great in practice.[36] It also increased the presidential term from five to six years and allowed the reelection of the president to a second consecutive term—under the old constitution, a president had to sit out at least two election cycles before running again. These changes resulted in a strong, centralized presidential system with fewer checks and balances. However, the constitution also created new institutions of "citizen power" and "moral power": a Supreme Judicial Court, a Moral Republican Council, a *Fiscal General*, and a *Controller General*, with the latter two representing citizen power. If allowed to function autonomously, such institutions had the potential to curb the excessive power of the central government. But

under the control of Chávez loyalists, they would merely be new instruments of control. Finally, the constitution extended the right to
vote to military personnel. This right is not unusual in democratic
countries, but it raised many eyebrows in Venezuela.

The real problem with the new constitution was not the specific
provisions it contained, but the fact that Chávez was in no hurry to implement it and to submit fully to the institutional constraints it imposed. Instead, he prolonged the transitional period until July 2000,
when elections were finally held for the presidency and the new National Assembly (Asamblea Nacional). (Chávez's Movimiento V
República won 76 of the 165 National Assembly seats, AD won 29, the
Movimiento al Socialismo picked up 21, and more than a dozen other
parties split the rest; COPEI won a mere 5 seats.)[37] This transition period gave Chávez a longer time to govern without an elected parliament, as the appointed *congresillo* did nothing to check his power. Reelected in July 2000 with 56 percent of the vote, against 35 percent for
his nearest opponent, he still wanted more power than the constitution granted him. Instead of accepting the constitutionally imposed
checks and balances, he convinced the National Assembly to give him
the power to legislate by decree in order to "modernize" the country.[38]
And he took advantage of the badly needed reform of the judiciary to
vet judges in ways that suggested that his real goal was to enhance political control rather than to upgrade the professionalism and efficiency of the judicial sector.

The president also sought to give the military a direct role in the
development of the country by launching Plan Bolivar 2000, which
put the armed forces to work building housing, distributing food, and
providing other services. Such a developmental role for the military,
which was often advocated by radical regimes in the 1960s and 1970s,
has proven a double-edged sword in many countries—the military
often makes a useful contribution to specific tasks, but it is also depro-
fessionalized in the process, and this readily leads to political interference. In Venezuela, Plan Bolivar 2000 created discontent within the
military, particularly among officers, and roused concern among
civilians. Chávez also appointed a considerable number of former military officers to political positions.

Chávez's vision was in many ways typical of radical regimes, particularly radical third-world regimes of the past. His admiration for

Fidel Castro and other leaders such as Saddam Hussein and Muammar Ghaddafi underscores this characterization. He envisaged a government willing to break with the status quo and to become an agent of rapid change. Like all leaders with a radical vision for their country, he was fundamentally illiberal and intolerant of dissent. He was interested in the outcome, not in the democratic process; a population tired of a nominally democratic system that had stopped delivering to its citizens largely agreed.

But Chávez did not govern a typical third-world country of the past. He had to deal with a country with a real tradition of democracy; with strong, independent media, labor unions, and business organizations; and with the citizens' expectations that power would be allocated by elections. He ranted and raved against the press, tried to control the labor unions' internal elections, and did not hide his lack of confidence in the labor unions, which he accused of corruption, and in the business community. But he did not have the capacity to repress and control all of these organizations. He harassed them, but they continued to operate independently of the government.

It took Chávez much longer than the promised one year to turn his attention to economic problems. Initially, this did not affect his popularity, because most Venezuelans were convinced that the economic crisis was rooted not in faulty economic policy but in faulty politics, namely, the corruption and unresponsiveness of the political elite. But eventually, the failure to deliver tangible economic improvement did affect his standing with his supporters. As for the business community, the relationship was marked by distrust and antagonism from the very beginning.

When Chávez finally did make a far-reaching attempt to put in place a program of economic reform, in November 2001, there was a quick response that almost cost him the presidency. Taking advantage of the powers granted him by the National Assembly, he issued by decree a series of 49 laws that raised the ire of the business community. Particularly controversial were the hydrocarbon laws, which increased royalties paid by foreign and private oil firms and made it mandatory for the government to have at least a 51 percent share in any oil ventures. Analysts and business leaders complained that these laws, coupled with a threat to nationalize banks that resisted controversial financial and legal reforms, would severely discourage private investment. Union leaders called for a twelve-hour national work stoppage in December 2001 to protest the decrees. During the strike, the sound of jet fighters roaring over Caracas to celebrate Air Force Day was drowned out by noise from thousands of residents banging pots and pans, the prototypical symbol of protest in Latin America. In late January, tens of thousands marched in the capital on the anniversary of Pérez Jiménez's ouster, calling for Chávez's resignation. [39]

Chávez did not back down. Instead, he caused further friction by replacing top managers in the Venezuelan oil company, Petróleos de Venezuela S.A., and continuing his verbal broadsides against any organization criticizing him. Again, labor unions and other groups took to the streets. In this climate of mounting disaffection toward the regime, on April 12 elements of the military, backed by the business community, tried to depose him, only to give up two days later. Chávez still had a lot of support among the poor and the unemployed, and they took to the streets this time—the choice of prominent businessman Pedro Carmona to become president undoubtedly helped mobilize Chávez's supporters. Carmona's decision to disband the National Assembly and suspend the constitution alarmed liberals. Most important, after some hesitation the majority of high-ranking military officers refused to support the coup and become involved in politics. Presented by its backers as an attempt to restore democracy, the coup was seen by others, domestically and internationally, as an even greater threat to democracy than Chávez posed. For all his populism, intolerance of dissent, and bombast, Chávez was an elected leader. He had slipped into semi-authoritarianism, it is true, but a military coup would be even worse.

Conclusions

Chávez's rise is part of a process of democratic decay that developed insidiously in Venezuela over a period of time, leading to a profound crisis in the 1990s. Chávez is a symptom of this decay; he was not its cause.

The Chávez regime shares the fundamental characteristic of all semi-authoritarian regimes, namely the existence of some democratic institutions and processes, and of open political space, alongside traits that are clearly authoritarian. Because of the country's long history as a democracy, however, semi-authoritarianism in Venezuela exhibits different areas of openness and closure, a situation that creates ambiguous reactions within the country and abroad.

The most striking difference between Venezuela and other semi-authoritarian states is the continuing integrity of the election process. There is no doubt that Chávez was elected democratically in fair elections—this is in stark contrast to the situation in most countries with semi-authoritarian governments, where electoral manipulation is a major tool of the incumbent regime. This crucial measure of legitimacy has put all those who oppose Chávez in the name of democracy in a difficult position. The foreign responses to the attempted coup of 2002 reflect the dilemmas involved in dealing with a democratically elected president who is no democrat. The Latin American members of the Organization of American States (OAS), committed to supporting democratic, elected governments and to preventing the return of the military to politics, rallied behind Chávez. They set aside their earlier concerns about many of his less democratic actions, which had prompted a week-long visit by the Inter-American Commission on Human Rights in early February; instead, they chose to condemn military intervention and to reiterate their support for the elected president. The United States, on the other hand, let its dislike for and suspicion of Chávez override other considerations, and only condemned the attempted coup when it was clear that it had failed and other OAS members had expressed their support for Chávez. One of the major democracy-promotion nongovernmental organizations in the United States, the International Republican Institute, went even further, issuing a communiqué that glossed over the role played by the military in the attempted overthrow and choosing instead to "applaud the bravery of civil society leaders . . . who have put their very lives on the line in their struggle to restore genuine democracy to their country."[40] Other U.S. organizations also came under suspicion because of the support they had been providing in the previous years to organizations involved in the anti-Chávez agitation, particularly the labor unions.[41]

Despite the continuing integrity of the election process in Venezuela and the frequency with which the president returns to it—in national elections, those for state and local authorities, and in referenda—Venezuela has been moving in the direction of semi-authoritarianism. Chávez suspended the Congress in favor of the Constituent Assembly in a move of doubtful legality, and he later delayed the implementation of the new constitution, thus continuing to rule unchecked. He shows no respect for the independence of the judiciary, which he tries to limit by vetting judges and putting his supporters on the bench. He prefers legislating by decree to respecting the separation of powers and letting the new National Assembly do its job. In general, he has little respect for institutions—he wants to get things done quickly and in his own way. The presence of the military in the government and administration has become pervasive. It is not a military regime, but in a country—and on a continent—with a history of military intervention in politics, the presence of a large number of military officers in political and administrative positions cannot be dismissed lightly. The image of Chávez in full military uniform presiding over the independence day celebration in July 2000 was disquieting to many Venezuelans. The image of Chávez in military fatigues standing alongside Fidel Castro in Havana a few months later did little to allay fears.

Another problem is that Chávez has done nothing to encourage reconciliation, contributing instead to the polarization of the society. While his support has remained considerable among the poor, members of the old political class and business elite have been unrelentingly hostile to him—a sentiment he has fully reciprocated. They complain endlessly about Chávez, dissecting his life experiences, defective education, and military career for explanations of what has led him to act as he has, rather than asking why he enjoys support while the old parties have lost theirs. Organized groups, including labor unions and the Catholic Church, also remain hostile and have organized large protests against Chávez.

Venezuelan democracy was based originally on a social compact that included the expenditure of oil revenue by the government in exchange for support for the dominant parties and sociopolitical stability. That compact was broken. The old political elite failed to grasp this quickly enough and was shunted aside. Chávez understood that the compact was broken but he has failed to forge a new one, relying instead on unorganized political support and direct appeals to the population. Until a new compact involving the political parties and other national organizations is reached, democracy is unlikely to be restored, and semi-authoritarianism is probably the best Venezuela can expect.

4

Senegal:
Democracy as *"Alternance"*

ON THE AFRICAN CONTINENT, where instability has been endemic for forty years and where governments have come to power more frequently through coups d'état than through free, competitive elections, Senegal has stood out as a stable and relatively democratic country—some have called it a semidemocracy.[1] The selection of Senegal as an example of semi-authoritarianism is thus bound to raise objections. This is, it can be argued, one of the few African countries to maintain a multiparty system for most of its independent history; and while the same party remained in power for forty years, it finally stepped aside peacefully when defeated in the 2000 presidential and 2001 parliamentary elections.

And yet, Senegal has been and arguably remains a semi-authoritarian state, although one that comes closer to the democratic end of the continuum than most. Beneath the democratic facade, Senegal reveals a long history of political manipulation by successive presidents and at times of outright repression. Furthermore, presidents have manipulated not only the electoral process, but also the constitution and institutions, thus calling into question Senegal's much vaunted commitment to constitutionalism and the rule of law.

It is easy to sketch the political history of independent Senegal. Between independence in 1960 and the 2000 presidential election, Senegal was ruled by the same party, most recently called the Parti Socialiste (PS).[2] In the same period, the country had only two presidents,

Léopold Sédar Senghor and Abdou Diouf, the latter handpicked by Senghor when he decided to retire from politics. And from 1978, when Senegal returned to multiparty elections after a period of de facto single-party rule, the country had only one significant opposition party, the Parti Démocratique Sénégalais (Senegalese Democratic Party, or PDS), led by Abdoullaye Wade.

This continuity spared the country the turmoil that has been common to other states in the region, but it did not bring with it any of the benefits stability is supposed to deliver. The lack of high levels of political violence and military intervention did not result in democracy or in more rapid economic development. Politically and economically, the country stagnated. It did not collapse in a dramatic fashion like others around it, but neither did it take off. The political system neither degenerated into full authoritarianism nor moved forward toward real democracy.

This pattern of stability to the point of stagnation was finally broken in 2000, when President Diouf was defeated by longtime opposition leader Wade in the presidential election. A year later, the long-ruling PS lost control of the National Assembly in parliamentary elections. The defeats represented the long-awaited *alternance*, the turnover of power from the old ruling party to a new one. Many hailed it as the beginning of full-fledged democracy. But the truism that "elections do not a democracy make" is particularly salient in the case of Senegal. The turnover has brought to power a politician and party that are very much part of the old political establishment; other conditions have not changed, either, and thus continue not to be particularly favorable to democracy. The *alternance* is beginning to look like a simple change of personnel or a rotation within the political elite, rather than a change in the nature of the regime.

After forty years of rule by the same party, and twenty years of that rule by the same president, the defeat of the incumbent president and party was an indispensable condition for a transition from semi-authoritarianism to democracy. There was simply no incentive for Diouf and his party to change a style of rule that had served them so well for so long. But the turnover was not a sufficient condition for real change. Democracy requires a system of constant checks and balances, and President Wade has explicitly rejected such ideas. Instead, he has interpreted democracy to mean simply periodic turnovers. A president and party must be allowed to govern for the period of their mandate without having to strike deals and compromises, so they can show what they can do; at the end of the period, new elections will give the voters the right to stay with the incumbents if satisfied or to reject them in favor of a new president and party. This is the view Wade put forth when campaigning for his party in the 2001 parliamentary elections. The outcome of the vote suggests that this might be what the voters are willing to give him.

Senghor and the Making of Semi-Authoritarianism

Members of the Senegalese elite express pride in the fact that their country has one of the best political records in postindependence Africa—only Botswana can boast a similar record. Democracy—Western democracy—has deep roots in the country, they argue. French occupation of some coastal areas of Senegal began in the eighteenth century, and Senegal even sent its own list of grievances to the French Estates General of 1789, thus participating in the process leading to the French Revolution. During the nineteenth century, four coastal towns in Senegal enjoyed commune status, which meant that their inhabitants were considered to be French citizens rather than colonial subjects. And as early as 1914, the first Senegalese was elected to the French National Assembly.[3] This long history, however, did not translate into an easy transition to democracy after independence.

Léopold Senghor started his political career in France, where he came to live in 1928, first as a student, then as a poet and a teacher, and eventually as a member of the French National Assembly representing the colonial subjects—as well as serving as the National Assembly's official grammarian.[4] He was a skilled politician and a very complex personality. He was a French-educated intellectual, but he was also passionate in his conviction that Africa had contributed considerably to civilization and must stay true to its identity. He embraced a philosophy of *negritude*, strongly asserting pride in the African identity and cultural accomplishments, but he also remained politically close to France. A Catholic in a predominantly Muslim country, he nevertheless managed to build strong political support in Senegal even while continuing to live in Paris for much of the preindependence period. His influence was long lasting. Senegal is a rare Muslim country where the concept of a secular, democratic state has faced remarkably little challenge, a fact that is almost always overlooked in contemporary debates about the compatibility of Islam and democracy.

But Senghor, who became Senegal's first postindependence president in 1960, was also a typical African leader of the time. He succumbed to the appeal of socialism, although calling for a more benign and not clearly defined "tropicalized" African socialism. The combination of the French tradition of a centralized, bureaucratic state and Senghor's own socialist and somewhat authoritarian inclinations combined to turn Senegal into a top-heavy system where the state controlled major infrastructure and industry, leaving room for private activity only in the farming and trading sectors. An arid country with few natural resources, Senegal faced a particularly difficult development challenge; under this centralized system that discouraged foreign investment and entrepreneurship, it simply stagnated.

Despite his long experience as a parliamentarian in a democratic system, Senghor was no more tolerant of dissent and compromise than other African leaders, and followed the trend toward strongman rule that was spreading rapidly through the continent in the aftermath of independence. The first constitution of independent Senegal prescribed the sharing of executive power between the president and the prime minister. Within three years, Senghor had the constitution amended to eliminate the position of prime minister and increase the power of the president. He also did his best to eliminate all political competition by moving toward a "unified" party—in other words, a single-party system. In the 1968 and 1973 elections, Senghor was the only presidential candidate, and his party presented the only slate of candidates for the parliament. Other political parties in this period were driven into semi-underground status, their members subject to arrest and imprisonment when they refused to be co-opted. Political liberties generally were severely curtailed.

Senghor nevertheless preferred political manipulation to outright suppression. Faced with domestic unrest, he sought to defuse discontent by again modifying the political system. Thus, in 1970 he reintroduced the position of prime minister, appointing to it Abdou Diouf, a young technocrat who had no power base of his own. Four years later, Senghor allowed the formation of one opposition political party, the Parti Démocratique Sénégalais (Senegalese Democratic Party, PDS) of Abdoullaye Wade, who thus started his career as the faithful and eternal opposition leader. In 1976, Senghor amended the constitution again to create a carefully crafted three-party system, in which each party had its own prescribed ideology. Inevitably, Senghor's party, renamed the Parti Socialiste (PS), was allocated the centrist position. The PDS was forced to recast itself as a liberal party, in the European sense—that is, pro-business and pro–free enterprise; Marxists were allowed to form their own organization on the left. Two years later, Senghor allowed the formation of a fourth, conservative party. Through much careful manipulation of the constitution and institutions, Senghor thus succeeded in crafting a political system that satisfied some basic democratic criteria without allowing his power to be challenged. Senegal had achieved semi-authoritarianism.[5]

The 1978 presidential and parliamentary elections were the first contested under the new system of controlled multipartyism. Wade ran for president, as he would do in every future election, but Senghor won, with over 80 percent of the vote. The PS also won a comfortable majority in the National Assembly, but Wade's PDS managed to win 18 seats, thus giving new democratic credibility to the National Assembly. Two years later the aging Senghor resigned voluntarily, transferring power to Diouf, as prescribed by the constitution.

Diouf and the Consolidation of Semi-Authoritarianism

Under the leadership of President Diouf the political system continued to evolve somewhat, but without losing the basic semi-authoritarian combination of formally democratic institutions and informal means of limiting political competition. As a result, Diouf remained in power for twenty years despite growing dissatisfaction with his rule, contesting three elections successfully before finally being defeated in 2000.[6]

This long presidential career got off to an inauspicious start. Too young to have been a leader in the independence movement and to be considered a father of the nation, Diouf did not have the same legitimacy enjoyed by Senghor. Nor did he have an easy relationship with the public. He has been invariably described as somewhat distant and lacking in charisma, a bureaucrat more than a politician. And he had not even come to power on his own, by winning an election or even carrying out a coup d'état. Rather, he was simply handed the presidency when Senghor retired. What allowed him to stay in power so long was his ability to revise the constitution and redesign institutions repeatedly—in this respect, Diouf was very much Senghor's disciple. He was also helped by the fragmentation of the opposition and the willingness of Wade, the head of the only significant opposition party, to join his cabinet twice.

At the beginning of his presidency, Diouf took an important step that both strengthened his democratic credentials and contributed to the longevity of his regime: He abolished the restrictions on the number and ideology of permissible political parties that Senghor had imposed. From a democratic point of view, the decision cannot be criticized—it is not the job of the president to prescribe the number of opposition parties and their ideological orientation. The consequences of the reform, however, were not good for democracy. A large number of political parties formed that represented nothing more than clientelistic groups gathered around a single personality. Voters, who under Senghor's system had been forced to choose among ideological orientations and programs, were left to choose among personalities. And since personality-centered parties found it very difficult to cooperate—as is always the case with such parties—the opposition remained highly fragmented. It is not clear whether Diouf was sufficiently Machiavellian to predict the outcome. It is clear that by allowing parties to organize freely, he made it more difficult for the opposition to mount a concerted challenge to the PS and the president. Despite this plethora of parties and candidates, only Wade and his PDS established themselves as a meaningful political opposition until the 2000 elections. None of the others ever succeeded in gaining more than three seats in the National Assembly or in garnering more than a few thousand votes in the presidential elections. Senegalese voters continued to support the party in power, largely because of patronage.

Patronage was an important part of the system, as is the case in many poor countries.[7] Patronage included, as it often does, the awarding of civil service and public-sector jobs to people in good standing with the ruling party. But it also included a peculiarly Senegalese trait, namely a cooperative relationship between the marabouts, the leaders of the Sufi brotherhood to which most Muslim Senegalese belong, and the ruling party. This relationship was first established by the French colonial authorities and was reaffirmed by Senghor and Diouf. In essence, the Senegalese government recognized the power of the marabouts, allowed them free rein in dealing with their followers, and increased their patronage and outreach by allowing them to control peanut cultivation and trade. In return, the marabouts recognized state authority and, most important, delivered to the ruling party the votes of their followers by issuing *ndigals*, or religious commands, instructing them how to vote.[8] Toward the end of the Diouf years, the marabouts stopped issuing such rulings when elections became more seriously contested, but their relationship with the government remained strong.[9]

Incumbency, patronage, and probably a degree of fraud, as the opposition alleged, ensured easy victories for Diouf and the PS in the 1983 and 1988 elections. Only Wade and the PDS managed to establish themselves as credible opponents in this period, with Wade receiving 26 percent of the vote and the PDS winning 17 of the 120 parliamentary seats in 1988, for example. The rest of the opposition was too fragmented to attract support. Although five presidential candidates contested the elections in 1983 and four in 1988, only Diouf and Wade were viable contenders.[10]

The real challenge to Diouf came not in the elections, which the PS had under control, but from the street. Both the 1983 and 1988 elections were followed by rioting and violence. Opposition parties did not exactly incite violence, but they contributed to the tension by accusing the government of electoral fraud. In 1990, when the government organized elections for local governments, the opposition parties further expressed their lack of confidence in the fairness of the process by refusing to participate.

With political tension rising inside the country, Senegal's democratic facade was beginning to show cracks. It was a particularly inopportune moment for Senegal to lose its reputation as a rare example of

African democracy, because efforts to make political systems more democratic were beginning to gather momentum in other African countries. Diouf moved to restore his legitimacy and refurbish Senegal's democratic reputation. He appointed a commission to study the reform of the electoral code and invited representatives of fourteen political parties to join. He also invited a team of experts from the National Democratic Institute for International Affairs (NDI) to conduct an outside assessment of the electoral code.

The two studies reached somewhat different conclusions. The NDI team expressed the opinion that the code by and large met international standards for democratic elections, identified some steps the government could take to improve the process, but also stated that the problems marring the Senegalese elections were not technical and procedural, but political—above all the lack of trust among political parties.[11]

The Senegalese commission recommended numerous changes. Many concerned procedures, particularly to safeguard against multiple voting and to protect the secrecy of the vote—Senegalese had voted previously by publicly dropping their paper ballot in the box of their preferred political party, but the commission recommended that the secret ballot be made mandatory. Other recommendations were more substantive: the imposition of a two-term limit on the presidency and the simultaneous extension of the presidential term from five to seven years; the lowering of the voting age to 18, a step favored by the opposition, which believed that younger voters would be more likely to opt for change; and the abrogation of a rule that kept political parties from presenting joint slates of candidates for the National Assembly elections—this rule had been part of Diouf's efforts to keep the opposition fragmented. The commission also recommended that a larger proportion of the seats in the National Assembly be filled on a first-past-the-post basis, rather than by proportional representation.

The government accepted the recommendations and the 1963 constitution was duly amended, together with the relevant sections of the electoral code. From the point of view of democracy, the reforms were a mixed bag. The imposition of the two-term limit was a step forward on paper, but the incumbent president was exempted from observing any such term limit. Increasing the number of parliamentary seats to be filled on a first-past-the-post basis also played into the hands of the dominant party. Although allowing electoral alliances helped the opposition, overall the changes probably helped Diouf and his party more than their opponents.

Diouf also sought to decrease political tensions by inviting Wade and other prominent opposition figures to join the cabinet. This invitation was widely seen as an effort to weaken the democratic opposition by co-opting key figures, since the country did not face a situation, such as an external threat, that justified the formation of a government of national unity. Nevertheless, Wade agreed to join the cabinet, dealing the opposition a setback. It was, however, a setback of short duration, because two years later Wade resigned in order to compete in the 1993 elections.

The Triumph of Semi-Authoritarianism

The 1993 elections were organized under heightened expectations of change created by the adoption of the new electoral code and constitutional reform. The level of voter participation was high. Among the new voters were some longtime political activists who had previously dismissed elections as meaningless rituals to confirm the PS in power. Wade and the PDS campaigned vigorously under the slogan "*sopi*"— change. But hopes were dashed when Diouf won again, with the help of the new rules that had raised hopes but actually helped the incumbent. The PS won 56 percent of the parliamentary vote but secured 70 percent of the seats (84 out of 120 seats), while the PDS, with 30 percent of the vote, won only 23 percent of the seats (27 out of 120), with small parties splitting the remaining nine seats. Support for Diouf, in the meantime, decreased sharply, from 73 percent of the vote in 1983 to 58 percent in 1993, with Wade's advancing from 26 percent to 32 percent. The elections thus confirmed the continuing weakening of support for Diouf and the PS, but did not bring about the hoped-for *alternance*.[12]

The elections of 1993 were followed by another period of unrest and violence. The opposition parties again accused the government of fraud. The labor unions mobilized, calling for an unusually large number of strikes. Adding to the tension, a bizarre charge was leveled

against Wade and other members of his party. They were accused of
having ordered the assassination of the Constitutional Council's vice
president. Although the accuser eventually retracted his statement,
the issue dragged on for months, with Wade arrested, released, and
then arrested and released again in a farcical cycle the public inevitably interpreted as a political maneuver to discredit him.

Public opinion was further soured by the devaluation of the CFA
(Communauté Financière Africaine) franc, the common currency of
the former French colonies, in 1994, which led to price increases and
more hardship for an already impoverished population. The devaluation of the CFA franc was a decision over which the Senegalese authorities had no control, but it happened on Diouf's watch and affected
his popularity.

Diouf reacted to the situation in predictable fashion: He tried to co-
opt the opposition by reaching out to Wade and the PDS, and indulged
in further attempts to manipulate the electoral rules and institutions.
In 1995, Wade accepted a cabinet post, with another four portfolios
going to PDS personalities. This second Diouf–Wade alliance was as
short-lived as the first, with Wade again dropping out of the cabinet to
prepare to run in the 2000 elections as an opposition candidate.

Diouf, in the meantime, continued to maneuver in order to increase his party's chances to win again in the 1998 parliamentary elections. He increased the number of seats in the National Assembly
from 120 to 140 and created an upper chamber, the Senate, whose
membership was in part elected by the National Assembly and regional and local government officials, and in part appointed by the
president. In protest of these changes, the PDS initially called for a
boycott of the parliamentary elections but eventually gave in.

Diouf's maneuver paid off. In the 1998 parliamentary elections, the
PS gained nine seats in the new enlarged National Assembly and the
PDS lost a few, with smaller opposition parties registering some gains.
The following year, the PS won all the elected seats in the Senate—
and, of course, Diouf appointed his supporters to the rest. Thus, by the
end of the decade Diouf was quite unpopular, and the population was
in a mutinous mood, but the PS grip on all institutions was firmer
than ever. Diouf had prevailed once more, but it would turn out to be
the last time.

The *Alternance*

The 2000 presidential election proved to be the turning point. Wade's victory was far from inevitable. The parliamentary elections had shown the strength of Diouf's grip on power, despite his diminishing popularity. Many analysts were predicting that Diouf would prevail again, with Wade being confirmed as the eternal front-runner among the challengers. Indeed, there were no major new factors either in the politics of the country or in its economy that made Diouf's defeat inevitable. No exciting new personality had entered the political fray, for example. The economy had neither improved nor deteriorated in a significant way; instead, Senegal struggled along, with modest growth in gross domestic product (GDP) that created few jobs and thus left the conditions for most of the population unchanged.

What explains Wade's victory is the convergence of several events. The most important was the defection from the PS of two well-known personalities and former ministers, Moustapha Niasse and Djibo Kâ. Both set up their own parties and decided to compete for the presidency. As a result of these defections, Diouf did not get the majority of the vote in the first round of the presidential election and was forced to compete against Wade in the runoff. In the first round, Diouf received 41 percent of the vote, with Niasse receiving 17 percent and Kâ another 7 percent. Wade, supported by the Front pour l'Alternance, which included the PDS and some smaller parties, did not do well, either, only gaining 31 percent of the vote in the first round, slightly less than in 1993. But the situation changed dramatically when Niasse rejected Diouf's advances and threw his support behind Wade for the second round, receiving in return a pledge that he would be named prime minister. As a result, Wade carried the second round by 58.5 percent of the vote to Diouf's 41.5 percent.

Another factor that made Wade's victory possible was the role played by a number of organizations of civil society—or perhaps more accurately a number of individuals—in mediating among the parties and preventing the usual postelection outbreak of violence. These groups also succeeded in restoring voters' confidence in the integrity of the election, thereby preventing a boycott or a low turnout, either of which would have played into the hands of Diouf and his machine.[13]

In order to best understand the significant roles civil society organizations played in Wade's victory, it is important to note the citizenry's mood at the time of the election. As the campaign started, the Senegalese were highly skeptical that the process would be fair. Many even expected violence. The most immediate bone of contention was the voters' register, which, according to opposition parties, was packed by the PS with multiple registrations and dead supporters. Wade increased skepticism and discontent with his often repeated assertion that he commanded such support in the country that he could only lose if the vote were rigged. Rumors that Wade was talking to elements in the military and courting their support added to the malaise. The rumors were unsubstantiated; the Senegalese military has an impeccable record of professionalism and noninterference in politics.[14] But in the prevailing atmosphere of fear and distrust the rumors were not dismissed; the example of Côte d'Ivoire, where a military with a similarly unblemished reputation had recently carried out a coup d'état, added credibility to the reports.

The mediation of several nongovernmental organizations (NGOs) dedicated to human rights issues restored some confidence in the integrity of the election process. Senegal's human rights NGOs are small, Dakar-based, elite organizations that can in no way be considered to speak for the majority of the citizens—they have been described by several skeptical representatives of donor organizations as permutations of the same thirty people.[15] But despite, or perhaps because of, their being part of the political elite, rather than being threatening mass organizations, the NGOs were able to mediate among politicians and reestablish confidence in the elections. In early 2000, two institutions that were supposed to ensure the fairness of the elections were in disarray, as well as at loggerheads with government and opposition parties. The first was the Observatoire National des Elections (ONEL), which was not an independent election commission—the Ministry of Interior maintained control over the organization of the elections—but merely a watchdog agency with unclear powers that was supposed to monitor the fairness of the process. The other was a committee set up to ensure equal access to the print and electronic media for all candidates.

With the two organizations unable to resolve contentious issues and restore public confidence, a number of NGOs coalesced in the

Front d'Action de la Société Civile (FACS). Preliminary contacts with the political parties led the group to conclude that the dispute over the voters' register was leading to a crisis. FACS then proposed the creation of a committee including representatives of government, opposition parties, and civil society to review the register, checking for multiple registrations and dead voters. The government agreed. The review eliminated only a few thousand names from the register, but this was enough to restore confidence and allow the process to go forward without violence. After the first round of the election, FACS again played an important part by helping Wade and Diouf agree on a common code of conduct—the essential point was the pledge by both candidates to accept the outcome without crying fraud and inciting their supporters to take to the streets. Diouf abided by the code. When the second round's results were announced, he conceded, then removed himself from the political scene by moving to Europe.

The Reproduction of Semi-Authoritarianism after the *Alternance*

Senegalese greeted the turnover of power from Diouf to Wade with a sense of relief that the change had finally taken place and that it had proceeded relatively smoothly. For the first time in well over a decade, the elections were not followed by disorder. There were no accusations of foul play and the new government, with Niasse as prime minister, was installed smoothly.

The ease of the transition is explained at least in part by the fact that the change, while momentous at the symbolic level, was actually quite limited in practice. The *alternance* was a change internal to the political elite that had dominated the country since independence. It was not a transfer of power to a leadership representing different social groups —in terms of class, ethnicity, religion, or any other indicator of social differentiation, the winners were not very different from the losers. Nor was it a transfer of power to a new generation of leaders, bringing to the table different experiences and a new political culture.[16]

Wade, the man who symbolized the long-awaited change for the Senegalese, was an integral part of the political establishment that had dominated the country for forty years. He had formed his political party not only with Senghor's permission but on his instructions, adopting the ideological position the president had assigned him in order to balance the three-party system. He had run for president in every election since 1978—he was the loyal opponent who lent a degree of credibility to elections the PS would inevitably win. He had served twice in a Diouf cabinet. And he was seventy-four years old. Prime Minister Niasse was also a quintessential member of the old political establishment, a PS dissident who nevertheless retained some ties to the party. And the cabinet Wade assembled contained many other familiar faces, as the president paid back various parties that had supported him in the elections. There were some younger members in the cabinet, but not enough to suggest that the leadership of the country was being transferred to a new generation.

Very soon, it also became clear that Wade's views and his political strategy were not substantially different from his predecessors'. Like Senghor and Diouf, Wade was a firm believer in democratic legitimacy and respect for laws and institutions. Like them, he also believed that laws and institutions could be changed and redesigned at will to suit his immediate political requirements. Diouf had kept himself in power in part by amending the constitution and the electoral laws for political gain. As Wade moved to consolidate his power after the election, he resorted to the same expedients.

As a result, Senegal got not only a new president but a new constitution. And within a few months of the constitutional referendum, Wade was getting ready to modify the institutions once again, following very much in Diouf's footsteps. Like most Senegalese politicians, Wade did not see the institutions and the constitution as a given framework within which politicians had to live, but as infinitely pliable devices. And it became clear from his declaration that he saw democracy not as a system of checks and balances that constrained the activity of politicians at all times, but as a system in which the leaders had the power to govern without constant compromise, subject only to the population's right to review their performance periodically and decide whether to renew or terminate their mandate.

During his first year in office, Wade faced a difficult political situation because the National Assembly was dominated by the PS, which controlled 75 percent of the seats to the PDS's 20 percent. Under the existing constitution, Wade did not have the power to dissolve the leg-islature, and parliamentary elections were not scheduled until 2003. While difficult for the president, the situation also offered the best op-portunity Senegal ever had to strengthen democracy. The tradition-ally rubber-stamp National Assembly had the opportunity to play an independent role and to force a debate of policy choices. It might have been the beginning of democracy as a system of checks and balances.

But Wade could not conceive of governing without having full con-trol of the National Assembly. At the same time, he was not willing to violate the constitution and risk a confrontation with the assembly by dissolving it. Instead, he resorted to the tried-and-true method of em-barking on a new round of constitutional and institutional reform. This was such a routine activity on the part of Senegalese politicians that there was no protest over his actions, except by a few legal schol-ars. Even the PS acquiesced, and in the end it accepted the new consti-tution. Wade also announced that he would not launch any new policy until the reform of the political system was completed, and thus that he would not send any bills to the PS-dominated National Assembly. Obediently, the assembly met to approve the budget as required and then adjourned for the rest of the session.

Senegal's constitution did not have major flaws that made its revi-sion imperative. The major problem, which Wade had denounced re-peatedly in his election campaign, was that it put a lot of power in the hands of the president, to the detriment of the National Assembly. Wade had pledged to establish a better balance between the executive and the legislature, but once in power he changed his mind. The new constitution actually added to the president's power by giving him the right to dissolve the National Assembly under certain conditions. Otherwise, the constitution largely reverted to what it was before Diouf's last changes: The presidential term went back to five years with a two-term limit, the number of seats in the National Assembly was again reduced to 120, and the Senate was abolished.

The paucity of change confirmed that the main goal of the consti-tution-rewriting exercise was to make it possible for Wade to dissolve the National Assembly and to call for parliamentary elections imme-diately, rather than wait until 2003. If further confirmation that the early elections were Wade's goal is necessary, it will suffice to notice that soon after the 2001 parliamentary elections, Wade started talking to his advisers about the advisability of new changes, particularly to restore the Senate, which had been abolished as being both expensive and useless, yet afforded ample opportunities for patronage.[17]

The new constitution was submitted to a referendum in January 2001, and was approved with the support of all important political parties. Wade immediately availed himself of his new power, dissolving the National Assembly and calling for elections in April. He campaigned very actively for the PDS, with the message to voters that, having elected him, they should also give him a solid majority in the assembly, so that he could govern without having to compromise, show what he could do, and be judged at the end of his mandate on the basis of what he had accomplished. Having devoted the first year to politics, the president envisaged spending the rest of his time on policy untrammeled by politics—democracy, in other words, was a ritual to be performed every five years.[18]

The population complied, though less enthusiastically than Wade probably had hoped. The vote for the multiparty Coalition Sopi fell just short of 50 percent of the total, but this translated into a very comfortable control over 89 of the 120 seats in the National Assembly. The Alliance des Forces de Progrès (Alliance of Forces of Progress) of Niasse, who had been dismissed as prime minister shortly before the elections and thus had moved again to the opposition, won eleven seats. The PS was reduced to a meager ten seats. Wade had obtained what he wanted, a National Assembly that would not question his policies and force compromises. The same electoral system that had magnified the power of the PS in the past had worked in his favor this time. The turnover was thus complete. The position of Wade and the PDS after the 2001 elections was remarkably similar to that of Diouf and the PS in previous years. Once again, Senegal had a dominant party with enough seats in the National Assembly to do what it wanted.

Senegalese whom I questioned about whether anything had really changed, besides the name of the president and the identity of the ruling party, had a standard reply: The most important change was in the mind-set of the voters. Previously, they had never believed that the incumbent party could be defeated. After the 2000 and 2001 elections, they understood that the vote gave them the power to remove the incumbents. But most admitted that Wade had acquired too much power; with such a large parliamentary majority, he could enact any policy and even change the constitution again. But Senegalese also appeared confident that Wade would not stay in power for twenty years, not only because of his age but because the voters were ready to judge his performance and remove him if necessary. The president and public appeared to agree that democracy meant first and foremost *alternance.*

Moving Forward

It is not necessarily a disaster that the *alternance* has reproduced a regime with the same characteristics as the old one. As I have argued, semi-authoritarianism in Senegal has been a relatively benign affair, with a fair amount of political space for expressing conflicting opinions and organizing. Presidents have manipulated elections and institutions regularly, but they have not thrown people in jail often, and Senegal has a fair human rights record. Even if the system remains unchanged, Senegal is still ahead of most African countries.

The possibility of further change, of a transition from this benevolent semi-authoritarianism to a system in which democracy means not simply *alternance* but constant checks and balances, is slim. Wade and his party are part and parcel of the old political establishment and the old mentality. He observed his predecessors for decades, learned how they kept themselves in power, and started using the same tactics. Given his age and the new two-term limit in the constitution, his tenure will certainly be shorter than Diouf's, but this is no guarantee that his departure will be the beginning of real political renewal in the PDS or in Senegal. Furthermore, the United States and other foreign countries interested in promoting democracy have been quite willing to define the *alternance* as democratization and to accept Senegal as is, without exerting further pressure.

There is not much vitality on the part of other organizations, either. NGOs devoted to human rights and democracy are few, small, and above all without a following, and it is difficult to see how they could become a political force. And while Dakar boasts some impressive think tanks, they are Africa-oriented groups that pay very little attention to Senegal, probably deliberately.[19]

The political parties remain as they have been in the past: clientelistic groups gathered around personalities, and thus inherently fragmented. It is not even clear at this point that there is a party that can establish itself as the leader of the opposition, as the PDS once did. The future of the PS is uncertain; dominant parties that have suffered an electoral defeat tend not to fare well in Africa.

Finally, Senegal is not subject to external pressure for further change. The donors, a pervasive presence in a poor country like Senegal, appear ready to accept the *alternance* as a sign of democratization, ignoring the great similarity between the Wade regime and the one that preceded it. Senegal is a small country, not a trendsetter for the rest of Africa, and from the point of view of the international community it has been trouble free.

The elections of 2000 and 2001 were political landmarks, showing Senegalese voters that elections can be an effective means of replacing political leaders. They did not, and could not, affect the underlying character of the Senegalese polity and the nature of the political system. Getting to the *alternance* was a significant achievement for Senegal. Going beyond it will require much deeper, and probably slower, change.

5

Croatia:
Toward a Second Transition

IN 1990, CROATIA, still a republic of an intact Yugoslavia, held its first multiparty elections, ahead of the federal government and of every other republic except Slovenia. A year later, the country declared its independence. These events marked the demise of the old Yugoslavia and its brand of communism, but they proved a false start for democracy in Croatia. Yugoslav communism gave way to Croatian nationalism and to a semi-authoritarian regime. The break-up of Yugoslavia also precipitated a war in which Croatia was both the victim of Serbian aggression and an aggressor in Bosnia.

In January 2000, the country took a significant step toward putting that difficult period behind it. President Franjo Tudjman, the father of Croatian independence and the linchpin of the semi-authoritarian government, had died in December 1999. Within a month, his party, the Croatian Democratic Union (Hrvatska Demokratska Zajednica, HDZ), was defeated in both the parliamentary and the presidential elections. Stjepan Mesić, a member of one of the smallest parties in the opposition alliance, became president. Ivica Račan, the leader of the Social Democratic Party (Socijaldemokratska Partija Hrvatska, SDP), which had emerged from the ruins of the League of Croatian Communists (Savez Komunista Hrvatska, SKH), became prime minister with the backing of a six-party coalition.

The elections and the ascent to power of Račan and Mesić signaled the beginning of a new transition in Croatia. The first transition, during 1990–1991, had been from a communist system to semi-authoritarianism.

The second transition is envisaged by the new leaders as resulting in democracy and, not coincidentally, full membership in the European Union. This second transition is proving to be a complex process, but there are reasons for optimism.

Historical Overview: Independence and War

Several concurrent processes explain the disintegration of Yugoslavia and the emergence of Croatia as an independent country in May 1991: the death in 1980 of President Josip Broz Tito, the leader who had cobbled the country back together after World War II and governed it ever since; the country's growing economic difficulties; the general crisis of communism around the world; and the resurgence of ethnic nationalism in Eastern Europe and the Soviet Union. Always a precariously balanced, deeply divided state, Yugoslavia could not overcome all of these problems simultaneously. The breakup was precipitated by Slovenia and Croatia, the two most economically successful and Europe-oriented of the Yugoslav republics. Having decided to chart their own courses, Slovenia and Croatia both held multiparty elections in 1990 and declared independence a year later.

The League of Croatian Communists had launched the reform process by calling for competitive, multiparty elections. By allowing a period of genuine political freedom, however, it engineered its own demise. The HDZ seized the opportunity to organize and campaign vigorously on a nationalist platform; the League, whose image was tarnished by its past policies and its enduring ties to the Yugoslav federation, could not compete, despite its efforts to recast itself as a social-democratic party. In the 1990 elections, the HDZ easily won 59 percent of all the seats in the tricameral legislature to the League's 21, as well as majorities in each of the legislative houses.[1] The parliament then elected Franjo Tudjman, the leader of the HDZ, as president of Croatia. Tudjman spent the following year preparing for Croatia's independence and securing popular support. After 94 percent of Croatian voters declared their support for independence in a May 1991 referendum, the Croatian Assembly unanimously voted for a declaration of independence on June 25; Slovenia did likewise the same day.

The largest republic, Serbia, objected vehemently to the disintegration of Yugoslavia. With Serb minorities dispersed through most of the Yugoslav territory, Serbian nationalism aimed at creating a Greater Serbia—in practice, a resurrected Yugoslavia. (This was reflected in the Serbs' decision to keep the name *Yugoslavia* to denote Serbia and the only other republic to remain in the federation, Montenegro.) Slovenia was a relatively minor problem for the Serbs, but Croatia had large Serb minorities in several regions. Shortly after Croatia declared independence, the Serbs of the Krajina (a region bordering Bosnia) declared a countersecession and the establishment of the Republic of the Serbian Krajina. For its part, the Yugoslav army occupied the easternmost part of Croatia, Slavonia, and mounted attacks in many other areas.

Serbia, which controlled the old Yugoslav army, quickly gained the upper hand in the fighting. Over the following year, tens of thousands died and hundreds of thousands became refugees. By the time a ceasefire was signed in June 1992, the Serbs controlled about one-third of Croatian territory, in the Krajina and Slavonia.[2] The conflict continued with varying degrees of intensity until 1995. Both sides were guilty of atrocities and of so-called ethnic cleansing. On both sides, conflict enhanced the influence of ultranationalist elements. And both sides became entangled in the conflict in Bosnia, with Croatian nationalists seeking to detach Herzegovina from Bosnia and annex it to Croatia. By 1995 Croatia had built up its army sufficiently to wage "Operation Storm," a campaign to regain full control of its territory. With the conclusion of Operation Storm, peace returned. But any hope that the independence of Croatia would lead to democracy was destroyed in the fighting. Instead, Croatian nationalism and the military conflict defined Croatian politics for most of the 1990s and were instrumental in fostering semi-authoritarianism.

The Croatian Democratic Union (HDZ) and the Making of Semi-Authoritarianism

The HDZ, many have suggested, was a movement more than a political party. It lacked a tight organization, and it was full of ideological inconsistencies and contradictions. Its founders were motivated by both nationalism and anticommunism. Many, including Franjo Tudjman, were longtime dissidents who had fallen out with the Communist Party in the early 1970s, when hard-liners within the organization crushed the so-called Croatian Spring, a movement that combined attempts to reform and liberalize socialism with the revival of Croatian nationalism. Some had spent time in jail as a result.[3]

The nationalism of the Croatian Spring was fueled by the perception that the Croatian language and culture were being destroyed, subsumed into the Serb-dominated "Serbo-Croatian" favored by the communist regime. More concretely, it was also rooted in Croatian resentment of the transfer of revenue from the relatively rich Croatia to other republics and of the overrepresentation of Serbs in government posts and in the military. The HDZ's nationalism went much further, aiming for the separation of Croatia from Yugoslavia. And the extremists went further still, seeking the annexation by independent Croatia of Herzegovina, a Bosnian region with a substantial Croatian population. Particularly vehement on this point was the so-called Herzegovinian lobby, which drew its support from returning émigrés and was led by Gojko Šušak, who would become Croatian defense minister. The Herzegovina lobby had considerable influence with Tudjman, who had raised more than $5 million dollars from the Croatian and—above all—Herzegovinian émigré communities in North America to finance his 1990 election campaign. Among the moderates opposing the annexation of Herzegovina was Stjepan Mesić, who left the HDZ over this issue.

The HDZ rose to power in Croatia on a wave of nationalism and anticommunism, and thus with strong popular support. Once in office, however, its leadership took no chances, seeking to insure itself against a possible change in public opinion by establishing control over all institutions and by manipulating the electoral process. Mindful of the expectations of the international community and of the Croatian public that the postcommunist system would be more open and democratic, the party sought to preserve a facade of democracy. Behind the facade, however, it established firm and pervasive control over Croatia.

Establishing Control over Political and Economic Institutions

Despite its opposition to the Communists, the HDZ shared with them a fundamental approach to governing, in that both sought to make all institutions an extension of the party. Although in theory he continued to respect the idea of multiparty elections, Tudjman manipulated them extensively to make sure he won by a comfortable majority. And by maneuvering party members and supporters into positions of influence, as well as by general intimidation, Tudjman also achieved control of the judiciary, the security force apparatus, the private sector, and the media.

Electoral manipulation was an important tool of the Tudjman regime. It timed elections adroitly, calling them, variously, at the height of the summer holidays, when people were distracted; right after military campaigns, when patriotism was at a peak; or with the shortest possible notice, to hamper the opposition.[4] It maximized its number of parliamentary seats and consistently achieved an overrepresentation of more than 10 percent by gerrymandering districts to give more weight to friendly rural constituencies. It even succeeded in redistricting the city of Zagreb, where the opposition had more support, so that its voters were redistributed among four mainly rural districts. Croats in the diaspora, who were staunch supporters of the HDZ, were not only given the vote but received special seats, which had the effect of overstating their representation.

The regime also promulgated electoral law to its advantage. One law, for example, required plurality, not majority, constituency victories and therefore favored incumbent HDZ politicians. Elections laws were amended before each election to provide the government with maximum advantage. And when all else failed, the regime resorted to the occasional act of electoral fraud. For example, when the Croatian Social-Liberal Party (Hrvatska Socijalno-Liberalna Stranka) vice president seemed set to win the Zagreb seat in 1995, the last-minute absentee ballots of seamen and prisoners pushed the victory to the HDZ.[5]

These maneuvers helped Tudjman's party gain large majorities. The vote for Tudjman increased from 57 percent in the presidential election of 1992 to 61 percent in 1997. Meanwhile, the HDZ secured about 60 percent of the seats in the lower house of parliament (the House of Representatives, Žastupnički Dom) in the 1992 and 1995 elections, and won a similar percentage in the 1993 and 1997 elections for the upper house (House of Counties, Županijski Dom).

Despite the large majority the HDZ commanded in the parliament, Tudjman did not trust the institution and did his best to sideline it. It was Tudjman, rather than the parliament, who chose prime ministers. He used strong-arm tactics to bully legislators into supporting his policies, speaking personally to HDZ legislators who showed signs of independent thinking. As a result, the parliament did little more than rubber-stamp Tudjman's decisions. In any case, Tudjman could bypass the parliament entirely, since the new constitution gave him the power to legislate by decree. Theoretically limited to emergency situations, the issuing of decrees became an almost routine way of governing; Tudjman resorted to these decrees even more frequently than the Communists had. Special councils, such as the Presidential Council and the Defense and Security Council, further augmented executive power.

Tudjman granted the minister of justice broad discretionary power over the appointment and removal of judicial personnel.[6] Almost all the judges and prosecutors in the higher courts were purged. In its first six months, the Tudjman government replaced 280 judges with new appointees with favorable political qualifications. The High Judiciary Council, responsible for judicial selection starting in 1994, consisted of individuals chosen by Tudjman. The president of the Supreme Court was dismissed in 1992 after refusing to bow to Tudjman's pressure on certain decisions. In 1996 the new president was also removed, for similar reasons. These interventions eliminated dissenters from positions of power and intimidated the other judges into toeing the regime's line. The constitutional court held out the longest, eventually buckling under in 1999, when the terms of eight of its eleven members ended. The government then appointed a slate of prominent HDZ officials, at least two of whom had no real judicial experience.[7]

The ruling party also penetrated the military, a task facilitated by the fact that Croatia had to reconstruct its armed forces almost entirely after independence, since the old Serb-dominated Yugoslav army had largely chosen to fight for Serbia. Locked in war, Tudjman needed a strong professional military, but his desire for control took precedence.[8] The Croatian military became a client of the regime, with close ties to the ruling party. Professional officers who dissented from the regime position were simply dismissed and replaced by ruling party leaders, who infused the armed forces with loyalty to the party rather than to Croatia, thus consolidating political control over them. The HDZ also secured control over the set of active intelligence-gathering and security services, which were collectively (and ominously) called the Bureau for the Defense of the Constitutional Order. An HDZ vice president served as the head of this bureau in 1992, and Miroslav Tudjman, the president's son, took over in 1993, in an explicit assertion of political and personal control by the president.

In the economic realm, Tudjman had to resort to more complex methods to establish control. With Croatia under pressure from the international community to enact market-based economic reforms and especially to privatize the vast public sector, the president could not simply install officials to run the state-owned enterprises. Instead, Tudjman manipulated the privatization process, transferring companies to political allies on the basis of his vision of Croatia "as a statelet that would be ruled by 100 rich families."[9]

Because of the characteristics of the communist system that evolved in Tito's Yugoslavia and the way in which privatization was carried out, the result of the process was to concentrate rather than broaden control and ownership of assets. Yugoslavia had developed a fairly unique system of "social ownership," which gave managers and employees control over their firms, although not ownership. The Tudjman regime used the plausible argument that the system of social ownership was incompatible with market principles in order to appropriate control of these firms and divide them up among its supporters. Legislation enacted in April 1991 gave socially owned firms about a year to submit their proposals for privatization and to secure the approval of a government bureau, the Agency for Restructuring and Development. Companies that did not comply would revert to state ownership and control. By the deadline, only 1,000 of the 3,500 socially owned firms had submitted plans, and only 119 of these plans had been approved. As a consequence, 97 percent of the socially owned firms were taken over by the new Croatian Privatization Fund, which proceeded to allocate them, in a thoroughly corrupt and clientelistic manner, to entrepreneurs with close connections to the HDZ. Banks, furthermore, only made credit available to supporters of the ruling party. The process created a very small elite made up of expatriate entrepreneurs (the basis of the Herzegovinian lobby) as well as local Croatian ones, all with strong ties to the ruling party. The privatization process thus contributed to the regime's consolidation of power.

The Tudjman regime also resorted to a variety of means to establish control over the media. Privatization provided an opportunity to install new management and editorial boards loyal to the government. The government maintained complete control of both the national news agency and Croatian Radio-Television (Hrvatska Radio-Televizija); these media outlets' reporters and editors were essentially civil servants executing government policy. Those who showed too much independence were marginalized or dismissed. Croatia Radio-Television banned opinion poll results unfavorable to the HDZ and refused to air some opposition advertisements. Its election coverage was extremely skewed, with Tudjman and the ruling party getting the most airtime. The little time left for opposition parties gave disproportionate attention to the most insignificant among them.[10]

In theory, the HDZ allowed independent television and radio stations to operate. But the licensing body for all electronic media, the Telecommunications Council, was composed of senior members of the ruling party who allocated concessions in a corrupt fashion and manipulated the procedure to the party's advantage. As a result, most critical voices in the so-called independent media were squelched. A major exception was the Zagreb station Radio 101, which survived an attempt to close it down when tens of thousands of people took to the streets.

The regime did not openly impose censorship, but relied on administrative and technical means to control the print media, which in any case only reached about half the population, particularly as a deteriorating economy made newspapers prohibitively expensive for many. A 1996 law, for example, called for criminal prosecution of anyone who caused mental anguish to the president, prime minister, speaker of parliament, and presidents of the supreme and constitutional courts, even if the statements were factually correct. This effectively silenced most direct criticism of such officials. Libel laws were also liberally applied. Between 1994 and 1997, independent newspapers and journalists faced about 700 libel suits. The cost of constant litigation was crippling to independent papers. In 1999 the outspoken *Feral Tribune* owed an estimated $2.22 million in legal costs, with more than a hundred cases still pending. Independent newspapers and magazines were also financially crippled by a combination of credit rejections by the state-controlled banks; extra taxes, including one on pornography; intimidation of potential advertisers; and the high distribution costs imposed by the government-controlled Tisak company, which held 75 percent of the distribution market and a monopoly on kiosk sales.

Exploiting Nationalism and War

Much of the strength of the Tudjman regime resided in its ability to exploit nationalist feelings and the war to reinforce each other and to close the political space for the opposition. Tudjman routinely denigrated his own opponents as traitors to the cause of Croatian independence; he was ready to sacrifice the country's unity in the face of the enemy for the sake of personal ambitions. This helped him win all elections by a wide margin, even though his policies were not popular. Many studies have concluded that the Croatian public resented the privatization process, as well as the government's overbearing control of the press and its refusal to devolve power to local government, especially in Istria and Zagreb.[11] Croats did not even want a strong leader, unrestrained by parliament—a 1995 survey found that only 5 percent of respondents favored that option.[12] By making each election into a virtual plebiscite on Croatian independence, however, Tudjman managed to weaken the opposition.

The military conflict that engulfed Croatia in the first half of the 1990s was critical to the HDZ's grip on power. The regime relied on "the first and oldest ... need to defend oneself from the enemy."[13] With the country's integrity and even its survival threatened, Croats were ready to support the regime. The ruling party was seen as the defender of Croatian statehood against the perennial Serbian threat, and this won it votes. Tudjman was extremely aware of the electoral benefits of heightened patriotic fervor and exploited it to the utmost. In January 1993, for example, Croatia launched an offensive only two weeks before the upper house elections. Two years later, the government launched Operation Storm to free Serbian-occupied territory only two months before elections for the lower house. In the wake of the victory, the government's standing in the opinion polls reached an all-time high, and in the elections the HDZ did particularly well in the regions that had suffered the most from the Serbian occupation. In the atmosphere of patriotic fervor, the opposition found it difficult to craft a message and dwindled into insignificance.

Playing the Ethnic Card

In addition to exploiting the war to solidify support, the HDZ manipulated ethnic nationalism in other ways, appropriating a set of symbols Croats could hardly reject and whipping up public sentiment against non-ethnic Croats. Tudjman freely interpreted history to suit his requirements. The ruling party portrayed Ante Pavelić, leader of the World War II pro-Nazi Ustaše regime, as a Croatian patriot. It also sought to downplay the massive Ustaše violence against Serbs in World War II, instead representing the Croats as innocent victims of Serbian violence. Tudjman even adopted many of the symbols used by the Ustaše, such as the red-and-white checkerboard "Savonica" flag, the name of the currency, and the national anthem.

Some of the measures taken by the HDZ government affected all ethnic groups. The new constitution set the tone by declaring Croatia the country of the Croatian nation. The government made a determined effort to distill a pure Croatian language from what the Communists had called Serbo-Croatian, even seeking to revive archaic or disused terms in the name of authenticity. But most measures hit the Serbs particularly hard. When the government made nationality an explicit criterion for government employment, most of those losing their jobs were Serbs. Their representation in the lower house of parliament decreased from thirteen members in 1992, to three in 1995, to just one in 1999. Most important, the total number of Serbs in Croatia was halved in the 1991–1996 period, particularly after the Croatian army started reconquering the territories Serbia had occupied, and the Serb population fled.[14]

The Collapse of the Tudjman Regime

During the 1990s, the HDZ's grip on power seemed beyond challenge. Bolstered by war, ethnic nationalism, control over institutions, and manipulation of the election process, the party that had led Croatia to independence appeared invincible. In the 1995 and 1997 parliamentary elections (for the lower and upper houses, respectively), Tudjman's party still won more than 60 percent of the seats. But by the following elections, the situation had changed suddenly. On December 10, 1999, Tudjman died of cancer. On January 2 and 3, 2000, a coalition of two major parties and four minor ones (which became known as the "two" and the "four") won 95 of the 151 seats in the crucial lower house of parliament, while the once all-powerful HDZ took only 46.[15] A month later, in the presidential elections hastily organized after Tudjman's death, HDZ candidate Mate Granić won only 22 percent of the vote in the first round, failing to even reach the second round, and victory went to Stjepan Mesić, running as the candidate of the small Croatian People's Party (Hrvatska Narodna Stranka). The HDZ had lost its grip on power, although it was far too early to write it off for good as a factor in the politics of Croatia.

There is no single explanation for the quick collapse of the regime. A number of factors converged to produce such results. Some of these were special conditions and developments prevailing in Croatia at the time—the end of the war, the moderation of nationalism, the continuing economic difficulties, and Tudjman's death. Another factor, and the most interesting from the point of view of the present study, was a weakness Croatia shares with other semi-authoritarian regimes, the fact that semi-authoritarianism cannot be easily institutionalized. Torn between the democratic form of government they have chosen and their own authoritarian proclivities, semi-authoritarian regimes end up fighting against the very institutions they have developed. Very few, foremost among them Egypt, succeed in maintaining stability over the long run, and above all in overcoming the crisis of succession. The Tudjman regime did not, and the death of the leader led not only to a change of personnel but to a change of regime.

The end of the war in 1995 was simultaneously a triumph for the HDZ and the beginning of its demise. Croats rejoiced in the return of the Serb-occupied territories and heaved a sigh of relief that the war was over, but then turned their attention to domestic problems and began to wonder "whether the government that they had supported during wartime was the sort of government they wanted now that peace was at hand."[16]

With the end of both the war and Serbian provocation, and a greater sense of comfort among Croats with their nationhood, Croatian nationalism mellowed. While Tudjman still won credit as father of the nation, the HDZ lost its unique appeal as the party of independence. At the same time, the Social Democratic Party started gaining legitimacy as a democratic political party, shedding much of its image as the successor to the League of Communists and also the reputation of being a "Yugo-unitarian" party, that is, a party supporting the reunification of the former Yugoslavia, as Tudjman had claimed. Other parties also found more room for growth as dissatisfaction with the former ruling party mounted.

Beyond its success in reconquering the territory occupied by Serbia, the HDZ could not claim many successes. Domestic problems, particularly economic ones, were considerable, and while in power the party appeared to do little to tackle them. Between 1990 and 1993, gross domestic product shrank almost 30 percent. While it recovered somewhat in subsequent years, by the end of the decade the economy was contracting again. The average monthly wage was half the prewar level. By the end of the decade unemployment was at least 20 percent, and, even according to the state employment service, 300 jobs were being lost each day. In addition, a disproportionate number of people had been forced into early retirement, with a considerable worsening of their standard of living.[17]

None of these problems were due solely to mismanagement by the Tudjman regime. Declines in production, a loss of jobs, and falling standards of living have been part and parcel of the initial phase of postcommunist transitions everywhere. Such problems have been accentuated where the breakup of a country has destroyed a once-integrated market, as in Yugoslavia or the Soviet Union. Finally, the war also contributed to economic difficulties. But to problems that were probably inevitable, however, the regime added many that were not, and this created much public resentment. The public was angered by the perceived unfairness of the privatization process, the blatant self-enrichment of the elite, the "widespread corruption" that media controls could no longer hide, and the bankruptcy of the many companies that could no longer pay employees on time.[18] As the country settled down after the war, furthermore, the large payments the Tudjman regime made to the Croatian nationalists in Herzegovina came to be seen less as a patriotic duty than as political adventurism that only served to impoverish Croats.

Ten years after the initial multiparty elections that led to independence, the Croatian public was not only more discontented, but politically more mature. The general public, civil society organizations, and the political parties had developed considerably during the previous decade, and approached the 1999–2000 elections somewhat more critically.

One of the consequences was that the HDZ had greater difficulty controlling the flow of information to the voters without totally losing its credibility. Government-controlled media were still biased in favor of the ruling party, but not as blatantly as in earlier elections, the Organization for Security and Cooperation in Europe reported.xix Faced with a relatively sophisticated public, which at least in the cities had access to non-Croatian sources of information, the party had discovered that obvious manipulation did not pay off. As early as 1996, a report by the Commission on Security and Cooperation in Europe noted an HDZ official's admission that "the party overplayed the media by making its control or influence so blatant that it insulted the intelligence of the average citizen who probably grew tired of seeing the same personages highlighted and praised every day."[20]

Civil society organizations had also grown, both in number and capacity, during the previous decade, and became significant actors in the 1999–2000 elections, mobilizing to get out the vote and monitor the elections. While the effort was theoretically nonpartisan, in reality it had the very clear goal of helping defeat the HDZ. With financing and sometimes advice from international donors, Croatian nongovernmental organizations (NGOs) joined in a coalition called Glas '99, which aimed at increasing voter participation, particularly among younger people who were known to have little love for the ruling party. A second organization, Citizens Organized to Monitor Elections (Gradani Organizirano Nadgledaju Glasanje), was formed to monitor the election process, successfully mobilizing thousands of volunteers throughout the country. The impact of these organizations is difficult to measure exactly—Glas '99, for example, estimated that its efforts increased participation among young voters by about 4 percent, with the votes going overwhelmingly to opposition parties.[21] Domestic election monitoring, coupled with international pressure, made it more difficult for the HDZ to resort to outright fraud. There were even some improvements in the election law that resulted in the halving of the number of seats reserved for diaspora representation, from twelve in 1995 to six in 2000.

Neither the growing dissatisfaction of the public nor the increasing sophistication of civil society suggest that the defeat of the HDZ in the 1999–2000 elections was a foregone conclusion. There is no simple, direct correlation between popular discontent and regime change in authoritarian or semi-authoritarian regimes. Had Tudjman not died, the ruling party would most likely have continued in power, most analysts concur.[22] His death truly changed the political dynamics in the country, all the more so because it had been anticipated; he had been known to be suffering from cancer for several years. The HDZ was left divided and in disarray; like all strongmen, Tudjman had not allowed space for other potential leaders to emerge, even when his health deteriorated. The opposition parties, on the other hand, had the time as well as the incentive to prepare a new strategy, and this made all the difference.

The opposition political parties had had a poor track record during the 1990s. The two major parties, Dražen Budiša's Croatian Social-Liberal Party (HSLS) and the Social Democratic Party (SDP), distrusted each other and would not cooperate, even to defeat Tudjman. The HSLS, furthermore, was internally divided, and in fact a faction split off to form its own party. The remote prospects for an election victory made it more difficult for the party leaders to overcome these problems.

But in 1999, with Tudjman dying, the possibility no longer appeared so remote. Opposition leaders thus made a determined effort to overcome the fragmentation and mount a united effort. While complete unity escaped them, the HSLS and the SDP managed to form a coalition, with four minor parties organizing another. Although they put up separate presidential candidates, the two coalitions worked together closely to fight the HDZ. The strategy proved highly successful.

Attempting a Second Transition

Rebuilding Croatia, politically and economically, is proving much more difficult than ousting an entrenched ruling party. While the new president and prime minister appear sincerely determined to move beyond the facade of democracy and turn the country into a fully functioning democracy, oriented toward Europe, the outcome of Croatia's second transition, from semi-authoritarianism to democracy, is not assured.

The new government swiftly changed the political climate of the country as well as the dominant political rhetoric. Both President Stjepan Mesić and Prime Minister Ivica Račan abandoned the strident nationalism of Tudjman. The independence of Croatia was no longer an issue—in October 2000 the government even pretended to be paying little attention to the drama unfolding in the streets of Belgrade after controversy over election results forced Yugoslav president Slobodan Milošević from power, on the grounds that events in Serbia had nothing to do with Croatia. A more important issue for the new government was the future accession of Croatia to the European Union; this would require adherence to political principles, economic policies, and legal standards at odds with the political rhetoric and hate mongering of the HDZ.

Domestically, the atmosphere relaxed immediately. News broadcasts on radio and television became less ideological, although there were no changes to the structure of ownership and control. Similarly, the independent newspapers gained more space to write and criticize. The government undertook a review of the privatization process, and some members of the new economic elite who had benefited from Tudjman's policies were indicted. However, the government also made it clear that it did not intend to challenge or reverse the entire process.

Fundamental reforms, however, were slow in coming. It took a full year for the constitution to be amended, and few other laws were enacted in that period. President Mesić refused to take advantage of the broad powers he had under the previous constitution to speed up the process of change, to the chagrin of many who wanted reform. With few concrete changes, the country continued to stagnate economically and began to sulk politically.

The Uncertainties of Democratic Politics

A major drag on change was the fragility of the governing coalition, which exposed the country fully to the worst aspects of democratic politics from the beginning. A six-party coalition is bound to be unstable and slow moving, and Croatia's lived up to expectations. While only one party has dropped out—the Istrian Democratic Assembly (Istarki Demokratski Sabor) in mid-2001—the country has been shaken by periodic rumors of an imminent government reshuffle. The parties have vied constantly for government posts. But the major political cost of the large coalition has been the slow pace of reform dictated by the difficulty of reaching an agreement among such an array of political organizations.

Another source of tension has been the relationship between the two major parties, the Social Democratic Party (SDP) and the Croatian Social-Liberal Party (HSLS). When the two formed an electoral coalition for the 1999–2000 elections, they assumed that they would share power, with the SDP's Ivica Račan becoming prime minister and the HSLS's Dražen Budiša taking over the presidency. This did not happen, because Stjepan Mesić, a member of a small party nobody had taken particularly seriously, unexpectedly emerged as the winner in the presidential election. This left Budiša without any government post despite the fact that his party was the second largest in the coalition. The problem has been exacerbated by the ideological tensions between the moderate SDP and the increasingly nationalist HSLS. (The HSLS mayor of Split, Ivan Skaric, actually spoke at a major right-wing protest against the government in February 2001.)

The relationship between the president and the prime minister has also been in flux. Outwardly, President Mesić has agreed, even sought, to limit the power of the presidency. He supported the reform of the constitution enacted in November 2000 that devolved much power to the prime minister and the cabinet—by the end of the year, the weekly *Nacional* could report that "the President of the Republic is no longer the decisive factor in the political life of the country."[23] Nevertheless, Mesić and Račan have frequently disagreed on the precise boundaries of power. Most notably, they have fought over control of the military and intelligence services, with Mesić insisting that those areas are under his jurisdiction.

The new government has also been constrained by the survival of many of the old HDZ structures. Because the former ruling party penetrated every Croatian institution, its appointees controlled the security services, the judiciary, the bureaucracy, the broadcast media and some of the print media, and the major private and state business enterprises. This means that much needs to change, and that change will be difficult. It will be particularly difficult for a government that wants to act democratically. The government has been reluctant to fire a large number of people from public offices lest it be accused of a political witch-hunt, and it has also been unsuccessful at cleaning up the private sector, where corruption is rife as a result of Tudjman's privatization. Investigative and prosecutorial offices have proven weak, incompetent, and sometimes complicit. The financial police, for example, failed to expose a single major case of fraud or corruption after the new government took office, and was eventually disbanded.

The list of political reforms that needed to be tackled following the regime change was daunting: the revision of the constitution, the complete overhaul of the judiciary, the rebuilding of the parliament as a functioning institution independent of the executive, and the decentralization of governmental functions. But this was only the beginning: The military needed to be depoliticized and professionalized, the security services needed to be restructured and brought under the supervision of elected officials, and new regulatory agencies needed to be created to supervise a privatized economy. In dealing with these problems, the government needed to tackle the legacy of Tudjman and the much longer one of the communist regime. Indeed, even going back to an earlier time, Croatia simply had no historical experience with even a more moderately democratic government. Many of the reforms, furthermore, would cost money the government did not have. For example, the parliament had been inactive for political reasons, but as it started to play a more active, democratic role under the new regime, it immediately faced a critical shortage of office space.

It is easier for a government to redefine its foreign policy, and change in this realm has been swifter. Anxious to be accepted by the international community, particularly the European Union, the government has tried to recast Croatia as an excellent international citizen. President Mesić moved to improve relations with Bosnia early on, visiting there and announcing that the Croatian government would no longer support Croatian nationalists in Herzegovina, but would channel all aid to the Croatian community through Bosnian authorities. The government has also mounted a major effort to demonstrate its willingness to comply with the requirements of the international community, turning over many suspected war criminals to the International War Crimes Tribunal in The Hague and putting others on trial at home. The government also became much more willing to work closely with international agencies on the issue of the return of Serb refugees to their former homes. With an eye to the future, it has even set up an agency to vet all new legislation to make sure that it is in compliance with European Union standards.

Economic Reform in a Second Transition

The economic issues the new government faced were equally complex. It needed to revive the slumping economy and deal with the legacy of both the Tudjman and the communist regimes—one aspect of this legacy is that by the time the new administration took power, the government was consuming about 55 percent of gross domestic product.[24] The reforms were bound to create more hardships for a population that felt it had suffered enough during the war and was not in the mood for more sacrifices. The early months were devoted almost exclusively to studying the legacy of Tudjman's privatization program and his economic policies. Repeatedly, government officials declared that what they found was much worse than anticipated. They had expected mismanagement and corruption, but they also found unlimited off-budget spending by all ministries and gross overstaffing of all public institutions, which drove public expenditure to unmanageable levels. According to a variety of experts, the military needed to be reduced by about 30 percent and the police by 20 percent. The civil service also needed to be cut—analysts pointed out that 11.5 percent of gross national product (GNP) went to public-sector wages, twice as much as in Poland or Hungary and three times the average for transition economies—but the Mesić government refused even to undertake a serious study of the problem. And, in a microcosm of the bigger picture, government-controlled television employed about 6,000 people where, according to internal reformers, 400 should have sufficed.[25] Further reductions in personnel was also likely to take place in the privatized sector as soon as the parliament enacted the long-awaited bankruptcy law, giving moribund enterprises the opportunity to restructure and downsize their personnel.

With the unemployment rate already at about 20 percent of the labor force, and an even larger percentage not receiving wages regularly, the government was obviously scared of taking steps that would aggravate the problem in the short run, even if they might alleviate it in the longer run. Croatia was simply running out of safety nets. The informal sector already supported a large part of the population, and the pension system, forced to absorb large numbers of new entrants who had chosen early retirement over unemployment, was itself in dire need of rescue.

The litany of economic reforms Croatia needed to undertake, according to the World Bank, included the classic list of structural adjustments all postcommunist systems face, ranging from completing privatization to rewriting all commercial legislation, with the added difficulty of bringing it all in line with European Union standards. The government appeared to be overwhelmed by the number and complexity of the issues confronting it. At least in the economic field, Croatia was facing the limits of what goodwill and a theoretical commitment to change can accomplish.

The International Community and the Second Transition

The international community was both helping the government and making things more complicated. The new government was surrounded by bilateral and multilateral donors, each bearing assistance but also an extensive list of requirements or outright conditionalities. The World Bank, the Commission on Security and Cooperation in Europe, the European Union, and the United Nations High Commissioner for Refugees, all active and engaged, had different priorities, as befits specialized agencies. They all had model solutions for the country's problems, from the restructuring of the pension system to the restructuring of Croatia into a genuinely multiethnic society. Bilateral donors had their requirements as well, some of them very parochial and not very timely under the circumstances. Italy, for example, was insisting on a solution to the problem of Italian properties confiscated by the government of the former Yugoslavia.

There was, at the receiving end of these demands and requirements, only one Croatian government, anxious to show its willingness to live up to high standards and to comply with requirements, but also overwhelmed by the magnitude of the problems and the multiplicity of simultaneous demands. And this government, as donors were inclined to forget, was a coalition that needed to keep its members happy in order to keep the alliance intact. It was also an elected one, which in a few years would be judged by voters according to their standards and requirements, not those of the international agencies and foreign donors. The government would be judged by its success at creating jobs, not the degree to which the size of the public payroll measured up to international norms, and by what it did to improve the lives of Croats, not by how many Serb refugees had returned to the country.

The Dilemmas of Democratic Reconstruction

The success of Croatia's transition from semi-authoritarianism to democracy is not a foregone conclusion. There are many elements that suggest the possibility of success, including the government's commitment to democratic change, a rising level of maturity among political parties and civil society, and the allure of eventual membership in the European Union. Nevertheless, several factors are present that, in combination, create contradictions and tensions that could lead the Croats to turn to another strongman: a population disillusioned by the pace of change, persistent economic difficulties, the growing assertiveness of some organizations of civil society, a fragile governing coalition that reaches decisions slowly and with difficulty, the need for tough economic choices, and the seemingly infinite requirements of the international community. The example of Venezuela provides a reminder that in polarized societies facing difficult problems, the possibility of nondemocratic choices cannot be dismissed out of hand. Paradoxically, the more democratic climate that now prevails in Croatia is making it more difficult for the government to reconcile the multiplicity of conflicting internal demands and disparate foreign requirements.

Additionally, the increased assertiveness of civil society in Croatia is not necessarily a good thing. Civil society includes organizations such as those that helped defeat the HDZ in the 1999 and 2000 elections, human rights groups, NGOs working to reestablish the integrity of the judicial system, and others that embrace a variety of worthy democratic causes. But it also includes increasingly vocal war veterans' associations, which are strongly nationalistic and close to the HDZ. Such groups regard the suspected war criminals the government is extraditing to The Hague or trying at home as heroes who should be honored for saving the motherland rather than prosecuted in courts of law. Nationalist sentiments and resentment against the Serb refugees returning to Croatia is rife among other groups as well. One should not forget that Tudjman and the HDZ enjoyed genuine support.

More important, the former ruling party is not a spent force. In the local elections of May 2001, it won pluralities in fifteen of the twenty-one counties—a remarkable recovery from the 2000 parliamentary and presidential elections. Even the new right-wing party of Tudjman's son Miroslav won five of Zagreb's fifty-one seats. Although the HDZ has had trouble finding the necessary coalition partners and thus governs in only five counties, election results show that voters are deeply frustrated with the new government and its failure to deliver tangible results. The decrease in voter turnout from 70 percent in previous legislative and local elections to a meager 46 percent in the 2001 local elections confirms the extent of voters' malaise.

Croatia's ability to complete the second transition, from semi-authoritarianism to democracy, does not depend solely on the commitment of the new political elite to democratic ideals. The problem is unfortunately much more complicated. As the elections of 2000 in Croatia—and many other elections around the world—demonstrate, a new political elite committed to democracy can come to power very suddenly. But a democratic transition also requires a lot of elements that can only emerge slowly: the will and capacity to embark on a program of political reform to institutionalize changes, the ability to develop an economic policy that leads the country to sustainable economic growth without pushing the population to embrace extreme solutions or populist leadership in the short run, and, not least, the ability to steer among the inchoate requirements of the international community to develop a workable plan. All are long-term issues, and while there are reasons for optimism in Croatia, there are also signs that it is far too early to announce the triumph of democracy.

If Croatia's second transition succeeds, the semi-authoritarianism of the Tudjman period will appear to be a transitional phenomenon, a relatively harmless and possibly even necessary step between communism and democracy. This, however, would be a very misleading interpretation of historical events. Working deliberately and systematically, Tudjman did his best to build a lasting semi-authoritarian regime. His was not a regime forced by circumstances to impose restrictions on its population as even democratic governments often do in case of war. The fact that he eventually failed to build a lasting semi-authoritarian system should not obscure the fact that this is what he was trying to do. There is no difference in this respect between the semi-authoritarianism of Croatia under Franjo Tudjman and that of Azerbaijan, the other postcommunist country in the present study, under Heydar Aliyev. Tudjman, however, tried to develop his semi-authoritarian regime in a country where conditions were much more unfavorable to goals such as his than they were in Azerbaijan.

PART II

Why Semi-Authoritarianism?

Introduction to Part II

THE FIVE COUNTRIES discussed in the first section of the present study differ from each other considerably in terms of history, geographic location, stage of development, and cultural background. They nevertheless share the same essential political characteristics, namely the uneasy blend of democratic facade and authoritarian traits I have labeled *semi-authoritarianism*. Semi-authoritarian regimes are becoming increasingly common; indeed, they are one of the most noticeable outcomes of more than a decade of efforts to promote democracy by the international community. The rise of semi-authoritarianism has unfortunately been a more frequent occurrence than the emergence of democratic regimes on their way to consolidation.

The challenge of democracy promotion in the future is going to be, above all, how to deal with semi-authoritarian regimes. There are not many countries left in the world to which the model that has guided donors' democracy promotion programs still applies. Most countries have already gone through the initial, formal steps of the democratic transition envisaged by donors. Those that have not are mostly countries mired in conflict, which presents a different challenge altogether, beyond the purview of the present study. But by and large the looming problem is that of dealing with countries that were expected to enter a period of democratic consolidation but are instead revealing themselves to be semi-authoritarian.

The first step toward dealing with such countries is to understand better how they manage to maintain the blend of democratic and authoritarian characteristics. In broad terms, the explanations fall into two categories: (1) Such regimes succeed because of the deliberate maneuvers of politicians, usually including those in the opposition, who rely on power networks independent of the formal democratic processes and institutions; and (2) these regimes succeed because underlying conditions reduce the saliency of democracy for a large part of the population, make physical and economic security more important than democratic goals, and furthermore make it very difficult for new organizations to generate power. Semi-authoritarianism, not surprisingly, is the result of a convergence of *agency* and *conditions*. There are many villains in the tale of semi-authoritarian regimes, namely people who simply do not want democracy; but there are also steep mountains to climb and rivers to ford that would be obstacles even under different leadership.

Democracy promotion programs address agency much more than conditions. This is not simply a question of neglect, but a deliberate choice. A fundamental tenet of democracy promotion since the 1990s has been that all countries can democratize, no matter what the initial conditions are, given sufficient political will on the part of the political class and sufficient political pressure and technical assistance from the established democracies. The assumption, however, is not validated by experience: Most of the countries that have undergone a political transition in the last decade or so have not become democratic, and conditions are very much part of the explanation for why this is the case. It is not an accident that the outcome of the political transition in the Czech Republic was quite different from that in Azerbaijan, for example.

Agency, however, is the most visible factor in both successful and unsuccessful transitions and in the rise of semi-authoritarian regimes. Furthermore, focusing on agency does satisfy the propensity of democracy promoters to look at the process in somewhat Manichaean terms, as a struggle of what is good and right against the tyranny of self-serving politicians. Blaming Heydar Aliyev, with his past in the Azerbaijan KGB and the Soviet Communist Party, for the failure of what some hoped would be a democratic transition in Azerbaijan, provides a more satisfying moral outlet for frustration than attributing the failure to low gross national product, for example. Furthermore, focusing on agency provides greater hope that something can be done to tackle the problem of semi-authoritarianism in a relatively short time.

It is relatively easy to make the case that semi-authoritarianism, or any other unsatisfactory outcome of political transition, is the deliberate result of human action. There are obvious guilty parties in all the countries I have discussed, with government and ruling party officials continuing to take deliberate steps to hamper free competition and to shelter themselves from the challenges of opponents. Some of the measures are quite obvious and not too subtle, for example, Hosni Mubarak's jailing of thousands of Islamists in Egypt or Franjo Tudjman's demonizing of opposition parties as treasonous to the cause of an independent Croatia. Other measures are much more sophisticated, such as the constant, carefully calibrated amending of the constitution in which all Senegalese governments, including Abdoullaye Wade's supposedly more democratic one, have indulged.

A degree of manipulation of government programs, democratic mechanisms, and public opinion to further the interests of the incumbent government is common even in democratic countries. Extravagant campaign promises and pre-election pork barrel projects were not invented by semi-authoritarian regimes, and even in democratic societies politicians learn to play institutions and rules to their advantage—by deciding when to dissolve a parliament and call for new elections, for example. The difference is that semi-authoritarian regimes go much further, and that the defenses against excessive, unlawful manipulation are much weaker in the states they rule.

Manipulation, however, does not occur in a vacuum. If the manipulation is more blatant and extreme in some countries, violating the spirit and often the letter of democratic behavior, it is not simply because politicians there are more authoritarian at heart, or less committed to democracy, but also because they can get away with it. In the most extreme cases, they are even encouraged by the population to behave in a nondemocratic manner. Hugo Chávez's personal democratic credentials are weak at best, but the majority of Venezuelans demonstrated that democracy was not their first priority, either, when they elected him to the presidency despite the fact that he had attempted earlier to seize power unconstitutionally. The voters sent a clear message in that election: They were more concerned about the content of government policies and their impact on everyday life than about respect for democratic process.

The democracy promoters' lack of interest in taking into account the importance of conditions results in part from fear that doing so would lead to a passive or defeatist attitude toward democracy promotion, encouraging a wait-and-see stance until conditions somehow improve. As I will show later in the present study, this does not have to be the case. Some of the conditions that impede democratic transitions and facilitate semi-authoritarianism or other undesirable outcomes could in fact be addressed by democracy promoters relatively easily. The issue is not whether donors should remain passive when faced with obstacles, but whether they should address different issues, and in different ways. Some conditions are probably beyond donors' capacity to address, but so (it must be recognized) are the actions of some nondemocratic politicians. No amount of high-level political pressure, support for civil society, or insistence that elections conform to accepted international standards makes a difference when leaders fighting for their political lives are truly determined to resist.[1]

6

Games Semi-Authoritarian Regimes Play

GAME PLAYING is an intrinsic part of democracy. Politicians may play clean or dirty games, and a lot of borderline ones, but they never just publish their platforms and sit back, letting the citizens decide in a rational manner which candidate they want to support. Democratic systems, Joseph Schumpeter lamented, tend to raise to prominent positions not benevolent statesmen who ponder what is best for the country while remaining above the fray, but vote getters who are willing to play the game of politics and are good at it.[1] Political consultants, campaign managers, opinion pollsters, focus groups, and political advertisements are just some of the weapons in the arsenal of the vote getters. Deliberate, rational weighing of political platforms and candidates' qualifications by the voters often appears to be the last thing politicians want, judging from the large amount of sloganeering and mudslinging that occurs in electoral campaigns. Such campaigns are an accepted exercise in manipulation of the voting public, and attempts to curb them run into strong opposition. Even in established democracies, outright election fraud is not unknown, and it was even cruder and more common in earlier years.

There is thus nothing unusual about the fact that politicians in semi-authoritarian states, particularly incumbents, indulge in political games. Some of these games are the familiar ones of democratic politics. Others go well beyond the limits of what is accepted elsewhere. And even the familiar games are played in a more extreme fashion in semi-authoritarian states, where there are few checks on the raw politics of power competition. Power distribution is unbalanced, with a dominant government party and a weak opposition; institutions in many cases exist in name only; and the culture of democracy is not well developed. Simply put, semi-authoritarian regimes play rougher games because they can get away with it.

Much of the game playing in democratic and semi-authoritarian states alike centers on three classic problems politicians need to solve: (1) how to manipulate features of the election process to the maximum permissible extent—by scheduling elections at an advantageous time, for example, or by mounting voter registration drives in some areas but not in others; (2) how to win voters' support; and (3) how to finance campaign activities. The five case studies provide many examples of how semi-authoritarian regimes deal with these problems. Election games are paramount. Although elections are only one aspect of democracy, and arguably not the most important in the end, in the short-run politics of a country, winning elections is all that matters. But even semi-authoritarian leaders cannot maintain power simply by manipulating elections; they need to generate some genuine public support. Opposition parties are even more dependent on such support. The battle for public opinion is thus as important in semi-authoritarian states as in democratic ones. Finally, money is crucial in the politics of all countries where politics is competitive. Politicians have to generate the revenue required to wage election campaigns and to fight the battle for public support.

Semi-authoritarian regimes do not limit their game playing to these classic areas of democratic politics. Since their real goal is to prevent competition that might threaten their hold on power, they devote considerable effort to issues that are not normal parts of the political process of democratic countries. In particular, they seek to prevent the emergence of competing political organizations, rather than just to defeat them in elections; they do their best to control the flow of information to the citizens, hoping to sway public opinion; they manipulate institutions and constitutions to their own advantage with remarkable frequency and thus undermine and distort them; and, in a growing number of cases, they seek to maintain political stability over the long run not by allowing institutions to consolidate but by manipulating the succession process in ways that are usually associated with monarchies rather than republics.

Dealing with the Classic Challenges
of Competitive Politics

In order to maintain a democratic facade, semi-authoritarian regimes need to engage in competitive politics, at least outwardly. They thus need to win elections, generate public support (the two are not the same in semi-authoritarian states), and find the means to finance their activities.

Elections

In any country that seeks to maintain a democratic facade, elections are the first test politicians must surmount on the way to assuming or maintaining power. For their part, donors consider elections to be a threshold that, if crossed with some degree of decorum, allows countries into the wider community of consolidating democracies, still imperfect but struggling toward success. Many of the games played by semi-authoritarian regimes thus center on elections.[2]

The methods used vary considerably from country to country. There are examples of outright, crude electoral fraud perpetrated on election day, although this is not the most important device used by semi-authoritarian regimes. Egyptian courts acknowledged that fraud at the polls was pervasive when they decided to put the polling stations under judicial supervision. International observers' reports on Azerbaijan over the years show that election day processes have never met even minimum technical standards of acceptability. But in most countries, observers usually find little evidence of violence on election day and little stuffing of ballot boxes, even when they conclude that the election process as a whole was neither free nor fair.[3] This is because flawed elections are engineered over time, through layers of marginally acceptable or outright fraudulent practices that started months or even years earlier. Indeed, one of the reasons why even troubled elections are often orderly and uneventful is that the damage has already been done by the time voters go to the polls or will be done afterward in different ways. Semi-authoritarian governments do not have to organize ballot-box stuffing if they can simply misreport the vote count; nor do they need to pay their followers to "vote early and often," as party bosses did in major American cities in technologically less sophisticated times, if they can program computers to do the cheating. This does not mean that what happens at the polling stations is irrelevant, but that the problem goes much deeper.

This is unfortunate, because the cruder the fraud and the shorter the period during which it is carried out, the easier it is to bring it under control. In Senegal, for example, honesty in the counting of rural votes increased dramatically when reporters for local FM radio stations armed with cell phones started calling in to their offices the preliminary vote counts posted at the polling stations; these results were immediately broadcast, making it difficult to change them later in significant ways. There are no similar quick fixes for problems that build up over time.

The conclusion that most of the problems with elections occur long before voters go the polls has led to significant changes in the policies of the international organizations and domestic and international nongovernmental organizations (NGOs) that help organize and monitor elections in countries in transition. Such organizations no longer deploy large international observers' delegations on election day. Instead, they dispatch teams to conduct early assessments of election preparations many months in advance of the actual voting and follow up with periodic reassessments. Coalitions of domestic NGOs formed to monitor elections and get out the vote also tend to organize much earlier than they once did.[4] These have been changes for the better, but they certainly have not been sufficient to eliminate electoral fraud and manipulation, because incumbent governments have at their disposal many ways to influence outcomes.

Manipulation of election schedules is one technique, perhaps less obvious than outright ballot-box stuffing or false vote counts, that semi-authoritarian regimes have embraced to maximize their chances of winning. Primarily, they like to hold elections when they can point to an achievement that increases their popularity. In Croatia, Franjo Tudjman sought to take advantage of military victories, particularly Operation Storm, which led to the reintegration of Serb-occupied territories into Croatia, to give his regime a new mandate. This is a common game even in those democratic countries where the constitution and electoral rules give the executive the power to disband the parliament and set the election date. Indeed, calling for elections at a particularly favorable time is one of the advantages of incumbency that few democratic systems have eliminated—the United States, with its rigid election schedule, is more the exception than the rule.

Semi-authoritarian regimes also make determined efforts to keep potential opposition supporters from participating in elections, often under the guise of ensuring fairness and eliminating fraud. Voter registration, crucial to an honest electoral process, affords ample opportunities for disenfranchising particular voters. Citizens in neglected areas of the country, bound to be dissatisfied with the incumbent government, can easily be bypassed in the registration process; they are difficult to reach in any case. Seemingly legitimate safeguards against fraud, such as requiring people to show a voter identification card before they can vote, can exclude a significant percentage of the population, particularly in rural areas. The problem is exacerbated when the registration process requires voters to travel some distance to register and perhaps to come back a second time to pick up their card.[5] Again, this can disproportionately disenfranchise the poor and those living far from official registration sites. Urban residents can also be disenfranchised through overly stringent registration procedures if the ruling regime views them as a potential threat. The electoral law in Zimbabwe required urban residents, many of whom were strongly opposed to President Robert Mugabe, to present proof of residence in order to register for the 2002 presidential election—a virtually impossible feat for the thousands who occupied rooms in another family's house, squatted in shacks, or did not pay utility bills because they had no electricity or running water in their home.

Even more insidious are rules that require voters to have proper government-issued identity papers in order to register to vote. This can create almost insurmountable obstacles for members of ethnic minorities, who can be denied formal identification and written off as citizens of other states—this is a favorite device in African countries. Conversely, semi-authoritarian regimes can, and often do, load the voter rolls with members of the country's diaspora. Liberal citizenship laws in many countries allow émigrés to maintain dual citizenship and even to reacquire their original citizenship in order to vote; experience shows that members of diasporas usually identify with and support the government in power. In Croatia, Tudjman went to great lengths to encourage members of the diaspora to vote. (Predictably, electoral rules discouraged ethnic Serbs who had fled the country from registering, since they were required to contact authorities in their original place of residence in order to be added to the new voter lists and were rarely informed of the proper procedures for doing so.) Senegal sets up polling stations for its citizens in major American and French cities where there are concentrations of Senegalese. On the other hand, governments that have reasons to fear the antiregime tendencies of their citizens abroad can easily exclude them. Venezuelan citizens residing in Miami are too likely to be opponents of President Hugo Chávez for their homeland's government to consider taking steps to facilitate their election participation. Refugees are another group many governments deliberately keep from voting.

Even if they succeed in registering, people can still be prevented from voting, or at least from voting as they would like, through intimidation. Violence is a common tactic, but it is not the only one. More subtly, semi-authoritarian regimes spread rumors about what happens to people voting for the opposition, or even issue outright warnings. A common rumor, which often gains some currency, is that the vote is not really secret and that the government has ways of finding out who votes for the opposition. Even more credible are government warnings that districts that vote against the government will receive little funding—this is not an empty threat in countries with a weak opposition.[6]

By decreasing the number of polling stations in opposition areas, the government can dissuade some potential voters from even trying to cast their ballots. Among voters who try, despite long distances and other transportation difficulties, some eventually give up in frustration after waiting for hours in barely moving lines; others persevere, only to find that the polling station has closed before their turn has come.

Electoral games played by semi-authoritarian regimes thus span a wide spectrum, ranging from those that respect the law but not the spirit of democracy to those that are clearly fraudulent. Cumbersome registration procedures, for example, are not illegal. They can even be defended as necessary to prevent fraud. But such procedures become undemocratic when they are used to keep citizens from exercising their constitutional right to vote. On the other hand, some measures are illegal, unjustifiable, and undemocratic under all circumstances, such as the intimidation of voters.

Gaining Support

Truly authoritarian regimes typically win elections by absurd majorities because they can simply proclaim whatever results they want.[7] Semi-authoritarian regimes do not have that option. They can indulge in a degree of fraud and manipulation, but they ultimately also need to win popular support. The examples of the two semi-authoritarian regimes in the present study that were ultimately defeated, Tudjman's Croatian Democratic Union in Croatia and Abdou Diouf's Parti Socialiste in Senegal, show that there are limits to what even a determined semi-authoritarian regime can do to win an election when popular support slips significantly.

All governments can win a measure of genuine public support by delivering public services and stimulating economic growth. Some semi-authoritarian regimes in well-administered countries with strong economies, for example Singapore, are successful in doing so. But for most semi-authoritarian regimes, including all those discussed in the present study, this method of generating support is out of reach. In that case, regimes have three options. They can (1) rely on the personal appeal of their leaders, (2) build patronage networks, or (3) play on the population's fears of instability and change. All these methods have their counterparts in democratic countries, but with significant differences. The image projected by the candidate is less crucial when institutions are strong, for example. Playing on the population's fears has a different impact when the specter being conjured is that of a tax increase rather than civil war or the imposition of shari'a.

Many semi-authoritarian governments enjoy real popular support at the outset. They represent an opening of the political system, rather than a closing, and thus arouse hopes for better times ahead. Even Chávez, whose rise to power in a country with a democratic history cannot be described as an opening, was hailed by a large majority as a much needed alternative to an old, ossified political class.

Some semi-authoritarian leaders, furthermore, have considerable personal appeal. It is not necessarily charisma, a personal gift for establishing an emotional link with the population.[8] Among the leaders discussed in the present study, only Chávez can be said to have charisma. But they all represent something the country wanted when they came to power. Hosni Mubarak was promptly nicknamed "*La*

Vache Qui Rit" by his fellow Egyptians, after his supposed resemblance to the laughing cow portrayed on boxes of the popular French cheese by that name. It is not a nickname for a charismatic leader, and Mubarak is not one. But he represented the stability and continuity Egyptians wanted at the time, and he was welcomed. Tudjman, stern and inclined to lecture and scold, was not loved, but he was respected as the father of Croatian independence. In Azerbaijan, Heydar Aliyev represented security after chaos. In different ways, semi-authoritarian leaders initially stand for something people value; paradoxically, they could probably win by fair means many of the elections they so assiduously manipulate.

But such personal appeal is political capital that dwindles unless it is replenished by concrete achievements. In all countries incumbent politicians, be they members of the executive branch or the legislature, have to show that they can deliver tangible goods. Members of parliament need to prove to their constituents that they have brought government money to their district or that they were instrumental in setting up popular programs. The executive has to convince the voters that the country has prospered, or at least improved, under its stewardship. In a democratic system, where elections are free, the benefits have to be widely distributed—the pork barrel has to be capacious, with something in it for as many as possible. Semi-authoritarian regimes, which can manipulate elections, are less concerned with spreading benefits widely than with maintaining the loyalty of a hard core of supporters through generous patronage. In Senegal, patronage meant government jobs for party stalwarts. In Tudjman's Croatia, patronage involved the systematic privatization of state assets into the hands of a small, politicoeconomic elite. In Egypt and Azerbaijan, economic benefits also go to major political supporters. Populist Chávez in Venezuela is somewhat exceptional in seeking to cast a wider net through social programs.

But semi-authoritarian governments also make an effort to reach broader circles. In keeping with their democratic facade, they are becoming adept at borrowing a page from democracy promoters and setting up their own networks of civil society organizations. While authoritarian regimes have traditionally relied on political parties and mass organizations, semi-authoritarian ones are learning to develop NGOs. Donors support NGOs because they see them as nonpartisan organizations, independent of both the government and opposition parties, that help promote citizens' involvement and thus democracy.

In countries with semi-authoritarian regimes, however, the world of civil society organizations is much more complicated. In addition to genuinely independent NGOs, there are at least three other types of organizations. First, there are NGOs that are fronts for, or at least closely related to, opposition political parties. Azerbaijan offers a particularly rich array of such organizations, while genuinely independent NGOs are rare. Such organizations are established both as a means to gain access to donor funds that would not be made available directly to political parties and as a way of extending the parties' reach in different sectors of society. Second, there are the civil society organizations established by the ruling party for the same reason. Often, these take the form of professional associations—journalists' unions, for example—or human rights organizations, set up as competitors for the independent ones. In some cases, semi-authoritarian regimes seek to establish control over previously independent organizations—the struggle between the Egyptian government and the professional syndicates is a case in point. Third, there are organizations that straddle the line between being tools of the incumbent regime and performing the functions of genuine civic groups. An example is the Egyptian women's organization funded by the government and headed by first lady Susan Mubarak. It is obviously not an independent organization, and one of its purposes is to increase support for the government among women. As a result, independent women's organizations consider it to be ideologically tainted and politically suspect. They grudgingly admit, however, that this tainted group is much more effective than they are in promoting the interests of women—Susan Mubarak's statements get national press coverage and the ear of the president, while their own pamphlets languish in obscurity. In sum, civil society organizations in semi-authoritarian regimes are found on all sides of the political divide. They can be independent organizations as well as cogs in the machines that governments use to generate support.

Finally, semi-authoritarian regimes seek to maintain support by playing on the population's fears of instability and radical change. Many of these fears are well founded. Reluctance to abandon a semi-authoritarian but stable government for the unknown does not necessarily denote a lack of understanding of democracy by the population, but can be the result of a sober assessment of a dangerous situation. Azerbaijanis did not vote for Aliyev because they mistook him for a democrat, but because they judged that he was the person most likely to see the country through a very difficult period. To be sure, the 98.8 percent support he claimed to receive in the 1993 elections was fictitious, but there is little doubt that the population was disgusted with the government of Abulfaz Elchibey, frightened by the turmoil, and willing to let a strongman take the helm.

The fear that a move toward democracy will be a leap from the frying pan into the fire is evident in many countries. Many Egyptians who express an interest in greater democracy and are critical of the present regime also argue that democratization must come from the top if chaos is to be avoided. They would like Mubarak to be more liberal and more tolerant, but they have no intention of fighting him to obtain the change, lest the outcome of the fight be instability. War-weary Croats in the late 1990s were happy that violence had abated and were not inclined to risk more turmoil in order to get rid of Tudjman, although they quickly took advantage of the opportunity to elect a more democratic president when he died. Even in Senegal, which has no experience with large-scale political violence, it took repeated elections before the voters finally took the decisive step of rejecting the familiar party and president. Indeed, voters must perceive the situation as desperate before they take the plunge into the unknown, as Venezuelans did when they elected Chávez.

Semi-authoritarian regimes play on these genuine fears, seeking in many cases to portray themselves as the only safeguard against chaos. Furthermore, they often do their best to guarantee that there is no appealing alternative to their rule. By placing obstacles in the way of even moderate parties, Mubarak makes sure that voters will be forced to choose between the status quo and change that could bring Islamic extremists to power. President Yoweri Museveni of Uganda plays the same game: To justify his continued refusal to hold multiparty elections, he reminds his fellow citizens that the parties that would compete are the same ones that in the past triggered the crisis that led to the rise of the infamous Idi Amin. At the same time, Museveni does his best to keep new parties from forming or the old ones from reforming themselves, thus ensuring that Ugandans will continue to face the choice between him and the discredited organizations of the past.

Of all the games in which semi-authoritarian regimes indulge, this playing with the population's fears is one of the most difficult for donors to handle, because in some circumstances greater democracy and freer political competition can lead to results that are threatening to the local population, to the international community, or to both. Free and fair elections in 1993 in Burundi appeared to be a great success initially, but eventually plunged the country into a turmoil that has yet to end. Elections in Algeria in 1992 would have brought to power a radical Islamist party, had they not been canceled at the last moment. Nobody really knows what the outcome of genuinely free elections would be with the participation of the Muslim Brothers in Egypt. Democratic process can lead to nondemocratic outcomes, and the international community is as fearful of this as the local populations—and usually less willing to admit it.

Generating Revenue

Without a well-filled campaign chest, no party or candidate can hope to make much headway in a democracy. In semi-authoritarian states, too, money is crucial. There is a fundamental difference, however. Where democracy prevails, the incumbent party or parties and those in the opposition have to raise money by the same means. In semi-authoritarian systems, the governing party enjoys a huge advantage, because it can dip into the state treasury to finance its election campaign.

In the world of ideal democracy, there is a clear distinction between the finances of the government and those of political parties. Government revenue derives from taxes and user fees paid by the citizens, and, in transitional countries, from the sale of public-sector enterprises. This revenue is devoted exclusively to financing services and programs decided upon by the executive and the legislature through a transparent budget process. Political parties must finance themselves through their own fund-raising efforts and, when the law so prescribes, government subsidies allocated to all parties in a fair manner on the basis of clearly stated rules.

The reality is somewhat different, even in democratic countries. There are always questions about the degree to which incumbents blur the line between their party role and their government position, charging expenditures made for the benefit of the party to the state budget. Some infractions are minor—for example, a U.S. government official occasionally making fund-raising calls from a government office rather than a party office. Other are quite serious—investigations into the finances of Italian political parties in the 1980s revealed that those belonging to the governing coalition routinely took a cut on the awarding of public works contracts, in effect financing party activities out of government funds. Despite minor and major violations, the rule is clear, however: Party and government finances should be, and in most cases are, kept separate.

No such distinction exists in semi-authoritarian states, where the boundary separating the finances of the government from those of the incumbent party is very permeable. Seepage of funds from the government to the party is difficult to stem whenever a party is in a dominant position and the institutions are weak. An additional source of ruling-party financing at public expense is provided by the liberal economic reforms undertaken by democratizing regimes or by those that want to appear as if they are democratizing. Privatization programs provide ample opportunities for building up the finances of the dominant party and those associated with it at the expense of the public.

This was particularly evident in Tudjman's Croatia, for example, where the privatization process was manipulated so as to transfer assets into the hands of Tudjman's inner circle, thereby benefiting both individuals and the ruling party. But Croatia is far from the only example. Starting with Anwar Sadat's Open Door Policy, economic liberalization in Egypt has led to the rise of a stratum of wealthy individuals with close political connections to the ruling party and the political elite.

Connected to the issue of party financing is the broader one of corruption. Government funds are diverted illegally both for political purposes and for personal enrichment—and the two are often difficult to separate, as in the examples just cited. In most of the countries discussed in the present study, with the exception of Senegal, corruption has been singled out by foreign and domestic analysts as a major problem with far-reaching repercussions. The new government in Croatia is still trying to sort out the corruption of the Tudjman era and is possibly adding new problems of its own. Azerbaijan has quickly gained a reputation as an extremely corrupt country—one of the most corrupt in the world, some would argue, although there are many competitors for that dubious honor. Corruption is a significant problem in Egypt, and it is spreading in Venezuela as well.

Corruption is most often discussed as an economic problem. It decreases economic efficiency and skims resources from public services that are already underfunded; worse, it severely hampers development by siphoning capital from the country, to be invested overseas or stashed in offshore accounts. And, of course, corruption is always an ethical problem. But the political consequences of corruption should not be neglected either, because corruption helps consolidate the hold on power of dominant parties and semi-authoritarian regimes by providing them with a level of funding the opposition cannot possibly match.

Corruption also alters the balance of power among the branches of government. A corrupt president gains access to assets that will make his or her position stronger vis-à-vis the legislature or the judiciary. Corrupt judges, on the other hand, enrich themselves and subvert justice, but do not increase the power of the judiciary in relation to other branches of government. Nor do corrupt legislators enhance the role of the parliament. Weak institutions, in turn, help perpetuate corruption, creating a vicious circle.

Preventing Transfers of Power

While outwardly committed to competitive politics, semi-authoritarian regimes devote time and resources to making the political environment less hospitable for those who would contest their power.

Limiting Competition

In theory, semi-authoritarian regimes recognize freedom of association, but they limit it in a variety of ways, both obvious and subtle. Even democratic countries impose some limits, such as banning violent and subversive organizations, but the laws are strict and the reasons for outlawing particular groups must be compelling. Semi-authoritarian regimes freely impose limits on both political organizations and political candidates.

States have a duty to protect their citizens and their institutions from disruptive groups, semi-authoritarian regimes point out. They have the right to prevent foreign groups from interfering with domestic political processes by banning foreign funding of political organizations. They cannot allow noncitizens to run for office. These arguments are reasonable, but the implementation of such policies in the semi-authoritarian context often is not. Under the guise of doing what is normal and justifiable in democratic countries, semi-authoritarian regimes do their best to eliminate meaningful competition.

In many deeply divided countries, for example, the authorities impose a ban on ethnic or religious parties; such bans exist in countries as different as Nigeria, Mauritania, Tunisia, and Uzbekistan. Given the potentially dreadful consequences of elections contested along ethnic or religious lines, such requirements can be construed as important measures to limit polarization and prevent civil war. In reality, the rules are misused to stymie competition rather than to prevent polarization. A common way to ensure that a party will be multiethnic, for example, is to require that it collect a certain number of signatures from a majority of the country's regions in order to qualify for registration. Such a rule may curb ethnic parties, but it also makes it extremely difficult for new parties to register, as it is virtually impossible for a new group to organize simultaneously everywhere.

Similarly, a ban on foreign funding of political parties, while often justifiable to control outside meddling in domestic politics, plays into the hands of incumbents by making it difficult for other organizations to compete. In extreme cases, the prohibition of foreign funding can make democratic competition impossible. In one of Africa's most successful postconflict transitions, that of Mozambique in 1994, the international community provided $18 million for the major opposition party, Renamo, and $3 million to help other parties become established.[9] Without such outside help, competitive elections and—even more important—peace itself simply would have been impossible. Renamo, the movement that had waged war against the government for fifteen years, had to become a competitive political organization or it would resume fighting. But without foreign support, Renamo would not have the means to emerge from the bush and remake itself as a viable political party. A ban on foreign funding would have amounted to a ban on competitive politics.

On the other hand, there is no doubt that foreign funding of political parties can subvert the meaning of democracy by making it possible for outsiders to distort the election process and put in power the leader favored by the funders. There was no distortion in Mozambique, because the countries and organizations that bankrolled Renamo took a truly neutral position toward the outcome of the elections. They wanted both parties to be well represented in the parliament, and both candidates to have a chance to compete, but they did not support one side over the other. Foreign funding of the opposition was a much more political undertaking in Serbia, because the international community wanted a specific outcome, the ouster of Slobodan Milošević.[10] Since it is now clear that the majority of Serbs also wanted his defeat, it is possible to argue that the international community's intervention was democratic because it allowed the popular will to triumph—when the support started, however, this was a hypothesis at best. But foreign funding and campaign support could also be used to thwart the popular will, leading to the victory of a candidate who is more popular with the international community than with his or her fellow citizens. Foreign funding of political parties in countries with semi-authoritarian regimes lies in a gray area between genuine democracy promotion and blatant political interference.[11]

Citizenship requirements are emerging as a tool of choice among semi-authoritarian regimes intent on excluding dangerous competitors. All countries, of course, require that candidates for political office be citizens, and in some cases even that they be born in the country. Semi-authoritarian regimes often go further, requiring that even candidates' parents be born in the country. Such requirements are particularly threatening to democracy in Africa, where most contemporary countries were not independent and in some cases were not even separate entities until the 1960s. A determination of the citizenship of one's parents can be quite arbitrary under such conditions, making it easy for a determined regime to refuse to qualify a potentially dangerous competitor. An extreme case is provided by Zambia, where Kenneth Kaunda, the country's first president and leader from independence in 1964 until his ouster in multiparty elections in 1991, was declared ineligible to stand for election in 1996 because his parents

were foreign born. Kaunda's reelection would not have contributed to
the democratization of the country—he had certainly been in power
far too long already. The citizenship issue, however, was a transparent
ruse by Kaunda's successor, Frederick Chiluba, to eliminate his main
competitor from the political scene.[12]

Managing Information

Under most semi-authoritarian regimes, state-controlled television
and radio, in particular, are used to mute or distort opposition messages. Even when rules are in place guaranteeing access to the air-
waves for all political parties, incumbent regimes manage to get much
more exposure simply by ensuring ample and sympathetic coverage
of what the government is doing. The print media are usually less
tightly controlled, and some genuinely independent publications survive in all semi-authoritarian states. The significance of these publications, however, is greatly limited by their small circulation, a consequence of the relatively high cost of newspapers and, in the least
developed countries, the low level of literacy and difficulties related to
distribution in rural areas.

Media control by semi-authoritarian regimes can be as crude as the
seizing of issues of newspapers and magazine containing articles the
government finds particularly offensive, and as sophisticated as trying
to bankrupt publications through frequent tax inspections and the resulting penalties. The latter was a favorite method in Croatia during
the Tudjman presidency. Governments have many ways to hamper the
distribution of independent newspapers and to limit their revenue. Independent publishers can be punished by artificially created shortages
of newsprint that force them to reduce press runs, if they can even publish at all. Government agencies with a monopoly over the distribution
of newspapers and magazines can delay or even scuttle the delivery of
publications that are deemed overly critical. In countries with a weak
private sector and, thus, a limited market for advertising, the government can add to the woes of financially shaky independent publications by refusing to place official announcements in their pages.

Semi-authoritarian regimes also use both carrots and sticks to exert
direct influence on what the media print or broadcast. Such regimes

intimidate, sue, and even arrest editors and reporters, but also woo others by establishing close relations that enhance these journalists' importance. Since the days of Nasser, Egyptian governments have mastered the art of ambiguous relations with the newspaper *Al-Ashram*, which succeeds in being neither government sponsored nor independent, and enjoys considerable prestige as a result. In many countries with semi-authoritarian regimes, a degree of self-censorship allows independent newspapers to exist but also limits their role.

There is no end to the schemes semi-authoritarian regimes will employ to manage the news media. In Croatia, Tudjman turned to privatization in an attempt to silence Radio 101, a municipally owned radio station in Zagreb that had established a strong, independent voice. His attempt to "privatize" the station by forcing its sale to a so-called business group controlled by his own son, however, was too obvious an attempt to silence an independent station and provoked a strong reaction by the residents of Zagreb. Faced with the outcry, Tudjman decided not to fight this particular battle, and Radio 101 survived. But Tudjman did fight other battles against free media with greater subtlety, and as a result usually prevailed. For example, he succeeded in preventing the emergence of a private national television channel—a politically dangerous development from his point of view—by insisting that one of the three frequencies allocated to Croatia be awarded to a network of small, local stations. (The other two frequencies are controlled by the state-run network, Croatia Radio-Television.) Under the democratic guise of championing the local media and the rights of small organizations, Tudjman prevented the emergence of a potentially critical national voice. Local stations have less political potential because of their narrow focus and are therefore less threatening to semi-authoritarian regimes.

The most insidious method of media control by semi-authoritarian regimes—and an increasingly common one—is the lawsuit. All democratic countries have libel laws to give individuals protection from unsubstantiated and damaging accusations. Libel laws must maintain a delicate balance between the rights of individuals to privacy and protection against defamation and the right of the public to information. There is scope for disagreement about where the balance lies, and different democratic countries have reached somewhat different conclusions in this regard. In countries with semi-authoritarian regimes, there is no balance. The government uses libel laws to muzzle independent media or bankrupt them through legal action if they do not cave in.

Admittedly, independent media do behave irresponsibly on many occasions, which is not surprising in countries with little experience with press freedom. There is much tabloid-style journalism and rumor mongering masquerading as investigative work. This provides governments bent on controlling the media with plenty of excuses to paint all inconvenient information with the same brush and to suppress legitimate news and the results of serious investigations along with outrageous allegations.

Efforts to control the flow of information reveal a lot about the nature of semi-authoritarian regimes. It is less clear how effective they are in practice and how much they actually contribute to the maintenance of semi-authoritarianism by depriving citizens of the information they need to participate meaningfully in the political process. People everywhere get their information from many different sources, and the closer a country is to an information-rich region, the less effective the efforts to control the media become. Access to international media is still relatively difficult in some countries, but practically universal in others, such as Croatia. Even in more information-deprived environments, the days when governments could monopolize information are long gone. By listening to foreign media, particularly the programs beamed to a region by major stations in Europe and the United States, citizens can learn a lot about what their government is doing and how it is regarded overseas. They can learn the same about major opposition parties in their country. On the other hand, they learn virtually nothing about newer or less prominent political organizations, and this makes it more difficult for such groups to become known. For example, it is possible, though difficult to prove conclusively, that the limited flow of information in Senegal in the past contributed to the survival of Abdoullaye Wade as the eternal opposition candidate. It is difficult to imagine that in a freer political climate a losing candidate could have remained politically viable for twenty years, but in Senegal, Wade had the advantage of name recognition, which others found difficult to achieve.

In addition to the broadcast and print media, informal channels, which exist in all semi-authoritarian states, diffuse a great deal of information. Islamist groups in Egypt cannot publish freely or hold political rallies, but they get their message across through the mosques. Much information travels from person to person, as it always has. The Internet, accessible to only a minuscule minority in many countries, nevertheless contributes to the general exchange of ideas by feeding information into the informal networks on which people rely.

From the point of view of democracy promotion, the availability of alternate channels through which information is diffused is important when donors are deciding how their invariably scarce democracy promotion funds should be allocated. The free flow of information is crucial in a democracy, but so are, for instance, strong parties or an independent judiciary. In the allocation of scarce resources, media operations do not automatically deserve priority if other sources of information are available to citizens.

Manipulating Constitutions and Political Institutions

Semi-authoritarian regimes are superficially respectful of laws and civil institutions, which provide their democratic cover. They do not abrogate or simply disregard constitutions as authoritarian governments often do, and by and large they implement policies through the institutions. The better-established semi-authoritarian regimes in particular would not consider disregarding the constitution, ignoring other laws, or dismantling institutions. Technically, the government of Egypt is punctiliously law abiding, as is that of Senegal. Croatia has also been imbued with respect for legality, both under Tudjman and today. Even Chávez, after attempting to seize power militarily, became president by running for office in a perfectly regular election. Azerbaijan, where not only the regime but the very state itself is new, is the only country among those considered in the present study where there is no sign of allegiance to constitutionalism and the rule of law.

Respect for the constitution and the laws, however, is rendered almost meaningless in some semi-authoritarian states by the ease with which these instruments can be amended or rewritten. In democratic countries, constitutions in particular are enduring documents, difficult to amend. As a result, they genuinely transcend the government of the day and impose meaningful restrictions on it. While laws are easier to change, the process still requires much discussion and bargaining among interest groups. In semi-authoritarian regimes, where the governing party controls not only the absolute majority in the parliament but often even the qualified majority needed to amend the constitution, it is possible for a government to respect due process and legality without being bound by inconvenient restrictions. If the constitution does not fit the political needs of the day, it can be changed. The constitution, the civil institutions, and the laws do not provide a restraining framework for the actions of the government because the government can alter them at will.

Senegal is the epitome of the semi-authoritarian state that always respects the constitution and the law but systematically guts them of their real function as constraints on government action. Senegalese politicians have consistently been conscientious about showing respect for the law and political institutions. Their discourse is replete with legal terminology. The idea of simply flouting constitutional provisions or acting outside the framework of institutions has been alien since the early days of independence. Indeed, respect for the law appears to be part of Senegal's cherished identity as the outpost of democracy in West Africa. But politicians have no qualms about engaging in a never-ending process of constitutional revision and institutional restructuring to further their political goals. Both of Senegal's first two presidents, Léopold Sédar Senghor and Abdou Diouf, amended the 1963 constitution repeatedly, and Diouf's successor, Abdoullaye Wade, promulgated a new constitution in January 2001, just months after his victory. In the past ten years, presidential term limits have been changed three times, the Senate has been abolished and reinstated, and rules on party formation have changed dramatically, among other modifications.

Senegal is an extreme case but not a unique one. In Venezuela, Chávez dedicated more than a year to rewriting the country's constitution and thus reforming its institutions. The resulting document abolished the Senate, thereby giving the president the right to appoint the vice president, and eliminated the rule barring a president from seeking consecutive terms. The sum of the changes will allow Chávez to stay in power legally for thirteen years if he wins reelection. Similarly, Egypt's constitution was amended in 1980 to eliminate presidential term limits outright, and Azerbaijan's 1995 constitution was notable for the substantial powers it vested in the president. There are, of course, cases in which constitutional reform must be the first step toward democracy—in countries where the constitution prescribes a single-party system, for example, or does not grant political rights to all citizens. It is the repeated amending of a democratic constitution that should be cause for alarm.

Dealing with the Problem of Succession

The problem of succession—how to transfer power in an orderly way when the incumbent steps down, dies, or becomes otherwise unable to remain in office—is a problem that historically has plagued all monarchies and remains a problem in today's remaining kingdoms. The issue of succession, for example, is central to the politics of Saudi Arabia and it is the object of endless speculation. However, it is not a problem normally associated with republics and certainly not with democracies. In such systems, the problem of succession should not exist, because power is supposed to reside in the position of the executive and not in the individual occupying that position, and mechanisms are in place to determine how the position must be filled. It is a telling commentary on the nature of semi-authoritarian regimes that succession is emerging as an issue in some of them. The presence of this issue highlights the extent to which power remains personal and non-institutionalized in such systems despite the trappings of democracy; it confirms the weakness of the institutions and the scant relevance of the processes to replace officeholders through elections. Succession is already an issue in Azerbaijan and Egypt, as well as in other countries in Central Asia and the Middle East with semi-authoritarian inclinations. Given the large number of semi-authoritarian regimes in the world, it may well become a major problem in the future.

The problem of succession emerges because semi-authoritarian regimes are not, and by and large cannot be, institutionalized. As I have argued, semi-authoritarian leaders need to maintain the cover provided by democratic institutions; thus, they cannot develop institutions that openly suit their goal of stifling competition and perpetuating their hold on power. As a result, power remains highly personal, concentrated in the hands of a ruling group adept at playing the games that perpetuate its power. On paper, semi-authoritarian regimes appear at times to have a lot of institutional strength because of the dominant role of their parties. In Egypt, Mubarak's National Democratic Party controls 85 percent of the seats in the National Assembly. Aliyev's New Azerbaijan Party nominally controls 75 out of 125 seats in the National Assembly, but some 30 additional seats occupied by so-called independents are in reality part of the machine. In Senegal, Wade's Coalition Sopi has 89 out of 120 seats, and Diouf's Parti Socialiste previously enjoyed a similarly large majority. Before Tudjman's demise, the Croatian Democratic Union controlled around 60 percent of the legislative seats in successive elections. Only in Venezuela is the picture less lopsided, with Chávez's Movimiento V República winning 76 of 165 parliamentary seats in the 2000 elections, but with the opposition extremely fragmented.

But the dominant parties in countries with semi-authoritarian regimes are often quite weak organizationally. These are not Soviet-style parties, with a strong machine that makes decisions and eventually controls the succession. On the contrary, they are often poorly institutionalized and organized and thus highly dependent on a leader. The National Democratic Party of Egypt has shown great organizational weakness in recent years, failing to ensure the election of the candidates it has vetted. An effort to revitalize the party is underway, but the outcome, particularly considering the troubled history of all Egyptian parties, including Nasser's, is an open question. Aliyev's New Azerbaijan Party is centered on his own figure—he made the party, not vice versa. Similarly, Venezuela's Movimiento V República is Chávez's creation, and it is difficult to imagine it continuing to be a political force without him. The weak performance of the Croatian Democratic Union in the presidential elections that followed Tudjman's death shows clearly how much such parties depend on personalities. These are not parties that can ensure orderly succession and thus the perpetuation of the power of the present ruling group beyond the tenure of the current president. Yet this ruling group wants to perpetuate its power, which is why the issue of succession looms so important.

There are examples of successful transfers of power from one personality to another in semi-authoritarian regimes. In Senegal, Léopold Senghor succeeded in transferring power to his handpicked successor, Abdou Diouf, mostly on the strength of his own personality and his image as the country's founding father. In fact, Senghor's influence over the regime extended even further: The long-awaited *alternance* has brought to power not a new player, but Abdoullaye Wade, a man also handpicked by Senghor to be a leader of the opposition. Egypt also succeeded in ensuring continuity after Anwar Sadat's assassination, largely thanks to the support of the military, the institution that has guaranteed stability and continuity in the country since 1952.

But such successions are exceptional. Even in Egypt there is now greater uncertainty about the succession, particularly because it is bound to entail a transition to a new generation or at least to a new age cohort. There are doubts about the present political importance of the military and about the balance of power between it and the security agencies. Nobody really knows what either the military or the security agencies would do if Mubarak died. It is thus not surprising that, with the president in his seventies, succession has emerged as a critical issue in the country.

Succession is an even more delicate problem in Azerbaijan, a young country where the regime is much more dependent on its leader than Egypt is. Heydar Aliyev has tried to solve the problem by designating his son Ilham as his successor. The officials of President Aliyev's New Azerbaijan Party have accepted the move, albeit with some reluctance, believing that only a successor anointed by Aliyev can perpetuate the weak party's hold on power.

Succession may prove to be the Achilles' heel of semi-authoritarian regimes, a point of maximum weakness that cannot be protected by the games they are adept at playing under normal circumstances. While successions can provide some unique opportunities to further the cause of democracy, they do not automatically lead to a new democratic opening. They simply represent a moment of instability that can lead equally easily to greater democracy, renewed semi-authoritarianism, or even greater authoritarianism.

Conclusions

Semi-authoritarianism is a political system deliberately created and maintained by a ruling elite through skillful game playing and maneuvering. Semi-authoritarian states are not simply unconsolidated and imperfect democracies, which, given time and judiciously administered foreign assistance, will blossom into full-fledged democracies. Rather, they are countries where the leaders have consciously chosen to limit the amount of transformation because it suits their interests to do so. Far from being a transitional stage, semi-authoritarianism is often an intended endpoint, a system leaders are determined to perpetuate, in some cases even beyond their death. Further change is not impossible; Croatia, I have argued, has started a second transition, although the outcome is far from certain at this point. But a second transition requires a break with the existing trend, not simply incremental changes.

The evidence that semi-authoritarian leaders deliberately engage in efforts to thwart democracy had led organizations concerned with promoting democracy to focus their efforts on preventing or at least limiting those games. There are programs to improve the quality of elections, to provide civic education so that the population will be less open to demagogic appeals or fear mongering, and to promote transparency so that it will not be so easy for incumbent governments to use public revenues for partisan political purposes. Other programs seek to improve the fairness of the laws regulating the registration of political parties and NGOs, and to improve both the freedom and the quality of independent media. These are all positive steps.

Limiting game playing is not enough, however. Leaders of semi-authoritarian states do not play their games in a vacuum. They are successful not only because of their political skills, which are often remarkable, but because underlying conditions in their societies allow and even encourage them to behave as they do. Understanding those conditions is crucial to explaining the rise and survival of semi-authoritarian regimes and to devising more effective ways of tackling the problem of semi-authoritarianism.

7

Beyond Games:
Looking at Structural Obstacles

THERE HAS BEEN much resistance among democracy promoters to systematic analysis of the structural conditions that impede the development of democracy. This resistance is problematic because it is not possible to explain the different outcomes of political transitions, and more specifically the rise of semi-authoritarian regimes, simply by looking at the games played by political elites. Nor can democracy promoters hope to help countries overcome semi-authoritarianism without addressing such underlying problems.

A definition is in order here for the term *structural conditions*. I am certainly not implying that there are some fundamental conditions or characteristics of a society that inevitably determine the outcome of political transitions. I am simply arguing that in all countries the political process is affected by conditions—be they economic, political, cultural, or anything else—that do not depend on the choices made by specific regimes or leaders and would influence the political process under any leadership. Ethnic polarization in Croatia, for example, is a structural condition that constitutes an obstacle to democracy, increasing the probability of a semi-authoritarian outcome. Ethnic polarization was a problem between the two world wars, in the Tito period, and under Franjo Tudjman. It still affects politics under the more democratic leadership of President Stjepan Mesić and Prime Minister Ivica Račan. The choices made by political actors can improve or exacerbate ethnic tensions in Croatia, but there is an underlying problem that constitutes a given of the situation. Income maldistribution and the rapid decline of living standards in Venezuela are structural conditions that impede the restoration of democracy there. Structural conditions can and do change, but they do not change quickly, or by government fiat. If Heydar Aliyev were to opt for honest political competition and the international community provided sufficient technical aid, Azerbaijan could hold impeccably free and fair elections the next time its citizens went to the polls, because what is at issue in Azerbaijan is political will and technocratic expertise. However, if Hugo Chávez suddenly became a committed democrat, economic polarization would not decrease, and it would continue to dim the prospects for sustained democracy in Venezuela.

The resistance to discussing structural conditions among democracy promoters is explained by three concerns. First, the admission that such conditions exist can be interpreted as a justification for or even a defense of semi-authoritarian regimes, something along the lines of, "It is really not their fault that they are not democratic, in that they cannot help it given domestic conditions." Second, any discussion of structural conditions that facilitate semi-authoritarianism is also a discussion of the structural conditions for democracy, and there is much ideological and political baggage attached to that debate. Third, structural conditions are difficult for democracy promoters to address, and bringing attention to their importance can be construed as a call for passivity in the face of daunting long-term problems.

The first concern can be put to rest quickly. The analysis, in the previous chapter, of the games semi-authoritarian regimes play shows clearly that such regimes are not the passive products of circumstances beyond their control, but that they are actively engaged in the promotion and maintenance of semi-authoritarianism. Still, it is important to acknowledge that there is more than misbehavior to the problem of semi-authoritarianism and that certain conditions facilitate game playing.

The second issue is more complex. The argument that the conditions for democracy do not exist in all countries has been used in the past in demeaning and condescending ways, with more than a whiff of racism. Colonial powers argued that colonized people, Africans in particular, were not ready for democracy when they denied them the right to vote in colonial elections and later when they resisted decolonization. Similar arguments were used to keep African Americans from voting in the United States. Also, during the Cold War, Western countries often justified their security-driven support for friendly authoritarian regimes by arguing that democracy was beyond the reach of Africans in any case. The concept of readiness for democracy imputed a certain intellectual and emotional immaturity or even inferiority to those "not ready," and deserved discarding. But structural conditions are not the same as readiness. The main factors that encourage the rise of semi-authoritarian regimes are not tied to the level of development or a country's political culture, but, as I will argue, to problems such as state formation or economic and ethnic polarization.

The third concern, that focusing on conditions leads to an abandonment of democracy promotion efforts, is based in part on a confusion between the idea of preconditions and that of conditions. I am *not* arguing that nothing should be done to promote democracy until certain specified preconditions are met—until a country reaches a certain per capita income, for example, or a certain level of education. I am simply stating that there are conditions that increase the likelihood of semi-authoritarianism. Furthermore, many of the structural problems that encourage semi-authoritarianism could and should be addressed by democracy promotion programs.

This discussion of the structural conditions that help explain the rise of semi-authoritarianism is mostly based on what the case studies indicate. I will single out those structural conditions that have emerged as problematic in the five countries and in other cases with which I am familiar, drawing only occasionally on the literature on democratic transitions. A larger number of case studies probably would call attention to additional issues—this is only a preliminary exploration.

The conditions influencing the rise of semi-authoritarianism are interrelated to some extent, but they can be divided for clarity into three broad categories: socioeconomic conditions, problems of state formation, and problems related to the nature of the political process.

The Impact of Socioeconomic Conditions

I will focus in this section on two issues. The first is the absence of vigorous economic growth and socioeconomic change, which makes transitions shallow political processes that do not reflect deeper transformations in the society. The second is the problem of ethnic and economic polarization. These conditions are not found exclusively in countries with semi-authoritarian regimes, of course. Lack of socioeconomic change can result in the survival of a modern authoritarian regime or a traditional monarchy as easily as it can lead to semi-authoritarian transformation. Countries can overcome the challenge of polarization and become democratic—in turn, decreasing polarization. Structural conditions thus should not be looked at as causes of semi-authoritarianism, but simply as factors that help facilitate its rise but can also lead to different outcomes.

Low Income, Stagnant Economies, and Shallow Transitions

Many studies of democratization have explored the links between democratization and levels of economic development. The conclusions of these studies can be summarized roughly in the following fashion: First, income levels have an impact on democratization, with richer countries being more likely to become democratic[1] and above all to remain democratic[2]; second, economic growth also has a positive effect, no matter what the initial conditions are—countries with growing economies are more likely to become and to stay democratic.[3]

Such conclusions relate well to the cases. These are low- or moderate-income countries with shrinking or stagnating economies. Azerbaijan and Senegal are classified by the World Bank as low-income countries, and Egypt barely makes it into the lower-middle-income category. All three, furthermore, have extremely sluggish economies. Venezuela is classified as an upper-middle-income country, but this classification is distorted by oil revenue and therefore does not reflect the true living conditions of most people. Furthermore, the Venezuelan economy has been contracting, with a considerable reduction in living standards. Croatia, which more genuinely falls into the upper-middle-income category, has suffered serious decline and continues to stagnate economically.

These conclusions suggest that low income levels and lack of economic growth probably facilitate the rise of semi-authoritarianism.

By themselves, however, such conclusions do not throw any light on why such correlations exist, or how low and stagnant incomes translate into political processes and behavior that lead to the rise of semi-authoritarian regimes.

A possible explanation for why low-income and stagnant economies favor semi-authoritarianism is suggested by studies of countries that democratized early, during what Samuel Huntington labeled the "first wave."[4] Such studies conclude that democracy is the result of very deep and complex processes of social and economic transformation, and in particular of the changes in the relations among, and the political importance of, social classes that result from economic change.[5] It is difficult to relate the specific conclusions of the historical cases to today's situation—exploring the relations between landlords and peasants in a country such as Azerbaijan does not hold much promise as an explanation of Aliyev's rise to power. Nevertheless, these studies call attention to a fundamental difference between these deep transitions and the shallow ones discussed in the present study. In deep transitions, new classes or new interest groups emerge, and the power dynamic shifts in ways that necessitate political change. But in the shallow transitions that have led to semi-authoritarianism, there has been little underlying change. Instead, political change is superimposed on economic and social structures that do not appear to be changing in significant ways. Change has been driven by discontent with regimes that have been in power too long, by nationalism, or by the contagion from events in other countries; change has not come from the emergence of new social groups clamoring to gain a political role. The lack of significant economic growth prevents such deeper transformations of society and economy and keeps political transition shallow.

These considerations lead to two tentative conclusions, the first being that political transitions, and even attempts at democratization, are not impossible in countries with stagnating economies or low incomes. But the absence or sluggishness of economic growth makes political transitions shallow, because they are not accompanied by socioeconomic change. These shallow transitions result in shallow democratic processes, which can lead not to genuine democratic transformation but to the facade of democracy that is typical of semi-authoritarian systems.

The Problems of Polarization

The case studies also suggest that another condition that favors the rise of semi-authoritarianism is polarization. With the exception of Senegal, the countries discussed in the present study are polarized along economic, ethnic, or religious lines.

Deep economic inequality is the most obvious and widespread form of polarization in all five case study countries. The income share of the poorest 10 percent of the population ranges from 1.6 percent in Venezuela to 4.4 percent in Egypt; the share of the top 10 percent ranges from 48.6 percent in Venezuela to about 29 percent in Croatia and Egypt.[6]

Economic polarization is a crucial factor in the crisis of democracy in Venezuela and the key to Hugo Chávez's rise. Venezuela suffered a period of rapid economic decline during the 1980s, and the social consequences were made worse by the measures taken to revive the economy. In the 1980s and 1990s, per capita income in the country declined by 40 percent, dragging 70 percent of the population below the poverty line. Most Venezuelans, furthermore, were convinced that the political elite was directly responsible for the decline because the oil revenue would have been sufficient to guarantee a decent life for all citizens if it had not been squandered by corruption and mismanagement. As a result, economic hardship and inequality turned into political polarization and the rejection of the old political class. From the beginning, Chávez was hailed as a hero by the impoverished and demonized by the business class.

The other countries discussed in the present study are also deeply divided economically, although the economic differences have not been politicized to quite the same extent as in Venezuela. In Egypt, inequality deepened in the 1980s and 1990s, following a period, initiated by Gamal Abdel Nasser, when the government sought to redistribute wealth and provide most Egyptians with a social safety net. The system was financially unsustainable, but while it lasted, it made life better for many, particularly the urban lower-middle class. Then came Anwar Sadat and the Open Door Policy, which favored growth over redistribution, with the result that the business class benefited at the expense of the lower classes. Making matters worse, the Open Door Policy was a half-hearted measure, sufficient to weaken Nasser's welfare state but not to unleash a vigorous free-market economy. The problems created by partial reform were not immediately evident, because Sadat's reforms were introduced at a time when the new wealth of oil-producing states, particularly those in the Persian Gulf region, was creating a large demand for Egyptian workers there. With more than two million Egyptians working outside the country by the late 1970s and sending remittances home, a high percentage of families experienced a considerable boost in income. But jobs outside Egypt started evaporating in the mid-1980s, and domestic income dried up right along with them. Similarly, in formerly communist Croatia and Azerbaijan, the 1990s brought not only greater and more visible income differentials and rampant corruption, but also the loss of economic security and predictability.

In Senegal, where economic maldistribution exists on a scale matched only in Venezuela among the five countries studied, the income gap may not be growing as rapidly, but is becoming much more apparent. The problem is less the sudden emergence of a wealthy class or the plummeting living standards of the urban middle and lower-middle classes than the transformation of hidden rural poverty into very visible urban poverty, as the exodus from a stagnant and drought-ridden countryside fills the shantytowns of major urban centers.

While economic cleavages are evident and apparently growing in at least four of the five case study countries, they do not have the same political consequences everywhere. In Venezuela, economic polarization is directly related to political polarization. Chávez and his supporters speak the language of class conflict, and the business class responds by hating and fearing him. The symbolism of many of Chávez's actions—particularly the flaunting of his relations with Fidel Castro and Cuba—worsen this polarization. But Chávez is an anachronism in today's world. In most countries, the language of economic polarization has fallen out of fashion, while the languages of ethnic and religious polarization and of nationalism are on the ascendancy. In Croatia and Azerbaijan, ethnic differences have been politically more salient than economic ones. In Egypt, political polarization now centers on the issue of Islam, while the parties of the Left, with their language of class conflict, are no longer able to attract significant followings.

Ethnic and religious conflicts are not economic conflicts in disguise. It is true that Egypt, Croatia, and Azerbaijan could have become polarized along economic lines, given those countries' growing income gaps. But it is ethnic or religious divisions that have become politically salient and that need to be addressed. The often voiced idea that it is poverty and inequality that leads to ethnic conflict or religious fundamentalism, or to terrorism and other assorted evils, is a gross oversimplification. The processes of ethnic and religious polarization have dynamics of their own.

Consider Egypt. Although economic conditions have not been irrelevant to the rise of radical political Islam there, rapid economic improvement in the country would not eliminate support for it. As mentioned earlier, sociological studies of Egyptian radical Islamist groups show that they draw their support predominantly from the lower-middle class, the very group that was beginning to get a toehold on a better life in the days of Nasser and has slipped back since. In an earlier period, before socialism waned as a viable ideology, such economic decline probably would have spawned a leftist political movement. An Islamist movement rose instead, seeking not the redress of economic grievances but spiritual salvation in a new political order inspired by a fundamentalist interpretation of Islam. Political Islam is now the ideology of the opposition in Egypt, and it attracts not just the poor in the slums of Cairo and the impoverished villages of Upper Egypt, but engineers and lawyers in the professional syndicates as well. Whatever the grievances that spurred the growth of Islamism originally, it is now a political ideology that attracts a broad following.

In Croatia, ethnic polarization was not the result of economic decline but instead was one of its main causes. Ethnic nationalism led to the partition of Yugoslavia, disrupting economic production and markets, and to war, which added new economic burdens and brought the destruction of much infrastructure. Mobilization along ethnic lines was not a spontaneous development—it never is—but the result of deliberate actions by political leaders, particularly Franjo Tudjman and, on the Serbian side, Slobodan Milošević. These leaders are now gone, but the population remains polarized along the ethnic lines of demarcation these men deepened.

In Azerbaijan as well, it is ethnic divisions, not economic ones, that are salient. The antagonism between Azeris and Armenians has led to war, the loss of 16 percent of Azerbaijani territory, the displacement of a large percentage of the Azerbaijani population, the demise of the government of Abulfaz Elchibey, and the return to power of Aliyev. The conflict is stalemated, with no fighting but no solution in sight, despite numerous mediation efforts. The prevailing state of no war/no peace creates a condition of uncertainty that makes a normal political process difficult, lending credibility to the government's claim that the country needs continuity and a strong hand to guide it through the crisis.

The case of Senegal shows something different, namely, that it is possible to have a society with great economic inequality and both ethnic and religious diversity that does not become polarized. There are several explanations for this: The most extreme poverty is well hidden in remote areas, and the alliance President Léopold Sédar Senghor, a Christian, formed with the marabouts served to decrease Muslim–Christian tensions and turned the marabouts into supporters of the status quo. A combination of good politics and good luck has kept the country from being torn apart by its social and economic cleavages.

Polarization and Semi-Authoritarianism

The impact of polarization on political transitions is evident in all five case study countries, creating conditions that are highly unpromising for democracy promotion and generating tensions that play into the hands of semi-authoritarian leaders.

Democracy requires pluralism, that is, the existence of a variety of organized interest groups; it also requires that interest groups be moderate and flexible in their demands, so that their different interests can be bridged by compromise. Democracy also requires that a proportion of citizens be willing to change their party allegiance depending on the issues of the moment, thus ensuring that there are no permanent majorities and minorities. Such conditions do not exist in polarized societies. If different groups believe that their interests are irreconcilable, pluralism leads to conflict. And if citizens never change their allegiances, permanent majorities are formed, making it difficult for the eternal losers to accept a system that guarantees defeat for them.

Ethnic and religious polarizations present the greatest challenges. It is difficult to compromise on issues of identity—typically, when differences have become politicized, people with mixed racial or religious identities tend to be rejected by all, or at least forced to choose sides. The appearance of ethnic and religious parties is a sure sign of polarization and bodes ill for the success of democracy. Ethnic and religious parties tend to have fixed constituencies, a situation that produces permanent majorities and minorities—the Serb parties of Croatia will never be able to collect votes outside their own ethnic minority group and thus will never significantly increase the number of votes they receive. Economic polarization, too, can lead to fierce political battles. Such polarization was a major factor in the formation of modern parties of the Left and the Right. But unlike conflicts based on ethnic and religious identities, those based on divergent economic interests can be reduced by compromise, which is what happened historically: Redistributive policies and the emergence of the welfare state reduced economic polarization, transformed communist parties into social-democratic parties, and ensured the survival of democratic systems by reducing differences and fostering inclusive politics and cultures of compromise.

As I have pointed out, polarization does not make semi-authoritarianism inevitable, and it does not constitute an insurmountable obstacle to deeper transformation. Ethnic divisions in the United States have not destroyed democracy, although they deeply affected it by keeping the franchise from being universal in parts of the country until the 1960s. Class divisions slowed democratization in Europe and halted it in Germany and Italy when the rise of radical socialist parties convinced majorities to support fascism. Eventually, in all these countries polarization decreased and, above all, became less significant politically.

The five countries discussed in the present study are a long way from overcoming polarization. While economic polarization is at present acute only in Venezuela, it is a potential problem in all four other countries. Furthermore, most of these countries are too poor to painlessly follow the classical route out of economic polarization, that is, by creating a strong welfare state (and the conditionalities imposed by the donors are too inflexible to permit this to occur). Ethnic tensions remain extremely high in Croatia, creating the possibility that the Croatian Democratic Union's influence will grow again. Azerbaijan is not only divided, it is in a state of war. In Egypt, the presence of radical Islamist fringe groups, as well as uncertainty about the true intentions of the Muslim Brotherhood, creates a climate in which not only the regime of Hosni Mubarak but also moderate Muslims and Coptic Christians have reasons to be deeply concerned about the outcome of truly free and fair elections. Such conditions play into the hands of semi-authoritarian regimes.

The Problem of State Formation

Democracy promoters focus greater attention on the political system than on the state itself. They see the process through which governments are formed and then formulate decisions as problematic, but they pay considerably less attention to the problem of state formation.[7] This is not surprising, because historically state formation preceded democratic transformation, so that the two processes were quite distinct. This is no longer necessarily the case. In many of the countries where processes of political transformation are now unfolding, from Central Asia to Africa, state formation is still an ongoing process. Some of these countries are new states, such as Croatia and Azerbaijan; others have existed for decades but either function very poorly or are failed states. Semi-authoritarianism in states that are still in the early stages of formation, such as Croatia and Azerbaijan, may have a salutary effect on the state even though it constitutes a setback for democracy. Where state formation is not an issue, however, there is no positive side to semi-authoritarianism.

In the early 1990s, Croatia and Azerbaijan were just emerging as states, and they still have problems defining their identity today. The issue of territory and borders is far from settled in Azerbaijan. As the successor to the Soviet republic of the same name, Azerbaijan lays claim to all the territory that republic once controlled. In reality, it only controls about 80 percent of it, because of the Armenian occupation, and it seems highly improbable that it will ever control all the rest. There is thus a fundamental problem of territorial definition in Azerbaijan. This is further complicated by the country's uncertain national identity, a consequence of the multiethnic composition of its population, and of the division between those who want Azerbaijan to be a secular state, culturally close to Turkey and part of Europe, and those who want strong ties with the Azeri population of northern

Iran, which adheres to Shi'i Islam. The Croatian state is more secure since the end of the war with Serbia and the political demise of Milošević. However, the reintegration of the Serbian minority remains extremely problematic; the presence of Croatian refugees from Bosnia is a constant reminder of the problems experienced by Croatian minorities outside the boundaries of the state and incites demands among radical nationalists for continuing involvement in Herzegovina. These problems could become much more acute if a new crisis erupts in Bosnia when international troops and administrators are eventually withdrawn. Considerably less threatening, but nevertheless indicative of the identity problems of the new country, is the continuing dissatisfaction of the Italian minority of the Istria region, which led to the withdrawal of the Istrian Democratic Party (Istarki Demokratski Sabor) from the governing coalition in June 2001.

The emergence of semi-authoritarian regimes in Azerbaijan and Croatia was an integral part of the formation of those states. In both countries, populations threatened by internal conflict with strong minorities supported by much better armed external allies initially turned willingly to strong leaders, as people do in all countries at war. The problem in these new countries was that civil and political institutions were too weak to hold leaders accountable, so that strong leadership became essentially authoritarian leadership.

Was semi-authoritarianism unavoidable in these new countries threatened by both domestic and exogenous problems? Should semi-authoritarianism even be considered a success of sorts, given the possibility of the emergence of fully authoritarian regimes? Can states ever be formed democratically? The historical record suggests that state formation has never been a democratic process. Reflecting on the experience of European states, Charles Tilly shows that coercive exploitation was a central factor in state building.[8] States have been formed and enlarged through conquest, international treaties that imposed settlements on the defeated, and colonial undertakings. They have never been formed peacefully, by democratic leaders through processes of consultation. The concept of democratic state formation is an idea of the 1990s without a historical precedent. This does not prove conclusively that states cannot be formed through democratic processes, but certainly helps put the rise of semi-authoritarian regimes into perspective.

The nineteenth-century ideal of the nation—a preexisting cultural, if not spiritual, entity finding its political expression in the building of a state—has been shown to be a fiction deliberately promoted by the state's power holders to consolidate their position.[9] The keys to state formation were war and violence, and the democratization of the state was a subsequent development achieved through a considerable amount of political strife. Even in the United States, where the spread of democracy and the process of state formation overlapped more closely than anywhere else, the state was built ultimately through war and conquest—the Revolutionary War, the conquest of the territory occupied by Native Americans, the Civil War, and war with Mexico.

Recent experiences are no different. Collapsed states that have managed to reconstitute themselves have done so through war. In Uganda, one of the most successful examples of the reintegration of a collapsed state, the military reconquest of the country by the National Resistance Army was the key to success. Among the states that emerged from the collapse of Yugoslavia, only one, Slovenia, has managed to do so under a reasonably democratic government and without serious domestic political upheavals. Slovenia was insulated from the turmoil in the Balkans by its peripheral geographical location and the absence of a large Serbian minority. The dissolution of the Soviet Union also calls into question the possibility of state building through democratic processes. The Baltic states are the only exception to the emergence of assorted strongmen, and all three had experience as independent, more liberal states prior to their annexation by the Soviet Union.

Even international intervention has not assured a democratic process of state building. The main attempt to set up new states that were also democratic took place in the period of decolonization, when France and Britain, having reluctantly accepted that the days of empire were at an end, tried to endow the new countries with democratic constitutions and elected governments. The attempt to hand off power to newly constituted democratic governments in newly cobbled states ended in virtually all cases in the failure of democracy. In many countries, it ended with the failure of the state as well, or its uncertain survival as a very weak entity. More recent attempts at democratic state building through outside intervention do not appear particularly promising, either. Six years of international occupation in Bosnia have succeeded neither in consolidating a multiethnic state that would not break apart without an outside presence nor in breaking the hold of the conflicting nationalist leaderships.

The failure of democracy in most new states facing conflict is not surprising in view of the fact that even in well-established democracies periods of war or domestic disorder create a real challenge to the democratic order. In wartime, citizens of democratic countries tend to rally behind the incumbent government and worry more about strong leadership than checks and balances. Security threats in general create a tension with democratic principles, as shown by the experiences of Germany and Italy in dealing with the Baader–Meinhof Gang and the Red Brigades, respectively, in the 1970s; of Britain dealing with the Irish Republican Army; and of the United States facing al Qaeda and other terrorist groups at present. Consolidated democracies can resist many nondemocratic pressures. Countries where democracy is new and to a large extent imposed from the outside are much more likely to slide into semi-authoritarianism or even authoritarianism when facing such threats.

A troubled and incomplete process of state formation is one structural condition that makes democracy an unlikely outcome of a political transition. Under such conditions, semi-authoritarianism may in fact be a positive outcome if it helps consolidate the state, solve the initial problems of survival, and create a stable situation that encourages citizens to look critically at the actions of the government rather than to turn to a strong leader for salvation. Unfortunately, by the time the state is better established and a degree of stability has been achieved, the semi-authoritarian regime is also often well-entrenched and quite capable of fending off challenges. State formation under a semi-authoritarian regime is not automatically followed by democratization. Democratization is a separate process and a separate battle. There are strong indications, however, that this battle is unlikely to be won when the existence of the state is still uncertain.

The existence of a semi-authoritarian regime does not always denote a weak state or an incomplete process of state formation. There is nothing weak or incomplete about the Egyptian state, for example, which has one of the longest histories of statehood and one of the strongest traditions of bureaucratic administration in the world, all within virtually unchanged borders. Unlike Egypt, Venezuela and Senegal cannot claim a history of statehood going back millennia, but Venezuela, which has been an independent country since 1830, is well beyond the process of formation, and even Senegal, despite the adventure of an attempted merger with Gambia and a residual problem with a separatist movement in the Casamance region, is not a weak or threatened state. The problems of semi-authoritarianism in these countries lie elsewhere.

The Nature of the Political Process

Many of the structural factors that encourage the rise and persistence of semi-authoritarianism are political. They are structural in that they are not the direct result of political choices made by the leaders but are the outcome of deeply ingrained political problems. I will single out three issues: the problem of asymmetrical power generation; the centrality of free-floating political elites without constituencies rather than of embedded elites with constituencies; and the new political obstacles that derive from semi-authoritarianism itself, making second transitions, or transitions from semi-authoritarianism, inherently different from first transitions, or transitions from authoritarianism.

Asymmetrical Power Generation

There is a fundamental dilemma in political transitions that hampers democratic outcomes: The sources of power open to democratic actors are much more limited than those that are available to actors who are willing to act undemocratically. The democratic parties are at a serious disadvantage when trying to generate power, because the process is essentially asymmetric. Nondemocratic organizations can use manipulation, coercion, and even open violence to further their goals. The democratic opposition can only try to win elections. Even democratic opposition parties that succeed in winning elections because of a temporary power vacuum can find it extremely difficult to continue generating the resources they need to govern, because democratic institutions are not developed instantaneously.

In semi-authoritarian states, power is not generated through formal political institutions and processes. Leaders are elected, but their power is rooted elsewhere (I will return to the special case of Venezuela below). Since power is not generated through elections, it cannot be taken away and transferred through elections, either. Semi-authoritarian leaders, as I have shown previously, do their best to manipulate elections, but this is only a part of the problem, and not the most important one. The greatest difficulty is a structural one, namely the conundrum of how to transfer, through a democratic process, power that is not derived from the popular will and that resides in individuals rather than in institutions. If power resides in a particular president, rather than in the institution of the presidency, it cannot be transferred to others—Aliyev may be able to install his son as president, but the son will not inherit the father's power. Instead, he will have to create his own network of support and consolidate power himself. In general, when power emanates from the barrel of a gun, the control and repression exercised by security agencies and political organizations, or the personal ties and loyalties the ruling group manages to forge, it cannot be transferred through elections. Rather, it must be broken before elections become meaningful.

The five case study countries show clearly the extent to which the power of semi-authoritarian regimes is generated by means other than democratic processes and institutions. Aliyev's power was firmly established before he was elected in October 1993. It was rooted in the network of contacts he had developed in the administrative apparatus and the political class during his Soviet-era political career, contacts he put to good use in getting himself formally elected speaker of the National Council. This power was further increased by his willingness to strike a deal with Surat Huseinov, whose militia forced the resignation of President Elchibey by threatening to march on Baku. By turning a potential enemy into an ally, and thus bringing the once threatening militia to his side, Aliyev essentially made it impossible for any other politician or organization to compete with him. By the time he organized presidential elections in 1993, his power was already well established outside electoral channels, and there was little the opposition could do to develop the clout to challenge him.

A similar situation exists in Egypt. After Sadat's sudden death in 1981, Mubarak's power was immediately ensured by the allegiance of the army and the security agencies. They were the real kingmakers behind the scenes. Mubarak's election by the National Assembly was simply a ritual, not the source of support that guaranteed him the presidency. In Senegal, Senghor became president because of his role in the independence movement, and nobody could challenge him in the elections. Most important, his power was such that he was even able to transmit some to his successor.

In the other two countries, Venezuela and Croatia, elections played a somewhat more important part in consolidating the power of the regime. Both Chávez and Tudjman were originally elected in entirely legal and competitive processes. But Chávez was also backed by at least a part of the military; behind his participation in the democratic process there was always an implicit threat that he could use an alternative avenue to come to power. Tudjman did not have special advantages in Croatia's first election, other than his popular nationalist message, but once in power he established other mechanisms of power, making it impossible for the opposition to compete.

Further change in countries with semi-authoritarian regimes can only take place if somehow the power derived from nondemocratic and noninstitutional sources is neutralized. Tudjman's death provides one example. Other factors could be a devastating military defeat or a popular uprising, both of which played a role in Serbia in 2000. Crises of this sort cause a breakdown of the mechanisms on which the incumbent government relies to generate power, creating an open situation in which others can compete. Under such conditions, it is possible that elections will be accepted as a mechanism for generating power.

Two examples illustrate the point that in semi-authoritarian states power will only be transferred by elections if something has forced the situation open. In Serbia in October 2000, Slobodan Milošević, whose power was not derived from democratic institutions and processes but from his control of the military and administrative apparatus, lost the popular vote to Vojislav Koštunica. What allowed Koštunica to actually become president, however, was not the vote itself, but the street protests that convinced the military not to back Milošević in his bid to retain power despite the election results. Deprived of military support, Milošević was forced to accept defeat. By contrast, in the Liberian elections of 1997, power was already firmly allocated, the voters knew it, and the vote remained an empty ritual on which the international community insisted. The elections pitted Charles Taylor, a military commander who had triumphed after years of brutal civil war, against Ellen Johnson-Sirleaf, an internationally known and respected former government minister just returned from exile. Taylor had an army and the proven willingness to use it to get his way. Johnson-Sirleaf had a good reputation based on past accomplishments and the goodwill of the international community. She was a more attractive candidate than Taylor, but many voters knew, and openly acknowledged, that an election victory by Johnson-Sirleaf would prompt Taylor to return to war. They thus decided to avoid a new crisis by voting in the man who controlled the guns.[10] They correctly assumed that elections do not generate power unless the situation is open in the first place. They knew that the situation was completely closed, and they had no means to force it open.

Theoretically, an open situation can also be created if the incumbent leadership simply decides to give up and withdraw from the competition. This is what Egyptians hope for when they state that democratization has to come from the top. But this does not happen often. It is possible to point at Ghana, where President Jerry Rawlings decided not to run for a third term despite the backing of the military and even allowed his party's candidate to be defeated in the December 2000 presidential elections. But such situations are rare. Furthermore, even the Ghana example is rather discouraging when one considers that by the time Rawlings stepped down, he had been in power for two decades.

In the absence of factors that loosen the grip of semi-authoritarian regimes, opposition parties are unlikely to prevail, at least not if they use democratic means—trying to attract voters through good party organization, running an efficient election campaign, and creating an attractive message. These are the tasks on which international assistance to political parties focuses. It is an uneven competition that the democratic opposition is bound to lose. If the opposition turns to nondemocratic means to level the playing field, on the other hand, symmetry is restored to some extent, but the outcome of the competition is unlikely to be democracy.[11] Cases like that of South Africa, where a conflict between a minority government freely using repressive methods and a nondemocratic opposition willing to turn to violence nonetheless led to democracy, are exceedingly rare.

Democracy promotion programs recognize the imbalance of power between government and opposition and try to apply some remedy to it. Democracy promoters have looked at civil society as the major source of countervailing power and have supported and trained thousands of nongovernmental organizations (NGOs) around the world. They have also provided some training for political parties, including those in power, in the techniques of organizing a party and waging an election campaign; some democracy promotion organizations now advocate a much greater commitment by donors to strengthening political parties.[12] On extremely rare occasions, for example in Mozambique before the 1994 elections, donors have even provided financing for opposition political parties in order to make competition possible. Programs focusing on political parties denote an increasing realism on the part of the donors about the limits of what civil society can accomplish. Nevertheless, donors still assume that the parties will eventually compete in an environment in which power can be transferred by elections. This is an unwarranted assumption in countries where power is generated through mechanisms that have nothing to do with elections. There are structural obstacles that cannot be overcome simply by providing opposition parties with more training and even with financing.

In a political transition, the problem of generating power goes beyond the initial step of defeating the opposition, and extends to the challenge of governing. It is possible for a new leadership to take the reins because the old regime collapsed on its own, but then fail to generate enough power to govern.[13] Generating power is an ongoing problem until a country stabilizes, and indeed until democracy consolidates to the point where other mechanisms for generating power become unthinkable. A new democratic government does not have the benefit of relying on institutions, because the institutions need to be developed and cannot generate power immediately.

The example of Azerbaijan demonstrates the difficulty some post-transition governments face in maintaining power. The Azerbaijan Popular Front was able to gain power in an election when the Soviet Union disintegrated and the local Communist Party leadership was thrown into confusion by the sudden change and lost its grip. But soon the front discovered that it did not have the resources to govern. It was unable to staff the government with reasonably competent people, it could not establish control of a civil service staffed by employees trained and promoted under the communist regime, it could not strengthen the military quickly enough, and it did not know how to build alliances with armed and civilian groups that would help it remain in power until democratic institutions could be developed sufficiently to become a source of power.

In a less dramatic fashion, Mesić and Račan face a similar problem in Croatia. Having won election to a large extent because of the slump suffered by the Croatian Democratic Union at Tudjman's death, they had to build a democratic apparatus from scratch, while nationalist organizations tried to reorganize and mobilize war veterans for mass protest. In contrast to erstwhile president Elchibey and the Azerbaijan Popular Front, the democratic parties in Croatia have a good chance of prevailing. The problems they face in developing the power to govern in a democratic manner, particularly when confronted with an opposition willing to turn to other means, are nevertheless significant.

Free-Floating Elites, Embedded Elites, and Semi-Authoritarianism

The political transitions that led to the rise of semi-authoritarian regimes were for the most part driven not by popular demand for greater political participation and democracy, but by political elites with weak popular constituencies and in most cases no clear political program or ideological message. All the elite groups involved in these transitions—both those that eventually won and are now in power and those that lost and now constitute the so-called democratic opposition—used the language of democracy. For some, it was simply lip service to ideas that had firmly established their primacy in the international political discourse of the 1990s; for others, there probably was a deeper commitment to the principles of democracy, although this is difficult to ascertain in the case of opposition groups, which are often democratic until they come to power. None of these elites, however, represented organized constituencies to which they were in any way accountable or responsive. This was true even of the leaders who initially had widespread political support. Tudjman, for example, took it upon himself to speak in the name of the entire Croatian population, but made sure that population would remain silent.

All political transitions are driven by elites, and all political ideals are articulated by elites. But transitions only lead to democratic outcomes if the political elites are *embedded*, that is, if they have ties to constituencies whose interests they represent and defend. (I am borrowing this concept of embeddedness from Peter Evans's characterization of the technocratic elites who successfully managed the economic transitions of several East Asian countries.[14]) Embedded elites may head large political parties or social movements, have deep roots in a particular social milieu or even region, or be part of religious organizations. In some way, however, they speak for significant constituencies that see them as acting in their interests. This does not mean that embedded elites literally represent constituencies in the sense of having received formal mandates, but they have strong connections to specific groups.

The five cases in the present study suggest that one of the factors in these transitions to semi-authoritarian rule was that the political elites who became involved in the process were for the most part not strongly embedded.[15] Furthermore, the elites who spoke in the name of democracy were—and remain—the least embedded of all. Some of the authoritarian leaders did succeed in establishing at least an emotional link with broad though unorganized constituencies through nationalist or populist appeals. Some of the nondemocratic opposition elites are also strongly embedded in certain social milieus—for example, Islamist leaders in Egypt are embedded in the society through the mosques, and radical nationalists in Croatia are part of a large milieu of war veterans' groups and their families. The advocates of democracy, however, remain by and large free-floating elites with little connection to the population; in many cases, they appear to be much better embedded in an international milieu of democracy advocates than in the societies they are trying to reform. The cases suggest, in other words, that one of the factors leading to semi-authoritarianism is the fact that democratic elites are not embedded but free floating, while embedded elites are not democratic.

The lack of embeddedness of prodemocracy elites is reflected in the idealized view of democracy they embrace. They portray democracy as a combination of abstract principles, formal political processes, and highly technical reforms. This is shown by the civic education publications they prepare, the meetings they organize, and even the way they explain their programs to visitors. On the other hand, these prodemocracy elites tend to be silent on the least noble aspects of democracy, namely the competition to influence government policies by self-interested groups seeking to further their individual goals. When these democratic elites without constituencies advocate policies, they focus on what could be called public-interest policies—constitutional reform, the restructuring of the judiciary, better laws on NGO registration, and the like. These are all important goals, but not goals that help democratic organizations become embedded. The international community has encouraged these free-floating democratic elites by sponsoring civil society organizations that depend on foreign donors rather than on the support of domestic constituencies. The strongest but also the least embedded supporters of democracy in semi-authoritarian states are found in some of these donor-created organizations.

Many opposition parties in the countries discussed in the present study, with the exception of Venezuela, are part of these nonembedded elites. Most appear to have no concrete message with policy implications capable of attracting support. Rather, they fall into two groups. The larger category consists of parties that are simply machines devoted to furthering the cause of a specific leader. Their message is essentially "X is a true democrat" and "X is better than the incumbent." These parties offer voters a choice between personalities, not programs—it is virtually impossible to classify most of these parties as belonging to the Right or the Left, for example. A smaller category consists of parties with an abstract democratic message that does not attract constituencies and leaves their leaders free floating—Egypt seems to be particularly rich in such parties. Venezuela is exceptional in that Chávez and the opposition are very clearly representative of constituencies with different interests. In the other countries, there is a paucity of parties and civil society organizations that seek to further the interests of specific groups; such parties and organizations, however, are essential to the pluralism of the political process and thus to democracy.

Several factors explain why the abstract and idealistic idea of democracy has become so prevalent in countries with semi-authoritarian regimes. Certainly, the fact that the transitions were started by political elites with weak constituencies contributed. The shallowness of these transitions is another contributing factor: Because there has been very little socioeconomic change in these countries, there are no new, significant interest groups seeking a political voice to advance their interests. Finally, by imposing multiple conditionalities, the international community has helped keep the debate abstract by removing from the domain of political discussion some of the most important policy choices confronting these countries.[16]

Governments in donor-dependent countries have their policy-making ability severely restricted by the economic and good-governance conditionalities imposed by international financial institutions and other donors. Even when the policies favored by the international community are not fully implemented, donor-dependent governments feel severely constrained in what they can propose. Few are the leaders who dare to make defiant statements to the international community, as Chávez does in Venezuela—not coincidentally, a country that is not donor dependent. Opposition parties also tend to be cautious in their statements, adhering to the prevailing orthodoxy in matters both political and economic. Conditionalities take policy out of politics, making policy a matter for the professional reformers rather than for politicians responsible to constituencies.[17] This development may ensure the formulation of policies in line with the prevailing international orthodoxy, but it reduces democracy to a set of abstract principles, thereby weakening its appeal.

This restriction on policy choices permissible for democratic governments and parties is a serious obstacle to democracy promotion. It limits debate and makes voters skeptical about the possibility of influencing government policies in the most crucial areas. In the end, the beneficiaries of forced policy orthodoxy are populist parties, nationalist parties, and parties based on religious or ethnic identities that appear to offer the public distinct choices. Such parties do not necessarily provide concrete economic and social benefits to their members—Chávez and Tudjman did little to foster economic growth or improve living standards for their respective populaces. But leaders of their ilk provide an emotional outlet and a promise of political salvation of one kind or another. Abstract democratic ideals, on the other hand, fire small numbers of intellectuals but do not have mass appeal unless they are coupled with other, more tangible issues. This is one of the reasons why NGOs that focus on democracy promotion, human rights, and civic education find it impossible to support their work through domestic contributions and are dependent on international donor funding, even in countries where citizens are willing to give to organizations dealing with concrete problems.

The separation of politics from policy makes democracy more relevant to the political elite than to the general public in countries with semi-authoritarian regimes. The formal democratic processes that are in place are a threat to the incumbents and hold out at least a vague hope for opposition parties; thus, they are important to all politicians. Democracy is also important to the intellectual elite. It provides a new intellectual home for the many who have become disillusioned with other political systems and ideologies, and it also provides reasonably well-remunerated employment in the new breed of democracy and human rights organizations for those whose jobs are threatened by re-structuring or no longer pay living wages because of budgetary restrictions.

A key to initiating further change in semi-authoritarian states (and indeed in all countries that are not yet fully democratic) is to make democracy relevant to the rest of the population. Unless a significantly larger segment of the population comes to see democracy as a valued means of achieving its goals, an instrument to protect and further its own interests rather than an abstract idea without much relevance to concrete problems, semi-authoritarian regimes will continue to prevail, making the most of the advantages afforded by incumbency.

The Fallout from Semi-Authoritarianism

Once in power, semi-authoritarian regimes create new conditions that make further transformation difficult. I am not referring here to the political games discussed earlier, but to the impact that semi-authoritarian regimes have on the society. Among the new obstacles to democratization that arise in semi-authoritarian states are the ambiguous nature of these regimes, transition fatigue, and the role played by the international community.

The political conditions in semi-authoritarian states are inherently ambiguous: not good, but not terrible enough to elicit a desperate reaction on the part of citizens. Even the most repressive among such countries—Croatia under Tudjman, or Azerbaijan and Egypt today— allow some space for political parties, NGOs, or an independent press. The space may be limited, but it exists, providing a safety valve for discontent.

In all the cases discussed in the present study, furthermore, economic conditions are a greater source of grievance than political ones for most people. Chávez's popularity among his core supporters has probably been hurt more by the continuing economic stagnation than by his erratic leadership. In Senegal, the rejoicing in the finally achieved *alternance* soon gave way to rumblings of discontent as people began to discover that political change was doing nothing to ameliorate economic conditions—on the other hand, only a few intellectuals expressed concern about President Abdoullaye Wade's manipulation of political institutions.

A second factor that compounds the difficulty of renewing the push for change is transition fatigue. The initial changes are usually accompanied by much optimism and enthusiasm. In the late 1970s in Egypt, and again in the period of liberalization that followed the beginning of the Mubarak presidency, there was an atmosphere of renewal and political optimism. In Croatia, the elections of 1990 were truly a turning point in the minds of most citizens, although the enthusiasm for independence was greater than that for democracy even at that time. And Chávez's election was a defining moment for his supporters, who saw his victory as the return to a political system more responsive to the needs of its citizens than the tired *"partidocracia"* of the 1980s. But semi-authoritarianism takes a heavy toll on enthusiasm. It is difficult for most people to be sanguine about renewed change when the transition they experienced has plunged the country into turmoil, war, or economic decline. In many semi-authoritarian states, citizens are exhausted by economic hardship and political turmoil, and are thus apprehensive about more change. This fear is reflected in the contention one hears constantly in Egypt, for example, that democracy must come from the top (and thus without conflict), or in the extraordinary willingness of the Senegalese to give Wade control over the National Assembly in order to ensure five years of peace and stability.

Unwittingly, the international community adds to the structural difficulty of change in semi-authoritarian states. International actors have become a major part of post–Cold War transitions, and their role is becoming more invasive as they gain experience and learn more about the problems that arise in the process. In the late 1980s and early 1990s, when international donors started underwriting and otherwise trying to influence the course of transitions from authoritarian regimes, they concentrated heavily on supporting multiparty elections. But donors have moved far beyond elections and now seek to promote comprehensive change. They have become more aware of the infinite number of steps that are necessary to make a country democratic, and they are increasingly convinced that it is necessary to link political and economic reform to make them both successful. Countries in transition are now burdened with impossible sets of demands and expectations on the part of international donors. Well intentioned as they are, these overly ambitious demands make true democratization more difficult, as the international community often requires that countries establish institutions that are truly representative of the people, only to then demand completion of a list of reforms that these institutions have had little or no say in developing.

The Example of Croatia's Second Transition

Croatia provides a telling example of how the conditions created by semi-authoritarianism, coupled with the more exigent demands of the international community, become in themselves obstacles to a second transition, this one away from semi-authoritarianism. President Mesić and Prime Minister Račan, although committed to reform, cannot possibly do everything they are pushed to do by international actors while doing what is necessary to maintain the political support needed to accomplish anything in a democratic system. They lead a rather unstable six-party coalition that can only reach decisions slowly and with difficulty—a typical cost of democracy. They have to solve the problems created by an incomplete and corrupt economic reform program, which has transferred valuable assets to private hands while leaving the public sector badly in need of streamlining. But they also face a population exhausted by the economic hardships caused by the war and the breakup of Yugoslavia and frightened by the prospects of new, painful reforms.

The logic of democracy would lead to a series of compromise solutions that sought to accommodate public demands, the government's need to maintain support, and the necessity of reform. This is how democracies work. But this is not the logic of the second transition in a semi-authoritarian state where the international community has its say. Croatia is bombarded with international demands. International financial institutions, anxious to bring the country in line with the practices prevalent in market democracies, are demanding drastic cuts in the public payroll that the tired population will not tolerate. Indeed, such action would probably renew support for the Croatian Democratic Union in the next elections. Furthermore, the foreign governments and organizations concerned about the future of democracy in Croatia have a different set of priorities. They want the government to devote its efforts to other difficult tasks, such as an overhaul of the constitution and all laws concerning political parties, NGOs, and the media; the complete rebuilding of the judiciary; the depoliticization and reprofessionalization of the military; and the reform of municipal government. Refugee agencies want Croatia to speed up the return of Serbian refugees, who remain highly unpopular within the country. The International Criminal Tribunal at The Hague demands that suspected war criminals be hunted down and extradited.

The government of Croatia cannot possibly respond to all these demands, certainly not immediately. It will inevitably respond to some and not others. What it does, however, will not follow the logic of democracy as normally conceived, that is, the balancing of conflicting domestic demands. Instead, it will be forced to follow a more complex logic of balancing internal demands and external impositions. It is not clear whether it can perform this balancing act and remain sufficiently accountable to its citizens to remain democratic.

Second transitions in semi-authoritarian states are affected by all the structural problems that led to semi-authoritarianism in the first place and by the additional legacies of the semi-authoritarian period. They are also affected by the growing number and complexity of international demands and the distortions these demands create in the democratic process. Ironically, these demands are at least in part a response to what the international community has learned from a decade of transitions that have not led to democracy.

Conclusions

The emergence of semi-authoritarian regimes is due at least in part to a variety of underlying structural conditions, which are extraordinarily complex and in general difficult for donors to manipulate. Accepting this reality does not mean absolving semi-authoritarian leaders of all responsibility for the character of their governments, or arguing that political pressure brought to bear on them might not make some difference in their behavior. It means, however, that democracy promoters should have no illusions that they can disregard conditions and rely on political pressure alone to further the cause of democratic transformation. One of the reasons for the proliferation of semi-authoritarian regimes since the early 1990s is that direct or indirect international pressures have pushed governments that did not face significant domestic demands for democracy toward giving themselves a democratic facade. If the international community fails to take a broader approach to democracy promotion, dealing with conditions as well as with the ill will of major political actors, the challenge of semi-authoritarianism will only grow more difficult in the future.

I have singled out shallow transitions in countries where the structural obstacles to democratic transitions include sluggish economies, deeply polarized societies, incomplete processes of state formation, asymmetrical mechanisms for generating power, nonembedded democratic elites, and the legacy of semi-authoritarianism. Not all of these problems exist in each of the five countries, but some are present in each.

Democracy promoters cannot remove these obstacles, but they can address them to some extent. But doing so requires greater willingness to admit that there are problems that cannot be corrected by imposing political conditionalities on leaders, providing more funding for NGOs, or improving the administration of justice. Such programs do not ease the polarization of a society, for example; nor do they necessarily make democracy more relevant to the average citizen. Indeed, because democracy promotion programs do not usually address underlying conditions, but seek rather to thwart the games played by the politicians of semi-authoritarian regimes, they simply embellish the facade of democracy without producing much substantive change. Training of Egyptian NGOs by a support center funded by the U.S. Agency for International Development will, if successful, ensure that NGOs that are part of the government patronage system will be better managed; this will not alter the fact that the political space within which independent organizations work continues to narrow. Training of political parties in Azerbaijan might have a marginal impact on the way in which the opposition organizes its election campaigns, but it does not change the fact that the parties as now constituted will not be even remotely able to generate sufficient power to counterbalance Aliyev's advantage. And donors will not bring government closer to the people by devising sophisticated programs to train people to participate in the preparation of local budgets that amount to only a few thousand dollars a year for a large area. There is a real risk, on the other hand, that such programs will generate cynicism about decentralization.

Addressing underlying conditions is the greatest challenge of democracy promotion in countries with semi-authoritarian regimes, requiring a departure from many of the programs honed by a decade or more of democracy promotion. Current programs are often useful, but they are never sufficient; furthermore, in some cases they are harmful. In most semi-authoritarian states, efforts to promote democracy must target conditions that stand in the way of a democratic transformation rather than seek to circumvent the games played by semi-authoritarian leaders.

Intervening in Semi-Authoritarian States

Introduction to Part III

The rapid increase in the number of semi-authoritarian regimes during the 1990s represents both progress and failure. In most countries, semi-authoritarian regimes are an improvement over their predecessors. Croatia, Senegal, and even Azerbaijan are better off today politically than they were in the 1980s, and so are many other countries where semi-authoritarian regimes are in control. But in some countries, represented in the present study by Egypt, semi-authoritarian regimes have long been entrenched and are disturbingly static, showing no sustained trend toward further democratic change. Finally, in some countries semi-authoritarian regimes represent a worsening of the situation, or at least the culmination of a process of deterioration that unfolded unobserved under earlier democratic regimes. This is the case in Venezuela, and the problem may well spread to other countries where the magnitude of socioeconomic problems is overwhelming the government's ability to cope, making the population more receptive to radical or populist appeals.

Even when it is an improvement on what preceded it, however, semi-authoritarianism represents the failure of the transition model envisaged and encouraged by the United States and other members of the international community since the collapse of communist regimes in Eastern Europe made democracy promotion a foreign-policy goal for all aid donors. Semi-authoritarian regimes are a stark reminder of the limits of external pressure. The international community has been successful at encouraging, cajoling, and at times coercing the political elites of these countries toward acceptance of superficially democratic processes and institutions, but has ultimately been unable to push them further.

In the last few years, awareness of this failure has grown. A consensus is developing that the latest wave of democratization has crested and that there will now be a hiatus before a new wave rolls in. Despite this new pessimism, democracy promotion organizations are not decreasing their efforts, and so far funding levels for democracy promotion have not been reduced. Nor does continuity of policy stop there. Disturbingly, democracy promoters continue turning to the same tools to promote transformation even in countries where those tools have failed to produce results. Democracy promotion activities continue to concentrate, predictably, on elections, institution building, civil society and the media, and the rule of law.

In the two chapters that follow I will discuss to what extent and how successfully democracy promotion organizations have addressed the games played by semi-authoritarian regimes and the structural obstacles to democracy that prevail in those countries. In the first of these two chapters, I will discuss what donors have done. My interest is not in evaluating how successfully specific programs have been implemented but in assessing how the donors' activities relate to the problems that contribute to the rise of semi-authoritarian regimes. In the subsequent and final chapter, I will suggest additional or alternative steps that donors should consider in order to address more specifically the problems posed by semi-authoritarian regimes.

8

The Record So Far

ASSESSING HOW SUCCESSFULLY democracy promotion programs
have addressed the problems posed by semi-authoritarian regimes is a
risky undertaking, because the answer to the question depends to a
large extent on the evaluative methods used. One approach would be
to evaluate the impact of individual programs in specific countries,
but this approach only reveals how successfully the program sponsors
achieved what they set out to do, without saying much about the impact on democracy. It is possible for a foreign government or nongovernmental organization (NGO) to implement its programs successfully in a country even if the overall political situation continues
to deteriorate. For example, in early 1998 the U.S. Agency for International Development (USAID) published a report showing that USAID
had "met or exceeded results expectations" in its democratization projects in Cambodia, although in July 1997 the country had experienced a
military coup d'état.[1] Since in this chapter of the present study I endeavor to ascertain how well democracy promoters address the challenges of semi-authoritarianism, not how well they implement their
self-designed programs, an approach focusing on individual programs in individual countries does not seem to hold much promise.
But it would not be particularly useful to jump to the opposite extreme
and conclude that the rise of semi-authoritarianism is in itself proof
that democracy promotion programs do not work. Since donor activities are only one of many factors that influence political transitions,

such a conclusion would be completely unwarranted. I will thus limit the discussion to identifying those problems of political transitions that democracy assistance has addressed in these countries and those it has overlooked. It should also be clear that in this analysis I am focusing on the democracy promotion activities implemented by aid agencies and NGOs—in other words, the "low politics" of democratization. I am leaving out of the analysis the impact on democratization— whether positive or negative—of the pressure brought to bear on the leadership of these countries through the "high politics" of diplomatic relations.

In the discussion that follows, I will focus primarily on four rather than five of the case study countries, because Venezuela has not received much democracy promotion assistance, and then only recently and on a much smaller scale than the other countries. At the time democracy assistance projects started being developed in the other four case study countries, in the early 1990s, Venezuela was still considered a consolidated, albeit troubled, democracy; thus, it was not a target for democracy promotion activities. Furthermore, Venezuela is a middle-income country and thus not a prime target for international assistance. USAID in particular does not provide assistance to Venezuela because of its comparatively high gross domestic product. However, NGOs that promote democracy—whose funds ultimately come from the U.S. government—have been active in Chávez's Venezuela. In particular, the National Endowment for Democracy has quadrupled its budget for democracy promotion in Venezuela since Chávez came to power, with the money going to support labor unions and build political parties and local government institutions.[2]

In the transition model that has gained ascendancy in the world of democracy promotion, there is no category so far for semi-authoritarian regimes. Rather, such regimes fall in the realm of the so-called consolidating democracies, that is, countries that have jumped through the hoop of the initial multiparty transitional elections and are now facing the process of consolidating their representative democratic institutions and norms. The worst cases, those countries where there seems to be little hope of further democratization, come to be seen either as backsliding states or victims of failed transitions. But classifying the countries discussed here as consolidating democracies does not capture their nature. Egypt and Azerbaijan are countries where the regime is doing its best to prevent democratic consolidation and to perpetuate instead its hold on power at any cost. In Senegal, President Abdoullaye Wade is following too closely in the footsteps of his predecessor, Abdou Diouf, to permit the conclusion that democracy is finally being consolidated. Among the five case-study countries, only Croatia can now be considered to be a consolidating democracy in the sense that the present government is genuinely trying to make democracy work, but even there the outcome remains uncertain.

The classification of these countries as consolidating democracies, however, does explain how the international community is approaching democracy promotion. The assistance offered to them is based on the assumption that they have already gone through the formal transition by holding "breakthrough" multiparty elections and now have governments that will accept further democratization. But these countries still need programs that seek to increase citizens' capacity to hold their government accountable, and they also need help in strengthening and further democratizing their political institutions. Consolidating democracies, like countries in the earlier stages of transition, are targets for programs that build prodemocracy civil-society organizations (meaning essentially professional NGOs advocating human rights and democratic reforms); for more tentative programs to train political parties in the techniques of organizing and campaigning; for continuing efforts to expand civic education; and for efforts to improve the quality of information available through the strengthening of independent media. In addition, democracy promotion agencies and NGOs target political institutions, particularly the parliament, the judicial system, the election commission, and local governments.

The assumption that these countries have already experienced formal transitions affects not only the type of democracy promotion programs that are implemented, but also their specific design. Consolidation programs are designed for an essentially friendly environment, where the main problem is the lack of know-how among organizations and institutions rather than the political ill will of the regime and its antidemocratic tendencies. For example, programs seek to improve parliaments' access to information, on the assumption that insufficient access is what keeps them from being more effective; in reality, the problem is often their overwhelming domination by the government party.

Programs based on the assumption that semi-authoritarian regimes are consolidating democracies are low-end programs; that is, they fall toward the least-invasive and least-coercive end of a continuum of possible interventions. In reality, semi-authoritarian regimes require programs that fall toward the high end of the continuum in order to be effective, because the major problem in such countries is still the distribution of power, not lack of knowledge and a need for training. Low-end programs are not adequate to address structural problems and are not always effective at thwarting the games played by semi-authoritarian regimes, either.

The distinction between low-end and high-end programs requires some elaboration. I classify as *low-end programs* those that are less aggressive, put little pressure on the incumbent government, are less invasive of the sovereignty of the recipient country, and are less likely to create a backlash against the countries implementing them by the government or other groups. Programs that provide small grants to NGOs, provide some training for the media, foster the introduction of civic education in public schools, or seek to strengthen the judiciary by printing compendiums of existing laws so that judges will know what they are supposed to uphold are examples of low-end endeavors. At the other extreme, programs that help organize and fund opposition movements under the guise of monitoring elections and getting out the vote, as the international community did when it backed opposition parties and civil society organizations in Yugoslavia, or that suspend all assistance until a government complies with political conditionalities, are *high-end programs*.

Democracy promoters' tendency to embrace low-end projects means that they have addressed only one aspect of the problem of semi-authoritarianism: They have sought to thwart the games played by the regimes, but have rarely addressed the structural problems that enable and encourage semi-authoritarianism. This chapter will begin with a discussion of this failure to address structural conditions, including shallow political transitions; ethnic, religious, and economic polarization; incomplete state formation; asymmetrical sources of power; and problems of nonembedded elites and the generally perceived irrelevance of democracy. Next, I will address the most common strategies for thwarting semi-authoritarian games, including civic education and political education programs, efforts to change structures of incentives through rewards and punishments, institution building, and promotion of free and fair elections.

The Failure to Address Structural Conditions

In the previous chapter, I singled out several structural conditions that impede democratic transformation and make semi-authoritarianism more likely. Among these conditions are the shallowness of transitions, the extreme polarization of society, the incomplete processes of state formation, the asymmetrical mechanisms for generating power, the absence of embedded democratic elites, and the fallout from semi-authoritarianism itself. With the exception of the latter, which I will not discuss in the present chapter because it has not been addressed at all by democracy assistance providers, all these issues go to the heart of democratic transformations everywhere. While they are difficult problems, they are not insurmountable. All successful democracies once had authoritarian regimes and had to overcome autocrats' stranglehold on power; in many, including the United States and the early European democracies, democracy was introduced by political elites and remained an elite process for years. Many new democracies faced early problems of polarization, and even weaknesses of state formation.

The Shallowness of Political Transitions

The democracy promotion programs of the years since about 1990 have done nothing to address the shallowness of most of the political transitions of this period. On the contrary, they have encouraged such shallow transitions by pushing all countries to adopt the same political institutions and the same path to transformation regardless of prevailing conditions. The international community essentially considers a shallow transition to be better than no transition at all. "Fourth-wave" transitions, those promoted from the outside, are shallow by definition.

The idea that it is possible to promote democracy even in the absence of socioeconomic change has taken hold only recently. During the 1960s and 1970s, the assumption that democracy would be a consequence of socioeconomic change was firmly established among experts and policy makers. Today, the opposite idea has become dominant, namely, that only democracy can unleash economic growth and social change. For example, the Alliance for Progress launched by President John F. Kennedy for Latin America in the early 1960s fastened on economic growth as the key to political change. Other donors also concentrated on economic development first. But at that time, both the donor community and the recipient countries were much more sanguine about the prospects for rapid economic change. They did not feel that by relying on economic growth to bring about democratization they would relegate the possibility of such political transformation to a very distant future.

After four decades of economic assistance, there can be no illusion about donors' ability to stimulate economic growth in most countries that is rapid enough to drive political transformations. In most countries, the prospects for a politically transforming economic miracle are essentially nil. This means that either these countries will experience a shallow political transition or that they will have no transition at all. But as an alternative to highly repressive authoritarianism, a shallow transition may be better than nothing.

Do shallow transitions inevitably lead to semi-authoritarianism? Is this the best that can be expected? Or can democracy assistance address the challenge of deepening the transitions? These questions have not been answered and, in many cases, have not even been asked. Democracy assistance has largely ignored the issue.

Polarization

There is an extensive literature on democracy in countries divided along ethnic and religious lines. All the writings in this genre recognize that polarization makes democracy risky, heightening tensions and possibly turning majority rule into ethnic rule. The prescriptions on how to avoid the perils of democracy in deeply divided societies vary widely. There are advocates of relatively simple systems of proportional representation that allow even small parties to gain a presence in parliament.[3] Others advocate the adoption of complex voting systems that provide incentives for political parties to build alliances and diversify their constituencies.[4] The most complicated solutions are set forth by proponents of consociational democracy, a system that institutionalizes ethnic differences and gives ethnic groups veto power over decisions that would impact on them unfavorably.[5] Until recently, however, the impact of economic polarization on democracy was a neglected issue. The question of whether countries with extremely skewed income distribution and very high levels of absolute poverty are capable of democracy has been getting more attention recently. Particularly in the wake of the attacks of September 11, 2001, the assumption that poverty and economic polarization breed extremism and terrorism, thus preventing democratization, has suddenly gained currency in policy debates, although the evidence is scant.

Democracy promoters, while recognizing in theory that ethnic divisions and other sources of polarization pose serious obstacles to democratic transitions, have been hesitant to address such problems openly and forcefully, in part because the international community is itself divided on this issue. The United States refuses to entertain the possibility that deeply divided societies require special institutional solutions, and it has consistently taken the position that as long as all citizens are guaranteed the right to vote and the protection of their individual rights, ethnic minorities do not need special protections and other distinctive provisions—a position consistent with its domestic policies toward minorities. European countries, which have been forced by vocal and at times violent minorities to adopt special provisions to protect the collective rights and identities of ethnic groups, are more inclined to believe that only regional autonomy or the protection of cultural and language rights can safeguard democracy in divided societies.

A commonly prescribed antidote to polarization in recent years has been the recommendation that government and the opposition in polarized societies enter into power-sharing agreements, particularly in postconflict situations. For example, the international community favored a power-sharing arrangement for South Africa while the negotiations to end apartheid were taking place in the early 1990s; in the end, elements of power sharing were incorporated into the transition. The Dayton agreement on Bosnia was based on an extremely complicated architecture of power sharing. Unfortunately, power sharing is an ambiguous concept, and applied to a democratic system it can be either redundant or curiously nondemocratic. It is redundant in the sense that democratic systems always entail a large amount of power sharing among the branches of government, among central and local governments, often among parties in a governing coalition, and, less formally, among the great number of interest groups that compete with each other to influence government policy and usually have to settle for compromise outcomes. Democracy is always a power-sharing system, and its normal rules circumvent the threat of the tyranny of the majority.

But the call for power sharing in transitional, deeply divided states goes beyond what is normal in all democracies. Rather, it is a call for the sharing of power between the party or parties that won the elections and those that lost. In this form, power sharing is a more questionable, nondemocratic idea. It may bring about reconciliation, but it also reduces accountability and increases the risk of corruption by co-opting the opposition into the government. When President Diouf brought Wade into his cabinet not once, but twice, Senegal did not become more democratic. On the contrary, it became less so, because the ruling party had succeeded in neutralizing, at least temporarily, its main challenger. Taken to an extreme, power sharing can create a de facto single-party system or at least a dominant-party system, in which the incumbents are undefeatable because they are all in the government together. Power sharing can be a crucial device in the initial stages of transition in a deeply divided society, easing fears and encouraging parties to find common ground. But it can also favor semi-authoritarianism rather than democracy and is thus no long-term solution to polarization, and certainly no antidote to semi-authoritarian rule.

Democracy promoters have stayed away from the more complex constitutional engineering proposed by some scholars for divided societies. Consociationalism, which sanctions the protection of group rights, is unacceptable to the United States. Complex voting systems are viewed by most democracy promoters as poorly suited to countries where there is still a lot of mistrust of election results. Nor do other experiments with ethnic power sharing appear more promising. The international community accepted such a system for Bosnia, but the outcome is not encouraging. Elections in that country's complex federal system have reconfirmed the competing ethnic nationalist elites and done little for the causes of democracy and ethnic reconciliation.

Among international NGOs involved in democracy promotion, considerable attention is paid to the issue of how to bring about reconciliation in divided local communities. These efforts seek to improve communication between various groups, to promote reciprocal understanding of each group's fears and needs, and to encourage cooperation in solving crosscutting problems. Locally, many such activities are successful. What remains more uncertain is the extent to which local initiatives, which never reach more than a small number of communities, affect the polarization that exists at the national level and thus improve the prospects for democracy.

In a surprisingly large number of cases, however, democracy promoters initially try to ignore the issue of polarization, be it ethnic, religious, or economic. In countries such as Burundi and Macedonia, they originally decided to hope that polarization would not derail the transition, instead of taking measures early on to deal with the problem overtly. This was a high-risk option, because ethnic polarization can have devastating effects on an attempt at democratization: Multiparty elections in Burundi, held in the absence of a well-thought-out agreement, a constitution providing guarantees for minorities, and an unambiguous commitment by the international community, led not to democracy but to bloody conflict.

The impact of economic polarization on democracy is also not explicitly addressed by the international community, or even by local players in most countries. For instance, there is widespread concern in international agencies about skewed income distribution as an economic and a humanitarian problem, and countries receiving World Bank loans and other international development assistance are now expected to emplace poverty reduction strategies. But there has been little discussion of whether skewed income distribution becomes an obstacle to democratization and whether the international community can take steps to mitigate this very real problem. The case of Venezuela offers a vivid illustration of how income inequality is a threat not only to human welfare but to democratic governance as well.

Polarization—whether ethnic, religious, or economic—is not the sole cause of semi-authoritarianism, but it is one of the conditions that encourage people to accept semi-authoritarian regimes and allow semi-authoritarian leaders to play on fears and anger to maintain power. Ethnic and religious polarization is addressed by the international community more in the realm of conflict management and peace-keeping than in the context of democracy. Thus, extreme polarization leading to violence is addressed by extremely high-end measures such as the dispatching of peacekeeping troops. Some low-end measures are used to reduce polarization at the local level. And semi-authoritarian regimes continue to take advantage of the fears and anger created by polarization.

State Formation

Democracy promoters usually take the existence of the state for granted, focusing their attention on supporting democratic transformation and increasing the state's administrative capacity. Only in countries just emerging from civil conflict, such as Afghanistan and Bosnia, has the issue of state formation received direct attention. Even in such cases, however, state formation has been conflated with the crafting of democratic institutions. The international community has embraced a democratic reconstruction model for postconflict situations, which is based on the assumption that state building and democracy building are part of the same process and must be carried out simultaneously.[6] This is an idea that developed during the 1990s; it has been tested in a few places—such as Haiti, Bosnia, Kosovo, and East Timor—but with very mixed and, above all, inconclusive results. For example, the attempted democratic reconstruction of Haiti has been a failure; there is yet no conclusive evidence concerning Bosnia and Kosovo, where both peace and a measure of democracy are maintained by a large international presence, or about East Timor, which was just emerging from international tutelage at the time of this writing. Furthermore, relatively few countries are targeted for state reconstruction. For example, despite the still-unresolved conflict with Armenia, Azerbaijan is not regarded as a postconflict country in need of special reconstruction efforts. There, the international community has implemented the same kind of democracy support programs that are implemented in countries whose recent past has been reasonably peaceful.

In postconflict countries, the international community acts on the assumption that successful state reconstruction depends on the immediate crafting of democratic institutions and the building of state administrative capacity. The emphasis on democracy as a tool of state reconstruction goes against historical evidence about state formation, as I have argued earlier. There is no doubt, on the other hand, about the crucial importance of administrative capacity to the survival of the state. It is less clear whether the particular institutions on which assistance focuses are those that are most important to the survival and consolidation of the state.

The democratic reconstruction model embraced by the international community today is a departure from past orthodoxy. Until recently, aid donors were as convinced that fragile states could not afford democracy as they are now that democracy is the only viable solution for them. The development literature of the 1960s and 1970s, and even more the policies implemented by all major bilateral aid agencies and international institutions, were based on the assumption that single parties and benevolent strongmen were more likely than multiparty democracies to succeed in holding together weak states.

The new model of how to promote state reconstruction and democratization simultaneously is a very high-end, interventionist approach, in contrast to the more cautious democratization programs implemented in supposedly stable countries. It is a maximalist approach, in that it calls for a large number of issues to be addressed simultaneously: state security, through a process of demobilization of former combatants and rebuilding of the military and the police; state administrative ability, through streamlining of the administrative apparatus, improved service delivery, and civil service reform; and state policy-making ability, through the strengthening of institutions, above all financial institutions. But the model also calls for things to be done about the problem of participation, through the building of electoral institutions, parliaments, courts, and other institutions of accountability. However, because of the supervisory role played by international organizations and the conditionalities imposed on aid, the model also introduces mechanisms of external accountability that weaken internal mechanisms. Conditionalities of this kind, imposed by the donors or even negotiated with them, weaken the accountability of the government to domestic institutions such as parliaments.

The democratic reconstruction model has been implemented fully in only a few cases. It is not only very invasive, it is also very expensive and very labor intensive. Nevertheless, it is the ideal that inspires donor activities in postconflict states. The few places where the model has been implemented—Bosnia, Kosovo, and East Timor—do not yet provide sufficient evidence that states can be constituted and consolidated through a democratic process. What is clear already is that even in these cases the attempt to build a democratic state has been made possible only by the coercion exercised by the international community. There is as yet no evidence whether these embryonic democratic states developed by outside intervention will survive without outside coercion, administrative support, and financial backing. The model makes demands that a state weakened by conflict, let alone one that has suffered real collapse, cannot possibly implement in short order or without substantial international assistance and oversight. It contains contradictions, such as the requirement that the state set up democratic institutions that will make the government accountable to its people while at the same time requiring it to be responsive to the donor community. In the end, the democratic reconstruction model prescribes too much and is likely to achieve little, particularly without sufficient external enforcement.

For most countries where semi-authoritarianism is at least partly related to the weakness of state formation, such as Azerbaijan and Bosnia, the democratic reconstruction model will not be the answer, because the international community favors it in theory but in practice hesitates to commit the needed resources. The challenge for the international community in the case of weak, semi-authoritarian states, then, is to devise a more modest approach, which sets priorities, and thus makes fewer simultaneous demands, and consequently has a real chance of being implemented. In some cases, state reconstruction may require a tolerance of semi-authoritarian regimes.

Asymmetrical Sources of Power

The most basic requirements for democracy include the existence of an opposition consisting of one or more parties and of an array of other independent organizations, including both self-interested lobbies and public-interest groups. Unless such groups are sufficiently strong to be competitive with the incumbents, the prospects for democracy are dim. No government is accountable unless it is faced with a credible challenge.

But the competition between government and opposition in semi-authoritarian regimes is unequal, and their sources of power asymmetrical. The opposition is expected to gain its power democratically at the polls, while the government has other means at its disposal. Support for democracy in these cases means taking measures that will help establish some balance of power. Steps the international community has taken or could take span a broad range, from the relatively nonpartisan low end to the strongly partisan high end.

Most of the democratization activities supported by the international community to deal with the issue of power distribution fall at the low end of the spectrum. Democracy promoters assume that it is possible for the opposition to generate power by playing the game according to the rules of democracy. If parties strengthen their internal organization, refine their message to the voters, master campaign techniques, and cooperate with other opposition groups, they can defeat the incumbents, or so the thinking goes. But this approach presupposes the existence of an open and at least somewhat level playing field, something that is supposed to exist in consolidating democracies but is absent in semi-authoritarian states.

The international community favors these low-end activities because they are the least controversial and allow the governments and agencies supporting them to claim that promoting democracy is a nonpartisan effort that does not constitute interference in another country's domestic politics. The political party training offered by international NGOs can be plausibly said to be politically neutral as long as it is open to all parties, including the governing ones. Support for NGOs can be defended on the grounds that such organizations are nobly prodemocracy and pro–human rights rather than antiregime. In reality, most donor-supported NGOs oppose the local regime, although there are some exceptions. For example, Venezuelan president Hugo Chávez received support for a time from human rights groups by inserting into the constitution language they had proposed. Another semi-authoritarian leader, President Yoweri Museveni of Uganda, deftly increased his popularity by supporting independent women's groups' demands for a new law on land ownership and inheritance.

Such low-end assistance projects that address the issue of power can be divided into three categories: (1) projects that seek to create countervailing forces by supporting civil society and, more rarely, political parties; (2) measures that aim at leveling the playing field; and (3) programs that seek to increase the power of democratic institutions by making them technically more efficient. Most of the efforts to create countervailing forces have been devoted to setting up organizations of civil society, in particular democracy and human rights advocacy organizations. The impact of these activities on semi-authoritarian regimes is open to question. While such groups exist in all countries discussed in the present study, they are invariably very small, often consisting of a leadership without a membership. Such organizations might be effective in countries with reformist governments actively seeking technical advice on the drafting of specific laws, for example, but they lack the muscle to force semi-authoritarian regimes to yield some of their powers—although, as I have noted, Venezuelan human rights organizations were consulted about and were able to influence the language on human rights in their country's new constitution, for example, they did not have much impact on the human rights record of the regime. Civil society organizations in semi-authoritarian regimes do not have the critical mass of support that would help establish a balance of power between the incumbent government and alternative political groups. Given the fact that they are mostly organized by nonembedded elites, they are unlikely ever to gain such weight. Donors, for example, have invested heavily in civil society organizations in Kenya, many of which are now competently run and well organized but still unable to outweigh the advantages enjoyed by the regime of President Daniel arap Moi.

Democracy promoters have also started working with political parties in at least some of the countries discussed in the present study. Party assistance remains more controversial than civil society assistance, since political parties are partisan by definition, while civil society organizations, which do not aim at gaining power but only at influencing the decisions of those who do, are seen as nonpartisan. (As mentioned previously, civil society organizations often have party affiliations—in Azerbaijan, for example, most NGOs are directly aligned with a political party, even sharing personnel and office space with them.) Low-end political party work is limited to training, as already mentioned. This teaches the parties to use democratic means more effectively, but provides little help when the government systematically blocks all democratic avenues to change.

The measures taken by democracy promotion organizations to level the playing field and monitor the fairness of election processes include support for independent election commissions, when they exist, and above all training and funding for domestic election-monitoring groups. There is little evidence that this often helps the opposition overcome its disadvantages, however. It is more likely to lead to the publication of a critical report that leaves the situation unchanged than to affect the election outcome. Similarly, the pressure the United States and other countries put on governments to improve access to the media for all parties, or to allow all organizations to hold public rallies and campaign meetings, usually has no significant impact in semi-authoritarian states.

Finally, technical assistance to democratic institutions has done little to increase their autonomy or power. Some of the clearest failures of democracy promotion in semi-authoritarian states fall in this category. For example, a program to provide technical support to the Egyptian parliament managed to be both controversial and ineffectual before being abandoned. A decentralization project in Senegal, which aimed to make local government more participatory, created an elaborate support infrastructure for increasing public participation in the budget-making process of rural governments, which only controlled a few thousand dollars a year. Court management systems everywhere have made it easier for judiciaries to keep track of cases but, unsurprisingly, have not increased their independence from ruling regimes. The primary problem for all institutions in semi-authoritarian states is power, not know-how. And, contrary to the old adage, knowledge in these cases is not necessarily power.

Although low-end programs have little impact on the distribution of power, most members of the international community usually hesitate to go further—particularly in semi-authoritarian states where the political situation does not appear to be sufficiently bad to justify more invasive programs. The reasons for this hesitation are primarily political. Strong measures to affect the balance of power between government and the opposition represent political interference without plausible deniability. They are not taken—nor should they be taken—in the absence of compelling reasons such as extreme domestic violations of human rights or threats to international stability. The actions of semi-authoritarian regimes do not normally fall into either category. Furthermore, in some cases semi-authoritarian regimes also serve the interests of the international community by maintaining stability in volatile areas, Egypt being a prime example.

In rare instances, the international community has turned to high-end activities—partisan, invasive, and risky—to reestablish the balance of power in transitional situations, although not in the five case study countries in the present study. These examples show what kinds of measures intervening countries can take to address the issue of power forcefully when this is deemed important. Such measures are not magic bullets, nor should they be automatically resorted to in countries with semi-authoritarian regimes. They are, nevertheless, examples of possible alternatives to the low-end measures usually implemented.

In 1994, Mozambique held its first-ever multiparty elections. A lot rode on the outcome, since failure would most probably mean the undoing of a difficult peace agreement that had put an end to fifteen years of civil war. The configuration of power in Mozambique was dramatically unsuited to a successful election. Frelimo (Frente de Libertação de Moçambique, or Liberation Front of Mozambique), the victorious liberation movement and then the country's only legal party for almost twenty years, was well entrenched though not necessarily well liked. Renamo (Resistencia Nacional Moçambicana, or Mozambican National Resistance), the main opposition group, was a guerrilla movement originally organized by the security services of white Rhodesia and later supported by white South Africa. It had a record of brutality against civilians, poor presence in the cities, no political experience, and an ethnic power base, to the extent that it had one at all. There was also a smattering of new parties formed to compete in the elections, but it was clear that they did not count and that the real contest was between the wartime rivals. Low-end activities would not have done anything to overcome Frelimo's enormous advantage. But if Renamo had no chance to compete, not only the prospects for democracy but the peace accord itself would be doomed.

The international community took a clear stand: Renamo had to be built up into a party capable of contesting the elections in a credible fashion. Donors did not offer training on campaign strategies or message development, but provided the financial support Renamo needed to open offices in the cities and bring its officials out of the bush and into Maputo, the capital. The international community rented houses, bought cars, and furnished offices. It built up Renamo, and to a lesser extent the other parties, and more or less bribed the leadership of Renamo to participate in the election. At the very end, the bribery became open: When Renamo threatened to withdraw on the eve of the election, the United Nations representative managed to conjure up an additional $1 million to prevent this from happening. The strategy paid off: While Frelimo won the elections, it did so by a very modest margin, and Renamo gained a strong presence in the parliament. Mozambique remained at peace.[7]

Since then, the international community has intervened forcefully and in a very partisan manner in other countries, abandoning all pretense at neutrality in the attempt to defeat particularly objectionable leaders. It did so in a fairly low-key fashion in Slovakia and Croatia, where it helped fund and organize coalitions of NGOs working to "get out the vote"—the opposition vote, that is—and monitor the elections. The approach was replicated on a much larger scale in Yugoslavia, where the international community mounted a concerted effort to help the opposition defeat President Slobodan Milošević in the fall of 2000.[8] The international community took a strongly partisan position in these elections, with the goal of getting rid of Milošević first and promoting democracy second. Support was provided both to political parties and to an openly partisan student organization, Otpor (Resistance), that was committed to mobilize voters in order to defeat Milošević. It was a high-risk strategy; when the first election results were announced and Milošević claimed victory, the opposition took to the streets, and Milošević called out the military. What saved Yugoslavia from massive violence was the army's refusal to move against the demonstrators who had surrounded the presidential residence and set the parliament on fire. In the end, however, the high-risk strategy succeeded—with much foreign funding, training, and a dose of luck. Later attempts by the international community to support the ouster through elections of Aleksandr Lukashenko in Belarus and Robert Mugabe in Zimbabwe failed.

The decision to resort to the type of high-end activities discussed here is a highly political one. It takes intervention out of the realm of promotion of the hallowed principles of democracy and into the gritty world of partisan politics. It represents blatant interference in the domestic politics of a sovereign country. And it is risky—Yugoslavia was as likely to sink into civil war as it was to elect a new, more democratically inclined government. High-end interventions thus cannot become a routine part of democracy promotion programs. This leaves policy toward semi-authoritarian states in a bind. Low-end activities do not overcome the asymmetry of power that characterizes these countries. High-end activities are too invasive and too openly political to be used routinely. The challenge is to identify effective steps that fall between the two extremes.

Nonembedded Elites and the Relevance of Democracy

Democracy promoters have failed to address, or have not addressed sufficiently, the structural problems that have encouraged the rise of semi-authoritarian regimes, but at least they have not created most of these obstacles themselves or made them worse. The only problem outsiders have worsened is the lack of embeddedness of the democratic elites. Democracy assistance programs have consciously adopted an elitist approach, which is particularly apparent from the roster of civil society organizations they have chosen to support. Funders have chosen to aid small, professional advocacy NGOs, whose main strength is knowledge, rather than membership-based associations or social movements, whose main strength is numbers.[9] Furthermore, by supporting professional advocacy organizations with grants and recognition, outsiders have made it possible for them to function even when they have little domestic support and have lost their incentive to develop such support. In a perverse manner, the international community has become the main constituency for a large number of civil society organizations. In order to survive, these groups must convince foreign funders of the importance of their projects. They are primarily accountable to these funders and write their reports for them. As long as they receive external support, civil society organizations can function without significant domestic constituencies.

The donors' preference for professional civil-society organizations led by free-floating elites is based in part on the conviction that democratic transitions are facilitated by pacts among elites, rather than by mass political participation, and in part on expediency. The concept of pacted transitions, derived from the experience of Venezuela and other Latin American countries, has had considerable influence on policy makers. The prototype of the pacted transition, as noted in the chapter on Venezuela in the present study, is the Pacto de Punto Fijo of 1953. Ten years earlier, the first attempted democratization of Venezuela had failed because Acción Democrática, then a leftist political party with mass support, frightened the military and conservative Venezuelans into carrying out a coup d'état. The second attempt in 1953 succeeded because the Acción Democrática leadership understood that it had to moderate its position. Instead of following the demands of its constituents, it entered into a series of pacts with other parties and organizations, with the Pacto de Punto Fijo being the most important of these. Pacted transitions, scholars concluded, were more likely to succeed than those in which change was brought about by mass participation.[10]

The elites that concluded the crucial pacts in Venezuela and elsewhere, however, were embedded, not free floating. The leadership of Acción Democrática had a large, organized constituency behind it, and it managed to maintain its support even as it moderated its position in order to conclude pacts with other groups. Other organizations involved in the pact-making process—such as the Christian Democratic party known as COPEI, the Catholic Church, and business groups —also had constituencies. Democratization was therefore the result of pacts among embedded elites.

Expediency encouraged democracy promoters to embrace the concept of pacted transitions, but to disregard the fact that the successful pacts were concluded among embedded elites. In most countries, alternative embedded elites simply did not exist. When they existed— for example, in the Islamist movements of Egypt—they appeared far too dangerous and undemocratic to be included in deals. The shortcut to the development of an alternative elite was the funding of NGOs. These organizations could be developed quickly, in great numbers, and with little funding. By supporting civil society organizations, international democracy promotion organizations succeeded in setting up an alternative elite capable of bringing new ideas into the discussion of the political future of the country. They did not succeed in conjuring into existence an alternative elite capable of bringing a meaningful constituency into a political pact; indeed, they did not even try.

For all their shortcomings, small, professional NGOs remain attractive to the international community because they are safe and unlikely to promote conflict. Large, popular movements are inherently more dangerous. They can lead to democracy, as in Poland and Czechoslovakia, but they can also bring to power authoritarian regimes, as they did in Germany and Italy between the world wars. Small, professional NGOs will never bring dictators to power, but they do not have the muscle to force authoritarian or even semi-authoritarian regimes to respond to their demands, either. Short of a personal ideological conversion to democracy, there is really no reason for President Hosni Mubarak to enter into pacts with the small and isolated NGOs that promote democracy and human rights in Egypt.

The current, low-end democracy promotion programs that bolster nonembedded elites have not created significant challenges to semi-authoritarian regimes. A more difficult, risky, but also potentially more productive high-end approach would be to support alternative elites who are better embedded because they link the idea of democracy to large constituencies' immediate, self-interested concerns, such as physical safety, access to employment, and decent health care. Some international donors, although not the United States, did that in the case of South Africa, following a policy that brought results but involved considerable risk at the time.

South Africa is considered one of the great successes of democratization in Africa, having undergone the transition from apartheid with less violence and having emerged with a much more democratic political system than many dared to hope. Behind the success, however, there is a story of mass mobilization and violence during the 1980s that suggests that democratic transitions are not always engineered by democratic elites inspired by high principles that foreign funders favor.

During the 1980s, the African National Congress (ANC) and its affiliate, the United Democratic Front, embraced a strategy to mobilize the population of the black townships by directly linking the comprehensive struggle for political rights to issues of immediate relevance to the daily life of ordinary South Africans, such as housing and electricity. Tens of thousands of people were mobilized in rent strikes and school boycotts, and the situation got very ugly, with growing violence on the part of the crowds and ruthless repression on the part of the government. The prospects for a democratic outcome appeared very dim at the time.

But in the end, the pieces fell into place. By linking the abstract issue of political rights to more practical issues, the ANC was able to mobilize more support than at any previous time. Faced with the evidence that the ANC was deeply embedded and could not be eliminated by repression, the South African government accepted that it had to negotiate a pact with the ANC leadership. After more than four years of negotiations, first between the apartheid government and the imprisoned Nelson Mandela and later among all political parties in the country, a pact was finally concluded. The high-risk strategy of the donors, particularly the Scandinavian countries and European NGOs, which had continued to support the ANC through a period of violence and with no certainty of a democratic outcome, eventually paid off.

It is difficult to find other instances in which at least one part of the international community was willing to take such a broad view of how democracy could be promoted. In the absence of a compelling argument for taking risks, such as that provided by the obvious injustice of the apartheid system, the international community is unlikely to take such risks. In most semi-authoritarian states, the argument for such high-end approaches is not compelling.

Dealing with Agency

Most democracy promotion programs in countries with semi-authoritarian regimes are directed at influencing agents and at thwarting the games played by the leadership. Democracy promoters do so either directly, by denouncing transgressions against democratic norms wherever they occur, or indirectly, by trying to build state institutions and civil society organizations capable of hemming in the leadership and forcing it to behave democratically.

Game-thwarting efforts are based on the assumption that the main potential impediment to effective transitions is the actions of the political class. It is thus important for the international community to ensure that those actions conform to democratic norms. This is usually done through three types of measures. Two of them are short-term: civic and political education of the population at large, and censure or even punishment of politicians who refuse to abide by democratic rules. The third type has a much longer timetable, even longer than democracy promoters are willing to admit: the building of institutions to circumscribe and restrain the actions of politicians in a systematic and transparent manner. Once institutions are in place, the personal proclivities of individual members of the political class should lose much of their importance. For example, if Egypt's National Assembly were strong enough to impose checks on the executive, Mubarak would not be able to maintain the state of emergency indefinitely, whether or not he was personally inclined to do so.

Educating for Democracy

Democracy promoters have directed civic and political education at both the general population and the political class. Programs addressing the general population are usually quite simple, starting with voter education before the first transitional multiparty elections, and then expanding into broader civic education programs, which are usually carried out by donor-funded local NGOs. Such programs seek to acquaint people with the functioning of the political system and with their rights. Programs are often also implemented in the schools. These are low-end activities, and in general are not particularly controversial. There are, however, many unanswered questions about their impact, with a number of studies questioning the long-term effects of abstract education when the contexts in which people live and have to act remain unchanged.[11]

Occasionally, democracy promoters also support more aggressive, action-oriented civic education programs, but these easily turn controversial and are opposed by semi-authoritarian regimes, particularly when they challenge the government. In Zimbabwe in the late 1990s, for example, some civic groups successfully convinced villagers that it was their right, indeed their duty, to vote out of office local councilors who were known to embezzle money, with the result that a majority of these politicians were defeated. The government allowed such action-oriented civic education programs at the local level, since local councilors were expendable pawns in the ruling party's game. But a few years later, when the opposition coalition known as the Movement for Democratic Change started educating the population about the wrongdoings of high government and party officials, the government used violence to thwart the efforts.

Democracy promotion organizations also devote many efforts to educating the political class and, above all, officeholders. Such programs rarely target high-level members of the executive; when executive agencies are involved, foreign organizations are more concerned with strengthening capacity than promoting democracy. Instead, they regularly target members of the legislature and the judiciary. Programs that provide training for judges and prosecutors as well as for legislators and parliamentary staff are common throughout the world.

The underlying assumption of most such programs is that a fundamental problem keeping the institutions of government from performing their appropriate roles in transitional countries is ignorance: ignorance of the standards they should meet, but more broadly lack of access to relevant information, such as the country's legal codes for the judges or relevant models of appropriate legislation to solve the problem at hand for members of parliament. In the least-developed countries in particular, there are many magistrates lacking adequate legal training and members of parliament with insufficient education to understand the bills on which they vote. But ignorance does not make judges corrupt or legislators subservient to the semi-authoritarian regime. In most cases, these problems are the result of rational choices on the part of political actors about the best ways to protect their own interests. Given the structure of incentives and rewards in semi-authoritarian regimes, behavior that is dysfunctional from the point of view of democrats makes a lot of sense from the point of view of individuals fighting for survival, in the political or even literal sense. Civic and political education is unlikely to have much impact under these circumstances.

Changing the Structure of Incentives through Rewards and Punishment

Democracy promoters are aware that civic education is not the answer to the unsatisfactory behavior of high officials in the executive branch of undemocratic governments. Ignorance about democracy is not a factor in the rise of semi-authoritarianism. Indeed, some semi-authoritarian leaders have mastered the concepts and language of democracy so well that they could easily become civic educators themselves. Azerbaijani president Heydar Aliyev, for example, can give masterful speeches about democracy. Changing the behavior of such leaders is not a matter of education, but of positive and negative incentives. The problem is that the international community can offer semi-authoritarian leaders no rewards that compare to ruling a country, and find it very difficult to mete out punishment that will hurt the leaders more than the citizens they rule.

For example, it is difficult to imagine what the international community could offer to Aliyev that would be more rewarding to him than ruling Azerbaijan and passing the mantle of leadership on to his own son. And in some cases, leaders themselves are only part of the problem. Even if the international community were to convince Hosni Mubarak to step aside, the military staff, security forces, and officials of the ruling National Democratic Party apparatus who back his regime would still have no incentive to cede power. Economic sanctions do not have much impact on semi-authoritarian leaders, because they are personally well protected from the hardships such punishments impose. It is ordinary citizens who lose jobs and income as a result of sanctions. Nor have the more recently devised "smart sanctions" proved more effective in forcing semi-authoritarian leaders to accept democracy. Smart sanctions are measures—such as blocking leaders' access to their foreign bank accounts or denying visas to top government officials and members of their families—that seek to do direct injury to the culprits while leaving the rest of the population unaffected. An example is provided by the unsuccessful international effort to press President Mugabe of Zimbabwe to open the election process and accept fair competition in 2002. Despite smart sanctions, constant public scrutiny, and no end of criticism, Mugabe brazenly and defiantly manipulated the elections and won a fifth term, demonstrating in the process the inability of the international community to create a new structure of incentives to alter his behavior.

Building Institutions

The long-term tool for thwarting the game-playing propensity of semi-authoritarian leaders is the building of institutions. With strong institutions in place, the personal tendencies of leaders become much less important. Probably no other expression is used as often and misused as regularly by democracy promoters as "building strong institutions." Unfortunately, there is a misconception among many democracy promoters about what institution building really means and thus about the capacity of the international community to build institutions in other countries.

When donors talk of institution building, they usually mean setting up an organizational structure that replicates what is found in democratic countries, writing the rules that will govern its functioning, and perhaps training the personnel to staff it. All of these measures are necessary to institution building, but they are only the first, quickest, and easiest steps. An organizational structure does not become an institution until it has proven its value in addressing concrete problems. Furthermore, an organization can only become an institution if it succeeds in fighting off attempts to deprive it of its functions or to have those functions discharged elsewhere.

An institution is not simply an organization. It is an organization to which the citizens, or at least a segment of them, attach a value, either emotionally, as is often the case with traditional institutions, or intellectually, because it has proven its usefulness. Parliaments are institutions in established democracies, but in nondemocratic countries they are simply organizational structures, to be set up and disbanded at will, and do not necessarily discharge real functions. If Diouf and now Wade in Senegal can eliminate the Senate and then set it up again at short intervals and with disconcerting regularity, it is clear that that body is not an institution and is not likely to become one, at least in the immediate term.

Democracy promoters routinely help countries, including semi-authoritarian ones, set up the organizations crucial to the functioning of democratic systems. They do not necessarily do it in the way most suited to the conditions of the country. Usually they follow the model of the institutions they are familiar with at home rather than try to develop something tailored to the specific situation in the recipient country. Nevertheless, setting up the structures is a relatively easy matter of transferring know-how and providing technical support. These are essentially low-end activities. Making organizational structures into institutions, however, is a different matter. Time is required for an organization to prove its value and become an institution, but time by itself is not enough.

Essentially there are two scenarios describing how outsiders can help a country develop an institution. One can be envisaged as a demand-side process: The leaders of a country are looking for an organization to address particular problems and turn to the international community for help. Technical advice from the outside helps them set up this organization, the leadership values what the organization does, and the organization becomes a durable institution. Outside assistance makes a contribution by providing the technical know-how, but the demand comes from inside the country. Given the importance the government of Croatia attaches to gaining early entry into the European Union, the commission set up to ensure that Croatian laws conform to European norms will probably become institutionalized. Sometimes, demand-side institution building can have unexpected results when the organization singled out for development becomes too powerful in relation to all others. For instance, Ethiopian emperor Haile Selassie once asked the United States for assistance in forming a modern, professional military. The project was so successful that the military became the strongest institution in a country where power was mostly exercised through feudal structures of fealty. The unexpected result was that this modern army eventually deposed the emperor and seized power.

The second scenario is a supply-side one. Members of the international community force a country to set up certain organizational structures even when the government does not really want them. A common example is that of election commissions. Intervenors want elections to be organized by independent commissions, and they often prevail upon the government to set up an organizational structure called an election commission. In many cases, the commission is not given the space to build up its capacity and power, and it thus never becomes an institution, although it may continue to exist. In other cases, a tug of war begins between government and democracy promoters that can lead incrementally to the institutionalization of the election commission. But this does not happen automatically or without strong pressure.

Ghana's election commission provides an example. Donors first insisted on such a commission in 1992, with mediocre results. The commission was not independent and the elections were heavily rigged. By 1996, with continued international support, the commission had established some independence, and the elections were accepted as fair even by the opposition parties, although they lost again. The independence of the commission and the fairness of the proceedings were reconfirmed in 2000, when the incumbent party finally lost. By that time, the commission had proven its independence and capacity, and it was probably as institutionalized as any organization can become in eight years.

This incremental, supply-side approach to creating institutions does not work often, and then only if in the end the government in power decides to allow the process to continue, as Ghana's then-president Jerry Rawlings did. An independent election commission probably never was high on the list of what he wanted, but he accepted it. He could have stopped the process of institutionalization at any time if he had wanted. In semi-authoritarian states, the cases studies suggest, the supply-side approach to institutions has been largely a failure. The organizations prescribed by the democracy promotion experts exist, but do not function. Making such organizations into institutions would require much more forceful, high-end intervention by the international community.

Elections and Games

Election assistance was one of the first democratization activities undertaken by the international community in the 1990s. It is also one area where international agencies have learned a lot from past mistakes and adjusted their programs most quickly. Assistance now starts much earlier in the election cycle, and assessments are carried out periodically. Monitoring by domestic organizations has become routine. Intervenors know what to expect and try to take corrective measures promptly. While election assistance has improved greatly, even sophisticated programs do not always improve the quality of elections— in some cases, periodic assessments serve to provide a good record of transgressions rather than to correct the problems. More important, it is not clear whether cleaner elections lead to democratization, or are themselves products of democratization. To be sure, elections in a democracy should be free, fair, and devoid of chicanery. Elections in many countries in transition, especially those with semi-authoritarian regimes, are marred by problems of all kinds. But do states become more democratic because they are forced to clean up their elections, or do they hold cleaner elections only when the incumbent's stranglehold on power has been broken and the situation becomes open? Like all chicken-and-egg conundrums, the question has no easy answer. Outsiders simply assume that they can encourage democratization by making elections fairer, and thus invest heavily in curbing the electoral games played by incumbents. In countries with semi-authoritarian regimes, such efforts rarely make much difference unless something else changes.

The five case studies in the present volume suggest that it is the balance of power in the country, rather than a better election process encouraged or imposed by the international community, that makes the difference. The rule of the Croatian Democratic Union did not end because elections became cleaner, but because the party lacked strong leadership after Franjo Tudjman's death and the opposition became able to assert itself. Elections were better because the Croatian Democratic Union no longer had the power to manipulate them. Conversely, clean elections in Venezuela could not prevent the rise of a semi-authoritarian leader once the old parties collapsed.

Furthermore, the international community's capacity to improve the quality of elections in a country where the government truly resists change is limited. Neither technical, low-end election support nor high-end steps such as sanctions work in such cases. The elections of 2002 in Zimbabwe provide an example. After nearly twenty years in power, by the late 1990s Robert Mugabe had become a very controversial figure both in his own country and abroad. Zimbabwe, once prosperous by sub-Saharan standards and reasonably open in the initial period after it became independent in 1980, had experienced steady economic decline and increased repression under Mugabe's rule. In the face of mounting socioeconomic problems, Mugabe tried to revive his flagging popularity by encouraging "veterans" of the war of independence—in reality, most often thugs far too young to have participated in that war—to seize white-owned farms. Domestically the policy gained him some support, because of the problems of unequal land distribution and income inequality, but it also caused much resentment, because the supposed veterans chased not only the white owners from the farms but the African workers as well. Internationally, these actions caused an outcry. In the meantime, a credible domestic opposition, which was headed by a trade union leader and drew much support in urban areas, started developing.

All sides saw the 2002 presidential elections as crucial. The international community openly sided with the opposition and put enormous pressure on Mugabe to allow a fair process. All the tools in the international kit were used—assessment missions, diplomacy, smart sanctions against Mugabe and high government officials, suspension of some aid, and international monitoring—with no effect at all. Mugabe played every trick in the book of unclean elections—fomenting violence to intimidate people, making voter registration difficult in areas where his political opponents were popular, packing the once highly independent courts with his own appointees in order to frustrate efforts by the opposition to win redress, and reducing the number of urban polling stations to prevent his opponents' supporters from voting. Naturally, he won handily, proving that when the distribution of power is lopsided and the incumbent is really determined, foreign and domestic pressures make little difference.

Elections in countries with semi-authoritarian regimes are heavily manipulated, as the cases described in the present chapter indicate; thus, the results cannot be taken to reflect the will of the people. Nevertheless, the evidence is unclear that the international community should always make better elections in these countries a major goal of policy. Semi-authoritarian rulers are masters of manipulation, and it is doubtful that the international community can achieve much simply by trying to outwit them at their own electoral games.

Conclusions

Democracy assistance and international pressure for political change are two of the main reasons why semi-authoritarian regimes exist, not because the international community has caused democratic transitions to fail, but because it has encouraged and even forced nondemocratic regimes to go through the motions of democracy even when the leadership has no intention of introducing democracy and does not face a real opposition challenge. To the extent that semi-authoritarian regimes are preferable to fully authoritarian ones, and that even the most coercive among them feel obliged to leave some areas of openness in order to protect their image, international pressure and democracy assistance have probably contributed to positive change in many countries with semi-authoritarian regimes. Such positive change falls far short of democracy, however.

Assistance to countries with semi-authoritarian regimes has failed to address the structural obstacles to greater democracy or has done so with low-end programs that do not seem effective. In particular, democracy assistance has decreased the need for elites, particularly those in civil society organizations, to build constituencies and become embedded.

Democracy assistance by itself is unlikely to change the nature of semi-authoritarian regimes. But as long as democracy promoters continue to work in states with such regimes and are determined to foster further change, they need to devise new approaches that deal more directly with the structural obstacles to further change, or, when that is not possible, they must try to work around the problems. In some cases, this will mean turning from low-end toward more high-end programs.

9

Looking to the Future

IN THE COMING DECADE, promoting democracy will increasingly
mean dealing with semi-authoritarian regimes. The number of countries that do not have the formal institutions of democracy and do not
hold multiparty elections has decreased rapidly, but the number of
states where democracy is only a facade has increased almost as quickly.
Countries that have had successful transitions to functioning democracies will no longer need support. The problem of semi-authoritarian regimes will continue to loom large, however. Democracy assistance by itself cannot bring about a second, democratic transition in
countries with such regimes; nevertheless, assistance would be more
helpful if it were based on a clearer understanding that these countries are not imperfect democracies, but political systems with special
characteristics and political dynamics. They are very different from
each other as well.

Democracy assistance is only one of the factors that influence political transitions, and it is not even the most important. Most countries
that are democratic today have become so because of domestic
processes and without the benefit of outside assistance. But external
aid can contribute significantly to political change, in both positive
and negative ways. In little over a decade, democracy assistance has
caused the diffusion of a new, standardized language of politics around
the world. With remarkably few exceptions, politicians everywhere
feel the need to talk about democracy and to use the same terminology

when doing so. Even in countries where democracy until recently meant "people's democracy" and "democratic centralism," politicians, including many who started their careers long before the days of democratic orthodoxy, now talk of transparency and accountability, extol the virtues of civil society rather than those of the broad masses, and in general try to show the world that they share in the values upheld by the established democracies. Actions rarely live up to the language, but the fact that the same language is spoken everywhere shows the influence of democracy promotion.

Such influence is also reflected in the similarity among the organizations of civil society that exist in all countries—from Latin America to Central Asia, one encounters organizations that resemble each other to an extraordinary degree and furthermore are unlike any that ever existed in democratizing countries in the past. Professional advocacy and civic education organizations are virtually interchangeable in terms of their language and way of functioning from Nepal to Zambia. At one level, such similarities are not surprising because civil society groups around the world are funded by the same countries, mentored by the same organizations, and belong to the same international networks. But if one considers the cultural differences among the countries of the world, the similarity among the organizations that supposedly represent these diverse societies gives one pause.

Democracy assistance has contributed much to the creation of the facade of democracy, but it is domestic factors that have determined the political realities behind that facade. The question is whether democracy promoters can now have a deeper impact on these transformations. I believe this is possible in many cases. Although internal factors will continue to be the most important ones, outsiders could have more effect than is currently the case. In order to achieve greater success, however, they have to refocus their efforts, rethink their methods, be willing to take greater risks by resorting to high-end approaches, be more selective about where they work, and take into consideration the differences among types of semi-authoritarian regimes. Taking the characteristics of specific countries into account does not mean making marginal adjustments to standard programs, as is most often the case now, but taking quite different approaches in at least some countries.

In this concluding chapter of the present study, which is essentially prescriptive, I will deal with two major issues. The first is whether and how democracy assistance can address the shallowness of the transitions that have led, not as many had hoped to democracy, but to semi-authoritarianism. Unless these transitions are deepened, the prospects for a further change leading to democracy are dim. Addressing the shallowness of transitions will require change in most areas of democracy promotion. The second issue I will deal with is how democracy promoters could address more pointedly the problems that are specific to the three types of semi-authoritarian regimes: those in equilibrium, those in decay, and those experiencing dynamic change.

Deepening the Transitions

Shallow transitions, I have argued, are attempts to craft new political systems out of the old social and political components. In contrast, deep transitions are changes in the political system that take place when economic growth, a modification of borders, the mobilization of new political groups into politics, or any other underlying transformation introduces new factors into the political equation. Deep transformations, in other words, are not purely political, but build on social and economic change. One problem of transition in semi-authoritarian states is that political changes generally far outpace any deeper transformation of the society. In some countries, for example Senegal, political changes have taken place without much social transformation at all. Furthermore, only in those semi-authoritarian regimes where a process of dynamic change is underway will the process have any chance of becoming deeper without outside intervention.

Democracy promoters cannot address the underlying problems of social and economic stagnation that keep these transitions shallow, or at least not quickly enough to make a difference in political transitions. It is simply not within their capacity to bring about in short order the socioeconomic changes that could underpin deep transformations. Half a century of development assistance has shown all too clearly that the international community's capacity to engineer socioeconomic development is limited. Countries that have developed rapidly enough for socioeconomic change to drive political transition—such as Taiwan and South Korea—are few and far between, and in any case they have not experienced this development as a consequence of foreign assistance. Thus, in the short run most countries will undergo an inherently shallow transition or no transition at all. Since democracy promoters cannot deepen transitions by affecting underlying conditions, they have no choice but trying to deepen the political process itself.

Outside intervenors could help deepen political transitions by abandoning the assumption that democracy is a natural aspiration of humankind and thus is automatically relevant to all people; by consciously promoting embedded elites even though it is much easier and less risky to work with free-floating ones; and by helping to reestablish the link between democratic politics and policy making that has been weakened by externally imposed conditionalities.

Making Democracy Relevant

In order to contribute to the deepening of transitions, foreign governments and organizations involved in the process need to devote more effort to making democracy relevant to the majority of the population in transitional states. This means, first and foremost, discarding the assumption that democracy is the aspiration of people everywhere and facing the fact that there are other ideologies that have a much more immediate appeal and are less abstract than democracy.

As a rhetorical device, the idea of democracy as the universal aspiration is hard to beat. As an assumption for guiding policy, however, it is highly misleading. What the five cases in the present study, and others, suggest is that while resentment of oppressive governments and a desire for a better life exist everywhere, these feelings can translate into different types of political demands, many of which cannot in any way be construed as representing democratic aspirations.

Even with the end of the Cold War, democracy is still competing with other ideologies. For example, nationalism is not a spent force. Western European countries appear to have put much of the problem behind them, and there is no reason to believe that other countries cannot do so eventually, but eventually is not now. In terms of immediate appeal to large numbers of people, nationalism gives democracy strong competition.

There are also political ideologies based on religion. Those based on Islam have attracted the most attention, because their adherents have become more strongly mobilized and are more willing to use violence in the pursuit of their goals. But there are faith-based ideologies in other cultures as well, and they all challenge democracy in some fashion, because religious values tend to be absolute, and democracy requires compromise. Even in an established democracy such as the United States, religious and democratic values do not always coexist comfortably.

Finally, democracy is challenged by leftist organizations, which have continuing appeal because they put the very concrete cause of socioeconomic justice ahead of the more abstract one of political and civil liberties. The Marxist-inspired socialism of the old Left has lost much of its luster, and it is difficult today to find many outside a small, die-hard intellectual elite who are willing to uphold those ideas. But broad attempts are underway to revive, in the name of antiglobalism, a socialist Left capable of addressing today's problems rather than those of the early Industrial Revolution. With about 50 percent of the world's people living on less than two dollars a day, the appeal of the Left cannot be dismissed as a thing of the past.

The movements that pursue these competing ideologies are headed by political elites who can become embedded more easily than those who advocate democracy, because they can appeal to concrete interests or to values that are part of the everyday experience of most people. The word *democracy* does not translate easily into many languages, but all societies have a word denoting a supreme being, and all draw the distinction between "us" and "them" on which nationalism is built. And globalization, while an abstract concept in theory, quickly becomes a concrete, bread-and-butter issue when local producers are put out of business by foreign imports or the privatization of utilities leads to higher costs for consumers.

The importance of political ideas that compete with democracy is clear in most of the case studies. Venezuelans chose to support President Hugo Chávez and his populist message over the old parties that represented democracy. Croats supported President Franjo Tudjman and his nationalism, and it took ten years and Tudjman's death for democratic ideas to start competing with nationalist ones—and this in a country that sees itself as an integral part of Europe. In Egypt, where a sophisticated, democratic elite already existed in the early twentieth century, the population has shown far more support first for President Gamal Abdel Nasser's socialist ideas and now for Islamist ones than for democracy.

What can democracy promotion organizations do to help make the idea of democracy more relevant and more competitive with other ideologies? Abstract civic-education programs are not the answer to this problem—experience so far suggests that their effects are limited and, even more important, brief. Making democracy relevant does not mean simply telling people that democracy is a good thing, but showing how it can be a means of influencing the government to address the issues people care about. At the same time, democracy promoters cannot promise people concrete results, because democracy is a process with open-ended outcomes. Finally, there is no direct correlation, particularly in the short term, between democracy and improved economic conditions. Democracy did not save the United States from the Great Depression, for example.

Developing a message about democracy that is concrete enough to resonate beyond the small circle of the urban educated class but at the same time does not make promises that cannot be kept is tricky business indeed, and has often been mishandled. Democratic parties in their election campaigns and even foreign supporters of democracy trying to get people to vote in transitional elections often link the idea of democracy to that of prosperity—the underlying idea is that democratic countries are likely to have inherently superior, free-market policies, more capable government, and less corruption. Unfortunately, a country that has just held its first democratic election does not suddenly acquire a more capable or even more honest government, and economic reforms tend to inflict pain before they lead to greater prosperity. When the promised democratic dividend fails to materialize, disillusionment sets in. "This is democracy" is a sarcastic, even cynical response to the government's failure to address some major problem that I have heard personally, or has been reported to me, too often for comfort.

It is probably not outsiders who can develop a message about democracy that makes sense for specific countries. This is indeed a job for local elites, but these local elites now speak a formulaic language about democracy, which is the same from Albania to Zimbabwe, that thus cannot go beyond general principles. This does not help deepen transitions.

The most important step that can make democracy relevant is the decision by organized interest groups, including those that are not committed to democracy as a matter of principle, to pursue their goals through democratic institutions and processes and not through other means. Prospects for the deepening of political transitions increase when socialist parties decide to compete in parliamentary elections rather than to organize underground cells to carry on the revolution, to use a historical example, or when Islamist organizations decide to do the same, to refer to a more contemporary challenge. It is only at this point that democracy stops being an abstract idea and becomes a means to a concrete end.

The decision to work through the democratic process, rather than outside it, is not one outsiders can make for local interest groups. Members of the international community, nevertheless, have a part to play. First, they need to be more open to dialogue with any embedded, organized interest group, no matter how unpromising, instead of relying solely on free-floating partners in the world of small nongovernmental organizations (NGOs) and prodemocracy organizations. Second, they need to reconsider the conditionalities and practices that, de facto, reduce the power of the very domestic, democratic institutions they promote, making it less appealing for organized interest groups to work through such institutions.

Dealing with Embedded Elites

Most of the organizations democracy promoters work with in countries with semi-authoritarian regimes are not membership based, or else have very small memberships. This is true not only of NGOs that are considered to represent civil society but of the opposition political parties, which are usually small, highly fragmented, and poorly organized. Yet in most semi-authoritarian states there are organizations with large memberships, or at least considerable emotional appeal and public support. These organizations could be a crucial element in deepening transitions even if they were not committed to democracy in principle, as long as they came to see its instrumental value.

In trying to increase support for democracy, democracy assistance providers have two options: either try to build the small, democratically oriented organizations of civil society into movements with mass memberships, thus making democracy more relevant to many and transforming the nonembedded elites who guide these organizations into embedded ones; or try to work with nondemocratic organizations that already have followings and steer them toward pursuing their goals through democratic means. The two approaches are not mutually exclusive, but the latter is the more important, because as long as organizations with substantial followings reject democracy, there will be no deepening of transition.

In some countries, democracy promoters have already been experimenting with a strategy of building small civil-society organizations into broad movements for democracy. They have recognized that only large organizations with massive support can generate sufficient power to force change in countries with semi-authoritarian or even authoritarian regimes. They experimented with this strategy in Slovakia, where they built an election-monitoring coalition into a catalyst for change, and then replicated the approach in Croatia, as mentioned earlier. They expanded this strategy in Serbia, backing what was essentially an insurgent movement that had the stated aim of defeating Yugoslav president Slobodan Milošević. Despite the enthusiasm generated by that success, democracy promoters still have a lot to learn about the conditions that made it possible to build small civil-society organizations into mass movements. They have even more to learn about whether such movements are ephemeral, disintegrating once their immediate goals are achieved, or can remain significant actors in a pluralistic, democratic system in which they are no longer the sole beneficiaries of donors' largesse. Building small civil-society organizations into mass prodemocracy movements is not a panacea; nor is it a substitute for engaging organizations that already have popular support.

There are antecedents that show how unpromising nondemocratic organizations can play a pivotal role in democratization. I have already mentioned the role of socialist parties in some European countries. Labor unions, despite a history of extremism and violence in certain periods of their development, have also helped consolidate democracy in some countries in the past by providing the needed link between broad constituencies and democratic ideals. Even in recent years, labor unions have played a crucial part in democratic transitions—or attempted transitions—in several countries, including Poland and South Africa. Several democracy promotion organizations recognize this and already work with labor unions in many countries. Other examples of the democratic role of nondemocratic organizations are offered by Catholic countries: Christian democratic parties with close ties to an authoritarian, hierarchical Catholic Church helped foster democracy by building a bridge between church and state. Such parties convinced conservative constituencies influenced by the Catholic Church to pursue their agendas through the parliament and other institutions.

It is unlikely that any of these experiences will be replicated in the same way in other countries today. The old socialist parties are a thing of the past, and labor unions are the product of industrialization, and thus have very limited importance in countries where the economy is dominated by subsistence agriculture and the informal sector. The specific organizations will be different. The general problem, however, is the same. Organizations with significant constituencies are crucial to democratization even if they do not embrace democratic platforms and are not internally democratic.

One aspect of all attempts to increase the relevance of democracy in any country should thus be the search for embedded organizations that can play that bridging role between the ideas and institutions of democracy on one side and the concerns, beliefs, and values that motivate important constituencies on the other. Such groups are more likely to generate enough power to defeat incumbents, or at least to compete with them on a reasonably level playing field, than elite organizations, parties with little popular appeal, and small, urban NGOs.

In all five countries discussed in the present study, there are groups and organizations that will obstruct democratic transformation unless they are a part of it. In Egypt, these organizations are primarily the Islamist groups. In Venezuela, they include the people who support Chávez, and who will continue to be a threat to democracy until they are drawn into parties that will provide them with effective representation. In Croatia, they are the nationalists who backed the Croatian Democratic Union (HDZ) and who remain a threat to the second transition. In Senegal this role is played by the Sufi brotherhood, once solidly tied to the government through patronage links but now more distant. This group must remain committed to democracy if the danger inherent in the radical ideas currently spreading throughout the Islamic world is to be avoided. Only in Azerbaijan is it difficult to identify a major, organized constituency that needs to be drawn into a democratic process lest it derail all prodemocratic change.

Reaching out to large, nondemocratic groups is difficult for outsiders. Many such groups are hostile by definition, particularly to the United States. All of them, however, include some moderate elements that may see the utility of working within a democratic system. Of course, these groups also include radical elements that will never accept democracy. There is also a risk that organizations will take advantage of the opportunity for victory that democracy offers them but will resort to undemocratic means if they win. For example, nervous white South Africans talked before 1994 about the danger of "one man, one vote, one time" elections. But there is an even greater risk in ignoring such organizations, or worse, cooperating with the incumbent government in continuing to repress them. The outcome is the perpetuation of semi-authoritarianism, at best (the price Egypt pays for keeping out Islamists), and a violent confrontation, at worst (the price Algeria paid). Of the two risky strategies, the only one that may lead to democratic results is that which seeks to bring organizations with mass followings into the democratic process, no matter how undemocratic these organizations' goals appear to be.

Reestablishing the Link between Politics and Policy

The organizations that could make democracy relevant to larger constituencies do not have to turn to democracy in order to pursue their goals. They have the option of using other avenues to obtain what they want, including violence. Nor do they need to embrace democracy in order to continue existing, unlike most donor-supported NGOs. They are thus unlikely to work within the framework of democratic institutions unless they believe that by doing so they can derive some benefits. In other words, they will accept democracy if they see it as an effective means of obtaining the policy changes they desire.

Unfortunately, democracy promotion has coincided with a process of erosion of the ability of many governments to make autonomous policy decisions in a range of crucial areas. The policy-making capacity of many governments, including those that are democratically elected, is severely restricted by the conditionalities imposed by donor agencies. For more than two decades now, donors have required regimes to carry out numerous policy reforms, originally in the economic realm but increasingly in others as well, as a condition for receiving assistance. The more a country needs such assistance, the more limited the sphere of autonomous policy making has become.

Technically, conditionalities are not imposed by international financial institutions and bilateral donors; rather, they are agreed upon through negotiation. But negotiations by and large focus on the details of policy, not substance—for example, how and how fast a government will privatize its parastatal companies, not whether it will privatize them at all. And these negotiations, furthermore, take place among technocrats on all sides, not in the kind of open processes that should be the basis for policy making in democratic countries. Increasingly, negotiations between donors and recipient governments formally require the participation of "civil society," but the individuals supposedly representing civil society are usually picked from the realm of NGOs—which are often not representative of the populations' desires, needs, or opinions—rather than from elected institutions. There is often a good reason for sidelining institutions elected in rigged processes, but this also creates a vicious circle: There is little incentive for any interest group to work through democratic processes if the institutions so formed have no power to make decisions. As a result, the institutions remain unrepresentative and often inactive.

Deepening transitions requires reviving the weakened connection between democratic politics and policy outcomes. Outside intervenors need to abandon the prevailing assumption that there are no contradictions between their efforts to promote democracy and their prescriptions for specific policy outcomes. Policy making in a democracy is a messy and conflict-filled process in which different groups—executive agencies, political parties, lobbies, and sometimes experts—push for different goals, with the outcome ultimately being a compromise dictated by the necessity to gather enough support for a decision. The international community wants democracy, but at the same time it wants policies based on a concept of "best practices," as defined by professional reformers rather than fashioned in political battle. (In reality, the concept of what constitutes best practices is itself far from apolitical, but it is influenced by the politics of the donor countries rather than those of the recipients.)

The tension between democratic policy making and technocratic policy making is most evident in regard to economic policies and the role of government in establishing a social safety net for its citizens. The idea that democracy and the free market go together—and consequently that democracy requires a small, streamlined government—is a dominant assumption that simply does not stand up to evidence. It is true that there has never existed (and it is impossible even to imagine) a state that put tight control of all economic activities in the hands of bureaucrats while at the same time allowing the civil liberties and free debate that are characteristic of a democracy. But democratic countries do not choose pure free-market economic models, either. European democracies until recently considered it necessary for their governments to control public utilities and key industrial sectors. Indeed, the post–World War II democratic reconstruction of Europe and Japan took place in a climate of strong statist economic intervention. Furthermore, all democracies have developed social welfare systems that, once in place, are difficult to scale back because of public opposition. And all interfere in domestic and foreign markets in many different ways, from subsidies for agriculture to the imposition of tariffs on goods that compete with domestic production.

All these departures from the free-market economic model, furthermore, are not aberrations. Rather, they are inevitable outcomes of democracy. A political system that allows interest groups to set forth their demands and mobilize the power of voters to sway the government's decisions will inevitably produce compromise policies that are responsive to the demands of mobilized interest groups, and thus that will modify the pure economic logic of the ideal free market with the political logic of the democratic marketplace.

Donors do not limit their policy prescriptions to economics. The range of what is prescribed is vast indeed, as I showed briefly in the discussion of Croatia's second transition. Many of these prescriptions are supposed to strengthen democracy by making countries that have adopted democratic institutions more similar to established democracies in all respects. In reality, however, policy prescriptions coming from the outside contribute to shallow transitions. They embellish the democratic facade rather than help institutions become tools citizens can use to pursue their goals in competitive processes.

Donors could go one step further to promote debate on important policy issues in the appropriate domestic institutions by requiring that all foreign assistance programs be discussed by relevant domestic institutions.[1] While such a requirement would in itself be another conditionality, it would be the imposition of a process of decision making, not of a policy outcome, and thus it would be more compatible with democracy.

Foreign donors negotiate their assistance programs with respective recipients' executive agencies, increasingly in consultation with civil society organizations, as I have mentioned. However, such consultations are exclusive processes, to which only a select few are invited. Donors should insist that assistance projects, which imply policy choices on the part of the recipient as well as a commitment of its own funds, be discussed in national parliaments. This would make a more significant contribution to the vitality of national legislatures—and show citizens the value of the democratic process—than, say, providing training for parliamentary staff.

Of course, from the point of view of donors, such debates would complicate matters greatly. They could result in the rejection of some programs, particularly those involving loans, and would force compromise on others. And it would not be possible to submit all assistance to parliamentary scrutiny in all countries; obviously, it would be more beneficial to vet programs in more plural parliaments, such as Croatia's, than in those heavily dominated by government parties, such as Azerbaijan's. Still, if the goal is to deepen transitions beyond the facade of democracy, donors should accept the utility of debate on foreign assistance within the institutions of recipient countries.

Making Choices

The suggestions in the present chapter about the steps members of the international community should consider in order to deepen democratic transitions lead to an inescapable conclusion: Meeting the challenge of semi-authoritarianism will require donors to make clearer and harder choices among conflicting goals in many countries, to engage more often in high-end activities that entail greater risks but also the possibility of greater payoffs, to decide when they are justified in intervening more forcefully in the deepening of transitions, and to do a better job of coordinating overall policy toward individual countries and the democracy promotion projects they fund in those countries.

Since the early 1990s, the international community has sometimes been able to avoid some hard choices and tough issues, in part because of numerous apparent successes in democracy promotion. But the rise of semi-authoritarian regimes, as well as outright reversals in countries that have suffered new military coups d'état or sunk into civil conflict, is dispelling illusions about democratization, fully revealing its conundrums. When the major obstacles to the deepening of transitions are structural, little difference can be made by low-end activities—such as creating more civil-society NGOs or giving civic education to a few thousand more people—directed at thwarting the games played by the incumbents. This means that democracy promoters need either to engage in high-end activities or, where that does not appear feasible under the circumstances, to disengage from democracy promotion for the time being. Not all semi-authoritarian regimes should be targeted for high-end intervention in the short run; nor should all interventions necessarily be directed at creating a democratic political system immediately. In many countries, identifying next steps is much more important than trying to figure out what the political system should look like eventually.

Even for governments that invest considerable effort and funds in democracy promotion, democracy is never the only consideration in the formulation of policy toward a particular country. This is inevitable and is not a problem in itself. What are problematic and counterproductive are the situations in which a donor continues to go through the motions of democracy promotion in a country with a semi-authoritarian regime, even as other interests make the donor reluctant to confront the government with high-end activities. By continuing to carry out low-end, ineffective democracy promotion activities as if there were no problem, outsiders help the semi-authoritarian regime maintain the facade of democracy. It would be less detrimental in the long run if they would simply cease democracy promotion activities and instead used their limited resources for other purposes.

The necessity of using high-end activities in semi-authoritarian states raises questions about the right of donors to interfere in other countries' domestic policies. Democracy promoters have avoided confronting this issue by pretending that democracy is such a universal value that its promotion is not a partisan political activity. This is never true—there are winners and losers in a process of democratization, and the fact that the losers are the undemocratic "bad guys" does not make democracy promotion less political or less of an interference in another country's domestic politics. Many low-end policies are not effective enough to constitute serious interference. But higher-end activities are inherently political. Do donors have the right to engage in them? Or is such interference in flagrant contradiction of the principles of sovereignty and the ideals of democracy? No single answer can cover all situations, particularly in semi-authoritarian states where violations of citizens' rights are not extreme. All forms of democracy promotion constitute interference to some extent. Whether they also contradict the very idea of democracy depends on the form of intervention. For example, attempts to encourage nondemocratic organizations to pursue their goals democratically constitute interference but do not hinder democracy. The decision by foreign governments to impose multiple conditionalities on a country without any consultation with its more representative institutions both entails interference and violates the idea of democracy.

Whether an outside intervenor decides to promote democracy through high-end activities or to step back until a more favorable time, a more focused effort to deal with semi-authoritarian regimes requires better coordination between diplomats in charge of the overall policy toward a country and democracy specialists in other agencies. For the United States, that means coordinating the high politics of diplomatic relations, which are in the hands of the Department of State and its diplomats on the ground, with those of the U.S. Agency for International Development (USAID) and its democracy and development specialists both in Washington and in the recipient country, and with the array of "partners"—both American NGOs and consultants—through which USAID implements its projects. Democracy specialists are highly suspicious of interference by State Department officials, believing that the diplomats' multiple concerns with security, economics, and domestic politics interfere with democracy pro-

motion. Indeed, they do. But if the high politics of the relations between the United States and semi-authoritarian regimes do not include democracy promotion, then low-end democracy promotion programs cannot possibly make a difference.

Dealing with Different Types
of Semi-Authoritarian Regimes

Each type of semi-authoritarian regime has special characteristics that
democracy promoters need to take into account. While the shallowness
of transitions is a problem characteristic of all such regimes, a deepening of the process poses quite different challenges in states in equilibrium, in decaying states, and in states where semi-authoritarianism is
accompanied by a dynamic process of change. Furthermore, even
regimes that fall within each broad category are far from identical to
each other. As a result, no single set of policies should be considered for
all semi-authoritarian regimes. I will return to the case studies to provide examples of how the problems of each country could be addressed.

Semi-Authoritarian Regimes in Equilibrium

Semi-authoritarian regimes in equilibrium pose the most difficult
problems. They are well established, stable, and have their own proven
methods of dealing with challenges to their stability. Semi-authoritarian regimes in equilibrium, in other words, are extremely good at remaining as they are. The allocation of power is closed in such regimes,
and elections have no impact. In Egypt, the extent to which people are
aware of this closure is reflected in the constantly heard assertion that
change can only come from the top, as the result of an elite decision that
might occur when power is transferred to a new generation—this, it
should be noted, is an optimistic view of what the future holds.

Democracy promoters have three options in such closed situations,
none particularly good: to do nothing and wait in the hope that more
enlightened members of the elite, probably younger ones, will decide
that democracy is a good thing; to continue with the present low-end

programs of support for civil society organizations and institutional strengthening in order to maintain the pretense that they are contributing to democracy; or to help mobilize a countervailing force capable of threatening the incumbent regime sufficiently to convince it to open up the political system.

The first, do-nothing alternative is defeatist and is also based on the unsubstantiated assumption that, with time, governments are bound to change. Given the stability attained by a state such as Egypt, this is probably wishful thinking, at least in the time span of interest to policy makers. With an economy that is growing too slowly to benefit more than the members of a small elite, Egypt is not soon going to experience the emergence of new interest groups that are anxious to control the government and influence its policies yet are also capable of mounting a real challenge. A wait-and-see attitude is an acceptance of semi-authoritarianism, not a strategy for long-term democratization. The high politics of the Middle East conflict and the imperative to combat terrorism may well lead the international community, particularly the United States, to decide not to rock Egypt's domestic political boat. This may be a justifiable decision in terms of the larger problems of the region, but commenting on that issue goes beyond the scope of the present study. But adopting a passive stance is not a decision that can be justified on the grounds that Egypt's political evolution will in any case lead that country to democracy. Egypt has had a semi-authoritarian regime for a quarter-century, and may be able to maintain it for a long time to come. The recent trend, furthermore, points to a hardening of semi-authoritarianism, rather than its relaxation, as a consequence of the rise of Islamist organizations.

The second option—continuing the present low-end programs—is counterproductive because it demeans the idea of democracy in the eyes of many Egyptians. To the opponents of the regime, the programs that fall into the U.S. democracy portfolio, such as the NGO Support Center, look like a form of assistance to President Hosni Mubarak because they are vetted by his government. European countries have been somewhat more daring than the United States in providing support to genuinely independent organizations, particularly in the human rights field, but these are small, free-floating groups that are too weak to make a difference.

The third option—working to develop a countervailing force—is the only one that holds any hope of influencing political change in Egypt. It is, however, a risky option. It requires high-level political decisions on the part of the governments embarking on that route, as well as coordination between the politics of diplomatic relations and the politics of assistance. Furthermore, the possibility of developing a countervailing force in Egypt by building up the existing organizations of civil society and parties that have democracy as their goal is remote. The government has made it clear that it does not want these organizations to grow, and they are too weak and isolated to resist. Already, many human rights organizations have disbanded, or at least have ceased functioning.

There is, on the other hand, a countervailing force the government cannot eliminate, namely the Islamist organizations. Repression has not worked against them, because they are embedded groups with broad support. Of course, these are not organizations that speak the language of democracy. Some, in fact, are far too radical to ever become amenable to being part of a democratic process. But others probably are already amenable. The position of the Muslim Brotherhood is ambiguous—it has followed the path of parliamentary politics when it has been allowed, and its leaders claim that they want to do so again. There are also smaller, moderate organizations spinning off from the Brotherhood that declare themselves in favor of parliamentary politics, but whether such groups by themselves could gather enough support to make a difference is not known.

There are a lot of unanswered questions about the potential role of Islamist groups in any democratization process in Egypt, but if the international community wants to make a difference it needs to open a dialogue with them, at least those willing to talk. Such a dialogue would have three purposes. The first would be to exert pressure on the government to likewise engage the Islamists in dialogue by putting the regime on notice that the international community would no longer accept at face value the contention that all Islamist organizations are dangerous to the stability of the country and the prospects for democracy. The second purpose would be to get to know the organizations and the differences among them, and ultimately to understand which ones could play a role in moving Egypt away from the present semi-authoritarianism, and how they could do so. The third purpose would be to stimulate change within the organizations themselves by showing that donors are not averse in principle to their participation in a more liberal political process.

Such dialogue needs to be undertaken at many different levels, not just with the leadership of the Muslim Brotherhood. There is, first of all, a vast world of Islamic organizations, which are more deeply part of the civil society than a lot of the donor-supported civil rights NGOs. Such groups need to be understood better, since they are part of the country's social capital. The question is whether they are a part of the social capital that can contribute to democracy.

There are also the professional syndicates, whose members in the early 1990s appeared to be on the verge of voting in new leadership affiliated with Islamist groups and were stopped by the government's freezing of their internal elections. Are these syndicates truly hotbeds of radical, dangerous political Islam? Or were they mostly guilty of rejecting the candidates favored by the government? Would freer elections turn the syndicates into agents of religious obscurantism, or would they contribute to the pluralism on which democracy is built? And what does it mean when the country's professional class, even one debased by two generations of government service at derisory salaries, is apparently ready to elect Islamists to head their associations? Engagement with the professional syndicates is crucial, because it is difficult to envisage how the country is ever to become democratic if its professional class is not part of the process.

Finally, there are the major political organizations, in particular the Muslim Brotherhood. Starting a process of exploration of and dialogue with such groups would require a variety of approaches and a lot of delicate balancing. International NGOs, professional associations, and party foundations would probably be in the best position to engage with their Egyptian counterparts, but they need enough backing from their respective governments to make it more difficult for the Mubarak regime to stop such contacts immediately. No matter how and by whom they are approached, many Islamist organizations will refuse, at least initially, a dialogue with the international groups, particularly those backed by the United States. It is equally likely that many Islamist groups will prove too radical to become part of the democratic process, or conversely too narrowly focused on charity and self-help projects to become part of that segment of civil society directly relevant to democracy. But there will undoubtedly be more moderate groups, which could play a constructive role if included and continue to be a negative force if excluded.

The approach I suggest is neither easy nor unproblematic. It would be resisted by the Mubarak regime, which has no interest in democracy or in taking steps that might increase the legitimacy of organizations that could command a significant following in a free election. But any significant democratization program in Egypt or any other stable semi-authoritarian state would be resisted by the government. Despite the difficulty and potential for controversy, however, democracy promotion projects in semi-authoritarian states in equilibrium will remain ineffective unless they engage groups with followings, because there can be no democracy without countervailing power.

Semi-authoritarian regimes in equilibrium are unlikely to change on their own, at least until new elements can be injected to alter this equilibrium. In theory, breaking the equilibrium should be the goal of democracy promoters in all such countries, but the opportunities might not always exist. Egypt affords opportunities because of the existence of organizations with considerable public support, which could change the balance of power and force the semi-authoritarian government to face competition.

Semi-Authoritarian Regimes of Decay

The semi-authoritarianism of decay is represented in the present study by Azerbaijan and Venezuela. Although I have grouped these two countries together, they are in some ways quite different from each other. Azerbaijan's semi-authoritarianism was a response to the chaos of a postcommunist transition for which the country was utterly unprepared; Azerbaijani president Heydar Aliyev is now trying to transform this emergency system into a regime in equilibrium similar to Egypt's, that is, into a machine capable of perpetuating itself beyond his own lifetime. Venezuela's semi-authoritarianism emerged from the decay of democracy. It is more complex and more unstable, with little likelihood of ever reaching equilibrium and consolidation. The two countries require different approaches.

Azerbaijan does not offer the international community many entry points for the introduction of change. Basic structural conditions are unfavorable. The country is mired in a no-war, no-peace situation, with no prospects for an early solution. The results include a large refugee population and a depressed economy. Aside from the problem with Nagorno-Karabagh and the Armenian minority, the country is not deeply polarized, at least not yet, but there are many fault lines running through the society, with religious and economic divisions becoming more pronounced.

Democracy has scant relevance to the majority of the population: None of the parties have been able, or have even tried, to articulate a program that gives content to the idea of democracy. Most parties are highly personal vehicles of their leaders, selling personalities rather than programs. The Azerbaijan Popular Front lost its best-known representative with the death of Abulfaz Elchibey, and the appeal of its original nationalist message has been blunted by the attainment of independence and by the festering problem of Nagorno-Karabagh, to which the party offers no solution beyond tough talk. Furthermore, the party endorses a Turkic identity for Azerbaijan that is not shared by all its citizens, particularly the non-Azeri minority and those Azeris living in the southern region of the country who have ties to northern Iran based on religion. The actions of the regime's opponents do not augur well for prodemocratic change, either. Attempts by the opposition parties to work together against Aliyev have faltered repeatedly because they are all headed by strong personalities who refuse to defer to each other in any form.

Civil society organizations also do little to spread a culture of democracy and to give the idea substantive meaning, even less than their counterparts elsewhere. Small, new, and not embedded in the society, these organizations are closely tied to the political parties—indeed, the distinction between civil society and political society has little meaning in Azerbaijan.

Democracy in Azerbaijan is a game played by the ruling party elite, the opposition parties, and the NGOs. This elite is divided, but not along lines that would favor an elite pact leading to a political transition. The dominant divisions are not between hard-liners and reformers with different ideas about what the country needs, but among personal factions that all want power. Without an organized popular force pressing for reform or otherwise manifesting its discontent, a reformist faction is unlikely to emerge, let alone prevail.

Democracy promotion in Azerbaijan is thus unlikely to bear fruit in the near future. The international community is faced with the unhappy prospect of either continuing with ineffective low-end activities, particularly support for civil society organizations, or suspending democracy promotion activities altogether. The chances that the country will move beyond semi-authoritarianism are probably equally dim, regardless of whether members of the international community continue their present activities or step back. Continuing to support civil society organizations that have no membership or that are simply part of the apparatus of a political party will not change the political equation; nor would suspending democratization programs jolt Aliyev into acting more democratically. Suspending democracy promotion programs has the advantage of sending other semi-authoritarian regimes the message that the international community will not continue indefinitely to accept at face value the fiction that these countries are democratizing. Such a move, however, would be of no more than marginal significance. High-end options are not open to the international community: There is no promising organization that could be built up into a popular movement to get rid of Aliyev. In any case, even if he were eliminated, the countervailing forces necessary for a democratic system to emerge are weak at best. Azerbaijan will probably continue to decay politically over the near term no matter what the international community does.

Venezuela presents a very different situation, rich with possibilities for change, although not necessarily for democratic change. The long-term extension of the status quo is not a likely scenario for a number of reasons. Venezuela has a tradition of democracy, and while the politics of the late democratic period disgusted a large part of the population into supporting Chávez, polls also show that a majority of Venezuelans believe that the problems of democracy could be fixed. Venezuela also has a pluralistic political system, even now. There is a tradition of political organization on a large scale in the old parties and the labor unions. Even if the old parties have faded, new ones have formed, and labor unions remain players. Furthermore, many analysts believe that the Acción Democrática party structures, although weakened, have not disappeared, particularly in the provinces. The country has a tradition of a free and critical press. Whatever Chávez's personal inclinations, this is not an easy country to coerce into quiescence. Venezuelan pluralism is real.

But pluralism can lead to conflict and further decay as well as to democracy. Socioeconomic polarization runs deep. Chávez has re-politicized the military, first with his own coup attempts and then, once he became president, by assigning it a social reform role that is inconsistent with the concept of a professional military and that has caused considerable tension among officers. In his effort to make the military an integral part of the society, Chávez has succeeded all too well, as was seen in the attempted coup of April 2002. While this new situation is counterbalanced by a tradition of military professionalism established over almost half a century, that tradition has been shaken along with the tradition of democracy.

In this fluid situation with its contradictory trends, the international community has an interest in preventing further decay and helping restore a democratic process. However, this is a country where the most common tools of democracy promotion cannot be used. The international community does not have as much leverage with Venezuela as it has with donor-dependent countries. The country receives some World Bank loans for antipoverty programs, but it is not eligible to receive assistance from most donors because it is an upper-middle-income country. Outsiders provide assistance to Venezuelan NGOs, especially human rights groups. The assistance provided by the U.S. National Endowment for Democracy has become somewhat tainted by questions about the ties of some of the grantees to the plotters of the April 2002 coup attempt, complicating matters. In any case, assistance to NGOs in Venezuela serves a useful role in supporting specific organizations but is of marginal importance in terms of the future of democracy; Venezuela is not a country where the population needs to be introduced to the concept of democracy or awakened to the possibility of political participation. Nor do Venezuelans need training in order to organize their parliament or run an independent press. They have done all this for a long time.

The threat to democracy in Venezuela does not come from the weaknesses democracy promoters normally address, but from the perception of a majority of the population that democracy is irrelevant to their problems. Chávez's decreasing popularity suggests that he, too, is coming to be perceived as incapable of providing answers. He has spent too much time on political reform while failing to deliver on economic promises. This provides an opening for democratic parties to show that they have answers.

To the extent that the international community can help convince Venezuelans that a democratic system can provide answers to the country's problems, it is not through the organizations that specialize in democracy assistance, but through those that deal with economic problems. Venezuela needs help in devising policies that address the issue of poverty in meaningful ways. More important, the crafting of such policies must result from the work of domestic democratic institutions, not from discussions among technocrats, because that will not restore confidence in the relevance of democracy. The discussion needs to be broader and more public, involving all political parties, the organizations of civil society, and the legislature. The international community has the capacity to encourage such a discussion, particularly by providing support for political parties and organizations that seek to address issues of economic policy. The real problem here is one of political will: whether the international community is willing to promote a dialogue that can help restore faith in the relevance of democracy but may have policy consequences the international community does not like. In order to help overcome semi-authoritarianism and prevent further political decay in Venezuela, the international community has to decide whether it values democratic politics more than its own policy prescriptions.

Semi-Authoritarian Regimes of Dynamic Change

Semi-authoritarian regimes in countries where change is being driven by internal factors are the most promising ones. It is important for democracy promoters, however, to understand the real nature of the change that is taking place and to take it into account in their programs. Croatia and Senegal, the examples chosen in the present study to illustrate the semi-authoritarianism of dynamic change, are not static states. Both recently experienced an important turnover of political leadership. In Croatia, the ultranationalist HDZ was defeated in February 2000, and the forty-year grip on power of the Parti Socialiste was finally broken by the victory of Abdoullaye Wade in Senegal just a month later. These turnovers do not guarantee that semi-authoritarianism is a problem of the past, because in both countries the change was extremely shallow, driven by highly contingent political events. It was the death of Tudjman that made it possible for the opposition parties to defeat the HDZ, while in Senegal the *alternance* was made possible above all by Moustapha Niasse's decisions first to break with President Abdou Diouf and then to back Wade in the second round of the presidential election. The challenge for outsiders in both cases is thus to help the transitions deepen and to perpetuate the change. Croatia offers considerably more opportunity to do so than Senegal. Croatia, however, is also the country where donors can do the greatest amount of damage if they continue asking too much, and in particular if they seek to impose policies that cannot be adopted democratically because the domestic political process would lead to other solutions.

A deepening of the political transition leading to a stable democracy is not impossible in Croatia, even in the short-to-medium term. The idea of democracy has more meaning for more people there than in some of the other countries discussed in the present study. Croatia has a more urban and better-educated population, for whom even abstract democratic principles mean something in practice—the ideas of freedom of speech and freedom of assembly resonate better in the streets of Rijeka than in the villages of the Sahel. Furthermore, the allure of membership in the European Union, for which a democratic political system is a precondition, gives a concrete meaning to democracy even for people who are not attracted to its principles. Political parties are becoming better organized, although factionalism remains a problem. Organizations of civil society have more capacity to organize and implement programs, although most are still free floating and donor dependent, while some of the better-embedded ones, such as war veterans' groups, are not democratic. The political scene is nevertheless active and pluralistic. Croatia is also changing economically. It is true that the economy is still stagnant and that the unemployment rate is high, and may well rise further as a result of cuts in the civil service. But reform and privatization are beginning to change the character of the economy, reducing the role of the state and slowly creating an entrepreneurial class.

But a revival of semi-authoritarianism leading to decay is not out of the question. The government has not been able to deliver much more than an improved political climate, and it needs to provide something more tangible or risk a backlash. Ethnic tensions remain high, particularly in the regions that were most affected by war and to which the Serb refugees are returning. The Croatian refugees from Bosnia, many of whom cannot return there, or are afraid to, add another element of uncertainty. The unexpectedly strong performance of the HDZ in the most recent local elections shows that much can still go wrong in Croatia. If the economy continues to stagnate or deteriorates further, ethnic tensions may increase again, and Croats might again be open to the appeal of nationalist organizations offering a different kind of salvation.

Intervenors can help deepen the transition that is underway and increase the prospects for a democratic outcome not by stepping up their democracy promotion efforts but by scaling down their demands on the country, interfering less with the domestic political process and allowing the many political forces in the country to work out solutions to major problems through their own institutions. The international community must accept that democracy will only take hold if the government and the parliament pick their own way among the multitude of problems and find solutions that are acceptable to the major political parties and interest groups. A democratic government needs to respond—and even more to be seen as responding—to the expectations of its citizens, not to the expectations of the international community. In a fragile transitional situation such as that prevailing in Croatia, it is particularly important for the government to be responsive: In a well-established democracy, a government that fails to respond to the expectations of the majority is voted out of office; in a transitional situation, it is democracy itself that could be rejected.

The international community can best help to deepen Croatia's transition by examining the combined impact of its demands and conditionalities on democracy there. There is an urgent need for better coordination among all the bilateral and multilateral agencies that are involved in promoting reform in Croatia. In particular, these agencies need to evaluate the extent to which their respective demands and pressures are compatible with each other and with the democracy to which all claim to be committed. Democracy promoters also need to reassess how they work with Croatia's institutions now that they have become more open and pluralistic, in order to make sure that they do not undermine these institutions by pursuing their own visions of how Croatia should reform. While such discussion is important in all countries, it is particularly so in a country such as Croatia, where these institutions are pluralistic and are still acquiring capacity.

Low-end assistance to civil society, political parties, and government institutions may be more useful in Croatia in the next few years than it has been in the past, particularly if the transition deepens further. Democracy assistance in Croatia in the past has been based on a supply-side approach—hoping to increase the demand for democracy by supplying organizations with funding and training. A deepening of the transition, however, could increase the demand for technical assistance by organizations and institutions that are already playing an active role in a democratic process but feel the need to acquire more know-how. Still-inexperienced political parties competing in open elections would probably find such training useful. Members of parliament actively engaged in drafting legislation or amending bills introduced by the executive could do their jobs more easily with the help of trained staff and with access to information retrieval systems. But such programs, however useful, have only secondary importance to providing decision making space for domestic political institutions.

The case of Senegal is less encouraging. The country is still stagnant economically and socially, and even the impulse toward political change seems to have exhausted itself with the *alternance*. With political parties and civil society still weak, and Wade very much a part of the old political elite, Senegal can easily slip back into the benign semi-authoritarianism that characterized it before the *alternance*. Indeed, there are indications that this is already happening.

Most low-end activities are probably not going to help much in Senegal. A little more funding for civil society organizations or a few more civic education projects will not create real countervailing forces or well-defined interest groups. On the other hand, high-end activities hardly appear justified in a country where the government is not particularly repressive and the human rights record is reasonably good. Donors should accept that, for the time being, democracy in Senegal will mean the *alternance*, and they should concentrate on keeping the possibility of further alternations of power open. Election assistance is thus particularly important for Senegal.

Conclusions

Semi-authoritarian regimes are today's major challenge to democracy, and fostering further change in countries with such regimes is the main challenge for the United States and other countries that make the promotion of democracy an important part of their foreign policy. In order to meet this challenge, these countries need to address more directly the structural problems that facilitate and encourage semi-authoritarianism. The measures I have suggested, both in general and for the five case study countries, provide indications of how democracy promoters could address some *structural* problems. In doing so, these measures depart considerably from the typical democracy promotion activities of the last decade. In some cases, I have suggested riskier and more intrusive policies; in others, I have argued that doing less would be a greater contribution to democracy.

The more typical democracy promotion programs are useful in some cases, but they should not be used indiscriminately. In particular, support for small NGOs should not be considered an all-purpose activity, helpful in all circumstances. Supporting nonembedded elites does not broaden political space in countries with semi-authoritarian regimes, although even small organizations that can provide specialized knowledge may be useful in countries whose political environment is already more open. Elections assistance is useless at best or even sends the wrong messages in semi-authoritarian regimes in equilibrium or those experiencing decay, where the problem is not the technical quality of elections but the repressive measures taken over a period of years or the absence of a credible challenge. But in a country such as Senegal, where democracy will probably only mean *alternance* for the foreseeable future, election assistance is an important activity. For this, and for any other type of program, it is the specifics of the situation that determine whether an outside initiative is helpful, pointless, or counterproductive. Conditions do matter, and they matter a great deal.

The rise of semi-authoritarianism is a disappointment. This is not what people committed to democracy in their own countries and outsiders seeking to assist democratic transitions hoped for in the early 1990s. Analysis of the outcome of the last decade shows that the number of new democratic regimes is much smaller than the number of new semi-authoritarian ones. It would serve no purpose to try to make this reality more palatable by pretending that semi-authoritarian regimes are just imperfect democratic ones. On the contrary, they are of an altogether different type that requires different approaches from democracy promoters. Even with different, high-end approaches, outsiders will not always be able to make a substantial difference. A transition to democracy is not inevitable in all semi-authoritarian states, and in most it is certainly not imminent.

The disappointment, however, should not overshadow the fact that the rise of these semi-authoritarian regimes in itself demonstrates the extent of the political transformation of the world since the end of the Cold War, one that has transformed the language of politics in most countries as well as the structure of their formal political systems. In many cases, furthermore, semi-authoritarian regimes are less repressive and allow their citizens somewhat more political space than their predecessors did. This is not enough, but it is a positive change nonetheless.

Notes

Notes to the Introduction

1. Rather than provide lengthy references here, I have included a short bibliography on the gray zone at the end of the book.
2. On democratic consolidation, see Juan J. Linz and Alfred Stepan, *Problems of Democratic Transitions and Consolidation* (Baltimore: Johns Hopkins University Press, 1996); and Larry Diamond, Marc Plattner, Yun-Han Chu, and Hung-Mao Tien, eds., *Consolidating the Third Wave Democracies* (Baltimore and London: Johns Hopkins University Press, 1997).
3. Todd Eisenstadt, ed., "The Neglected Democrats: Protracted Transitions from Authoritarianism," special issue of *Democratization*, vol. 7, no. 3 (Autumn 2000). Among the examples of protracted transitions discussed in the articles that make up this special issue are Mexico, Taiwan, South Korea, Indonesia (just embarking on the process), and, in Africa, the countries of South Africa, Ghana, Kenya, Tanzania, Uganda, and Zambia. Classifying some of these countries— where the prognosis is uncertain at best—as cases of protracted transition means prejudging an uncertain outcome.
4. David Collier and Steven Levitsky, "Democracy with Adjectives: Conceptual Innovation in Comparative Research," *World Politics*, vol. 49, no. 3 (April 1997), pp. 430-51; Steven Levitsky and Lucan A. Way, "The Rise of Competitive Authoritarianism," *Journal of Democracy*, vol. 13, no. 2 (April 2002), pp. 51-65; Nicolas van de Walle, "Africa's Range of Regimes," ibid., pp. 66-80. See also the gray zone bibliography.
5. Larry Diamond, "Thinking about Hybrid Regimes," *Journal of Democracy*, vol. 13, no. 2 (April 2002), pp. 21-35.
6. Francis Fukuyama, "The End of History," *National Interest*, vol. 16, no. 3 (Summer 1989), pp. 1-18.
7. Samuel P. Huntington, *The Third Wave: Democratization in the Late Twentieth Century* (Norman, Okla.: University of Oklahoma Press, 1991).
8. Larry Diamond, "Is the Third Wave Over?" *Journal of Democracy*, vol. 7, no. 3 (July 1996), pp. 20-37; Larry Diamond, "Is Pakistan the (Reverse) Wave of the Future?" *Journal of Democracy*, vol. 11, no. 3 (July 2000), pp. 91-106.

9. A similar argument has been advanced by Joel S. Hellman in relation to partial free-market transitions in postcommunist countries. He shows that such partial transitions are deliberate and that winners often seek to stall the reform in a "partial reform equilibrium" because it is to their advantage to do so. See Joel S. Hellman, "Winners Take All: The Politics of Partial Reform in Postcommunist Transitions," *World Politics*, vol. 50, no. 2 (January 1998), pp. 203-34.

10. Robert Putnam, *Making Democracy Work: Civic Traditions in Modern Italy* (Princeton, N.J.: Princeton University Press, 1993); Barrington Moore, Jr., *Social Origins of Dictatorship and Democracy: Lord and Peasant in the Making of the Modern World* (Boston: Beacon Press, 1966).

11. Guillermo O'Donnell and Philippe C. Schmitter, *Transitions from Authoritarian Rule: Tentative Conclusions about Uncertain Democracies* (Baltimore: Johns Hopkins University Press, 1986).

12. Robert Putnam, *Making Democracy Work*; and "Bowling Alone: America's Declining Social Capital," *Journal of Democracy*, vol. 6, no. 1 (January 1995), pp. 65-78.

13. A thorough analysis of the democratic transition model and the policies donors enact to promote democracy is found in Thomas Carothers, *Aiding Democracy Abroad: The Learning Curve* (Washington, D.C.: Carnegie Endowment for International Peace, 1999).

14. Marina Ottaway and Thomas Carothers, eds., *Funding Virtue: Civil Society Aid and Democracy Promotion* (Washington, D.C.: Carnegie Endowment for International Peace, 2000).

15. Samuel P. Huntington, *Political Order in Changing Societies* (New Haven, Conn.: Yale University Press, 1968), pp. 8-11 and 146-47.

16. Huntington's observation that regimes need to maintain the balance between the degree of institutionalization and the level of participation applies quite well to semi-authoritarian regimes (ibid., pp. 78-92).

17. Daniel Kaufmann and Paul Siegelbaum, "Privatization and Corruption in Transition Economies," *Journal of International Affairs*, vol. 5, no. 2 (Winter 1997), pp. 419-58; Michelle Celarier, "Privatization: A Case Study in Corruption," *Journal of International Affairs*, vol. 50, no. 2 (Winter 1997), pp. 531-43.

18. Sheri Berman, "Civil Society and the Collapse of the Weimar Republic," *World Politics*, vol. 49, no. 3 (April 1997), pp. 401-29.

19. "Silencing Citizens in Egypt," *New York Times*, June 7, 1999, p. A22.

20. Marina Ottaway, "Social Movements, Professionalization of Reform, and Democracy in Africa," in *Funding Virtue*, pp. 77-104.

Notes to Chapter One

1. A brief overview of this period is provided in "Great Britain and Egypt, 1914-1951," information paper no. 19 (London: Royal Institute for International Affairs), 1952. See also Marius Deeb, *Party Politics in Egypt: The Wafd and Its Rivals 1919-1939* (London: Ithaca Press, 1979).

2. For an interesting analysis of Egyptian society during this period of democratic experimentation, see Anouar Abel-Malek, *Egypt: Military Society* (New York: Vintage Books, 1968), part 1.

3. See Richard P. Mitchell, *The Society of the Muslim Brothers* (New York: Oxford University Press, 1993); and Gilles Keppel, *Muslim Extremism in Egypt: The Prophet and Pharaoh* (Berkeley, Calif.: University of California Press, 1993).
4. On this period, see John Waterbury, *The Egypt of Nasser and Sadat: The Political Economy of Two Regimes* (Princeton, N.J.: Princeton University Press, 1983); Richard Hrair Demejian, *Egypt under Nasser: A Study in Political Dynamics* (Albany, N.Y.: State University of New York Press, 1971); and P.J. Vatikiotis, *The History of Egypt from Muhammad Ali to Sadat* (Baltimore: Johns Hopkins University Press, 1980).
5. On the Sadat period, see Waterbury, *The Egypt of Nasser and Sadat*; Raymond A. Hinnebusch, Jr., *Egyptian Politics under Sadat: The Post-Populist Development of an Authoritarian-Modernizing State* (Boulder, Colo.: Lynne Rienner, 1988); Anthony McDermott, *Egypt from Nasser to Mubarak: A Flawed Revolution* (London: Croom Helm, 1988); and David Hirst and Irene Beeson, *Sadat* (London: Faber and Faber, 1981).
6. See Raymond William Baker, "Afraid for Islam: Egypt's Muslim Centrists between Pharaohs and Fundamentalists," *Daedalus*, vol. 120, no. 3 (Summer 1991), pp. 41–67.
7. See Gilles Keppel, *Jihad: The Trail of Political Islam* (Cambridge, Mass.: The Belknap Press of Harvard University Press, 2002), especially ch. 4; for a sociological analysis of radical Islamist groups, see Saad Eddine Ibrahim, "Anatomy of Egypt's Militant Groups," *International Journal of Middle East Studies*, vol. 12, no. 4 (December 1980), pp. 423–53.
8. See Muhammed Hasanein Haikal, *The Road to Ramadan* (New York: Reader's Digest Press, 1975).
9. Haikal published his view of Sadat's last months in *Autumn of Fury: The Assassination of Sadat* (New York: Random House, 1983).
10. On the Mubarak period, see Robert Springborg, *Mubarak's Egypt: Fragmentation of the Political Order* (Boulder, Colo.: Westview Press, 1989).
11. Larry Goodson and Soha Radwan, "Democratization in Egypt in the 1990s: Stagnant, or Merely Stalled?" *Arab Studies Quarterly*, vol. 19, no. 1 (Winter 1997), pp. 1–21.
12. Jon Alterman, "Egypt: Stable, but for How Long?" *Washington Quarterly*, vol. 23, no. 4 (Autumn 2000), pp. 107–18.
13. Saad Eddine Ibrahim, "Reform and Frustration in Egypt," *Journal of Democracy*, vol. 7, no. 4 (October 1996), pp. 125–35.
14. For more on the popularity of Islamism in Egypt, see Fouad Ajami, "The Sorrows of Egypt," *Foreign Affairs*, vol. 74, no. 5 (September/October 1995), pp. 72–88; Mary Anne Weaver, *A Portrait of Egypt: A Journey through the World of Militant Islam* (New York: Farrar, Straus and Giroux, 1998); and M. H. Hafez, "Explaining the Origins of Islamic Resurgence: Islamic Revivalism in Egypt and Indonesia," *Journal of Social, Political, and Economic Studies*, vol. 22, no. 3 (Fall 1997), pp. 295–324.
15. See Robert Springborg, "Egypt: Repression's Toll," *Current History*, vol. 97, no. 615 (January 1998), pp. 32–37; Max Rodenbeck, "Is Islamism Losing Its Thunder?" *Washington Quarterly*, vol. 21, no. 2 (Spring 1998), pp. 177–93; and Steven Barraclough, "Al-Azhar: Between the Government and the Islamists," *Middle East Journal*, vol. 52, no. 2 (Spring 1998), pp. 236–49.

16. See Eberhard Kienle, "More Than a Response to Islamism: The Political Deliberalization of Egypt in the 1990s," *Middle East Journal*, vol. 52, no. 2 (Spring 1998), pp. 219–35; and May Kassem, *In the Guise of Democracy: Governance in Contemporary Egypt* (Reading, England: Ithaca Press, 1999).

Notes to Chapter Two

1. On the concept of the petro-state see Terry Lynn Karl, *The Paradox of Plenty: Oil Booms and Petro-States* (Berkeley, Calif.: University of California Press, 1997).
2. Background information on this period is found in Audrey L. Altstadt, *The Azerbaijani Turks: Power and Identity under Russian Rule* (Stanford, Calif.: Hoover Institution Press, 1992).
3. Stephan Astourian, "In Search of Their Forefathers: National Identity and the Historiography and Politics of Armenian and Azerbaijani Ethogeneses," in Donald V. Schwartz and Razmik Panossian, eds., *Nationalism and History: The Politics of Nation-Building in Post-Soviet Armenia, Azerbaijan and Georgia* (Toronto: University of Toronto Centre for Russian and European Studies, 1994), pp. 41–94.
4. For details, see David Levinson, *Ethnic Groups Worldwide: A Ready Reference Handbook* (Westport, Conn.: Oryx Press, 1998), pp. 201–03.
5. Raoul Motika, "Islam in Post-Soviet Azerbaijan," *Archives de Sciences Sociales des Religions*, vol. 115 (July–September 2001), pp. 111–24; and Lawrence E. Adams, "The Reemergence of Islam in the Transcaucasus," *Religion, State and Society*, vol. 24, no. 2/3 (September 1996), pp. 221–31.
6. Edmund Herzig, *Iran and the Former Soviet South* (London: The Royal Institute of International Affairs, 1995); and Shireen Hunter, "Azerbaijan: Search for Identity and New Partners," in Ian Bremmer and Ray Taras, eds., *Nation and Politics in the Soviet Successor States* (Cambridge, England: Cambridge University Press, 1993), pp. 225–60.
7. On this period see Audrey L. Altstadt, *The Azerbaijani Turks*, especially ch. 12; Elisabeth Fuller, *Azerbaijan at the Crossroads* (London: Royal Institute of International Affairs and Radio Free Europe/Radio Liberty Research Institute, 1994); Audrey L. Alstadt, "Azerbaijan's Struggle toward Democracy," in Karen Dawisha and Bruce Parrott, eds., *Conflict, Cleavage and Change in Central Asia and the Caucasus* (Cambridge, England: Cambridge University Press, 1997), pp. 110–55; and Edmund Herzig, *The New Caucasus: Armenia, Azerbaijan and Georgia* (London: Royal Institute for International Affairs, 1999). The Caucasus Report of Radio Free Europe/Radio Liberty, available online at <www.rferl.org/caucasus-report>, also provides excellent coverage of this period.
8. Fuller, *Azerbaijan at the Crossroads*, pp. 5–12.
9. See Audrey L. Alstadt, "Azerbaijan's Struggle toward Democracy," p. 125.
10. Organization for Security and Cooperation in Europe and United Nations, "Report of the OSCE/UN Joint Electoral Mission in Azerbaijan on Azerbaijan's 12 November 1995 Parliamentary Election and Constitutional Referendum," January 1996. Available at <http://www.osce.org/odihr/documents/reports/election_reports/az/azer1-1.pdf>.

11. National Democratic Institute for International Affairs, "Statement of the National Democratic Institute for International Affairs (NDI) International Observers Election Delegation to Azerbaijan's October 1998 Presidential Election," September 11, 1998.

12. Organization for Security and Cooperation in Europe, Office for Democratic Institutions and Human Rights, "Presidential Election in the Republic of Azerbaijan, 11 October 1998." Available at <http://www.osce.org/odihr/documents/reports/election_reports/az/azer2-2.pdf>.

13. National Democratic Institute for International Affairs, "Statement of the National Democratic Institute (NDI) International Observer Delegation to Azerbaijan's November 5, 2000 Parliamentary Elections." Baku, November 7, 2000. On the 2000 elections, see also Svante E. Cornell, "Democratization Falters in Azerbaijan," *Journal of Democracy*, vol. 12, no. 2 (April 2001), pp. 118–31.

14. On the period of consolidation, see Mahran Kamrava, "State Building in Azerbaijan," *Middle East Journal*, vol. 55, no. 2 (Spring 2002), pp. 216–36.

15. Terry Lynn Karl, "The Perils of the Petro-State: Reflections on the Paradox of Plenty," *Journal of International Affairs*, vol. 53, no. 1 (Fall 1999), p. 34.

16. "Azerbaijan Country Brief, August 1999," and "Azerbaijan Country Brief, September 2001" (Washington, D.C.: World Bank); and "Azerbaijan: Enhanced Structural Adjustment Facility Policy Framework Paper, 1999–2001," January 8, 1999 (Washington, DC.: International Monetary Fund).

17. "Azerbaijan: Enhanced Structural Adjustment Facility, Policy Framework Paper, 1999–2001," January 8, 1999 (Washington, DC.: International Monetary Fund).

18. "Poverty Reduction Strategy Paper," May 2001 (Baku: Authorities of Azerbaijan).

19. Transparency International, *Global Corruption Perceptions Index 2001* (Berlin, 2001). On a 0–10 scale, Azerbaijan received a score of just 2. One should note that the index measures how countries are perceived; it is not intended to provide an objective measurement of corruption.

20. Lawrence E. Adams, "The Reemergence of Islam in the Transcaucasus," *Religion, State and Society*, vol. 24, no. 2/3 (September 1996), pp. 221–31.

Notes to Chapter Three

1. Michael Shifter, "Dictator or Democrat," *International Economy*, vol. 14, no. 2 (March/April 2000), p. 47.

2. See Michael Derham, "Undemocratic Democracy: Venezuela and the Distorting of History," *Bulletin of Latin American Research*, vol. 21, no. 2 (April 2002), pp. 270–89, for a critical discussion of Venezuelan democracy.

3. For a discussion of consolidation, see Scott Mainwaring, Guillermo O'Donnell and J. Samuel Valenzuela, eds., *Issues in Democratic Consolidation* (Notre Dame, Ind.: University of Notre Dame Press, 1992); and Andreas Schedler, "What Is Democratic Consolidation?" *Journal of Democracy*, vol. 9, no. 2 (April 1998), pp. 91–107.

4. Juan J. Linz and Alfred Stepan, *Problems of Democratic Transition and Consolidation: Southern Europe, South America, and Post-Communist Europe* (Baltimore: Johns Hopkins University Press, 1999), esp. pp. 3–15.

5. Enrique A. Baloyra, "Public Opinion and Support for the Régime: 1973–83," in John Martz and David Meyers, eds., *Venezuela: The Democratic Experience* (New York: Praeger Special Studies, 1986), pp. 54–71.

6. Andrew Templeton, "The Evolution of Popular Opinion," in Louis Goodman, Johanna Mendelson Forman, Moisés Naím, Joseph Tulchin, and Gary Bland, eds., *Lessons of the Venezuelan Experience* (Baltimore: Johns Hopkins University Press, 1995), pp. 79–114. Other surveys give somewhat different results. A 1993 survey, for example, found that only 48.4 percent of the voters judged democracy to be either good or very good, while 35.8 percent found it bad and 15.7 percent very bad. However, 71 percent of the same sample thought that democracy could be fixed. See Valia Pereira Almao, "Venezuelan Loyalty toward Democracy in the Critical 1990s," in Damarys Canache and Michael R. Kulischek, eds., *Reinventing Legitimacy: Democracy and Political Change in Venezuela* (Westport, Conn.: Greenwood Press, 1998), pp. 79–114.

7. Baloyra, "Public Opinion and Support for the Régime."

8. The term was first used by Terry Lynn Karl; see "Petroleum and Political Pacts: The Transition to Democracy in Venezuela," in Guillermo O'Donnell, Philippe Schmitter, and Laurence Whitehead, eds., *Transitions from Authoritarian Rule: Latin America* (Baltimore: Johns Hopkins University Press, 1986), pp. 196–219.

9. See Judith Ewell, *Venezuela: A Century of Change* (Stanford, Calif.: Stanford University Press, 1984), pp. 118–20.

10. For more on the Pacto de Punto Fijo, see Terry Lynn Karl, "Mexico, Venezuela, and the Contadora Initiative," in Morris J. Blachman, William M. LeoGrande, and Kenneth E. Sharpe, eds., *Confronting Revolution: Security through Diplomacy in Central America* (New York: Pantheon, 1986). For more on the "partyarchy" in Venezuela, see Michael Coppedge, *Strong Parties and Lame Ducks: Presidential Partyarchy and Factionalism in Venezuela* (Palo Alto, Calif.: Stanford University Press, 1993).

11. Terry Lynn Karl, *The Paradox of Plenty: Oil Booms and Petro-States* (Berkeley, Calif.: University of California Press, 1997).

12. Moisés Naím, "The Real Story behind Venezuela's Woes," *Journal of Democracy*, vol. 12, no. 2 (April 2001), p. 21.

13. Karl, The Paradox of Plenty, p. 101–11.

14. Moisés Naím, *Paper Tigers and Minotaurs: The Politics of Venezuela's Economic Reform* (Washington, D.C.: Carnegie Endowment for International Peace, 1993), p. 19.

15. Ibid., p. 24.

16. Ibid., p. 20, figure 1.

17. Naím, *Paper Tigers*, p. 24.

18. Naím, *Paper Tigers*, p. 24.

19. Naím, "The Real Story behind Venezuela's Woes," p. 21.

20. Javier Corrales, "Why Citizen-Detached Parties Imperil Economic Governance: Venezuela in the 1980s, 1990s, and Beyond," *David Rockefeller Center for Latin American Studies News*, Harvard University, vol. 2, no. 3 (Fall 1999), pp. 26–29.

21. Corrales, p. 27.

22. See Karl, The Paradox of Plenty, p. 98–101, and "Petroleum and Political Pacts: The Transition to Democracy in Venezuela," *Latin American Research Review*, vol. 22, no. 1 (1987), pp. 63–94.

23. David J. Myers, "The Venezuelan Party System: Regime Maintenance under Stress," in John D. Martz and David J. Myers, eds., *Venezuela: The Democratic Experience* (New York: Praeger, 1986), pp. 109–147.
24. Corrales, "Why Citizen-Detached Parties Imperil Economic Governance: Venezuela in the 1980s, 1990s, and Beyond," *David Rockefeller Center for Latin American Studies News*, Harvard University, vol. 2, no. 3 (Fall 1999), pp. 26–29.
25. Karl, "Petroleum and Political Pacts," p. 66.
26. Julia Buxton, "Venezuela: Degenerative Democracy," *Democratization*, vol. 6, no. 1 (Spring 1999), p. 253.
27. Myers and Martz, "Venezuelan Democracy: Performance and Prospects," in Martz and Meyers, *Venezuela*, p. 462.
28. See Daniel H. Levine, "The Decline and Fall of Democracy in Venezuela: Ten Theses," *Bulletin of Latin American Research*, vol. 21, no. 2 (April 2002), pp. 248–69.
29. For more on Venezuela's economic situation and Pérez's decision to implement reforms, see Naím, *Paper Tigers and Minotaurs*, pp. 31–57.
30. Ibid., pp. 62–69.
31. Pérez was convicted in 1996, not for enriching himself at the public expense but for using government funds to send National Guard troops to provide personal security for Nicaraguan opposition leader Violeta Chamorro during her presidential campaign—an improbable and incongruous conviction given the political situation in Venezuela.
32. On La Causa Radical, see Margarita Lopez Maya, "New Avenues for Popular Representation in Venezuela: La Causa-R and the Movimiento Bolivariano 200," in Canache and Kulischek, *Reinventing Legitimacy*, pp. 83–96.
33. For a profile of Chávez from an American point of view, see Jon Lee Anderson, "The Revolutionary," *New Yorker*, September 10, 2001, pp. 60–79. For Venezuelan views, see the review essay of eight books on Chávez: Maxwell A. Cameron and Flavie Major, "Venezuela's Hugo Chávez: Savior or Threat to Democracy?" *Latin American Research Review*, vol. 36, no. 3 (2001), pp. 255–65.
34. For overall analyses of the Chávez period, see Daniel H. Levine and Brian F. Crisp, "Venezuela: The Character, Crisis and Possible Future of Democracy," *World Affairs*, vol. 161, no. 3 (Winter 1999), pp. 123–65; Steve Ellner, "The Radical Potential of Chavismo in Venezuela," *Latin American Perspectives*, vol. 28, no. 5 (September 2001), pp. 5–32; and Leonard Vivas, "Why Chavez in Venezuela?" *Fletcher Forum on World Affairs*, vol. 25, no. 1 (Winter 2001), pp. 109–114.
35. Jennifer L. McCoy, "Chávez and the End of 'Partyarchy' in Venezuela," *Journal of Democracy*, vol. 10, no. 3 (July 1999), pp. 64–77.
36. The old constitution did not give the president excessive power. The formal powers of the president, on the contrary, have been defined as "sparse"; see Brian Crisp, "Presidential Behavior in a System with Strong Parties: Venezuela, 1958–1995," in Scott Mainwaring and Matthew Soberg Shugart, *Presidentialism and Democracy in Latin America* (Cambridge, England: Cambridge University Press, 1997), pp. 160–98. Rather, the power of the president was based on his capacity to respond to interest-group pressures in the way in which a Congress bound by tight party discipline could not, and to appoint members of special commissions charged with studying reform in various sectors or even draft legislation. This meant that the president had great capacity to set the agenda for the Congress. Finally, the president's power was increased by the large percentage

of government spending carried out through off-budget special agencies, of which hundreds existed. By 1980, off-budget expenditures had reached 70 percent of the total, reducing the power of the Congress, which could only control on-budget expenditures; see McCoy, "Chávez and the End of Partyarchy." For a general analysis of the constitution, see Janet Kelly, "Thoughts on the Constitution: Realignment of Ideas about the Economy and Changes in the Political System in Venezuela," paper presented at the 2000 meeting of the Latin American Studies Association in Miami (March 16–18, 2000).

37. On the elections, see Jose E. Molina, "The Presidential and Parliamentary Elections of the Bolivarian Revolution in Venezuela: Change and Continuity (1998–2000)," *Bulletin of Latin American Research*, vol. 21, no. 2 (April 2002), pp. 219–47.

38. José de Cordoba, "For Venezuela's President, a Long Leash—Assembly Grants Chávez Broad Powers, Prompting Fears of a Dictatorship," *Wall Street Journal*, November 8, 2000, p. A22.

39. On protest in the 1990s and more recently, see Margarita Lopez-Maya, "Venezuela after the Caracazo: Forms of Protest in a Deinstitutionalized Context," *Bulletin of Latin American Research*, vol. 21, no. 2 (April 2002), pp. 199–218.

40. "IRI President Folsom Praises Venezuelan Civil Society's Defense of Democracy," Statement by George A. Folsom, President of the International Republican Institute, April 12, 2002.

41. Christopher Marquis, "U.S. Bankrolling Is under Scrutiny for Ties to Chávez Ouster," *New York Times*, April 25, 2002, p. A6, col. 1.

Notes to Chapter Four

1. Christian Coulon, "Senegal: The Development and Fragility of Semi-Democracy," in Larry Diamond, Seymour Martin Lipset, and Juan Linz, eds., *Democracy in Developing Countries*, Volume 2: Africa (Boulder, Colo.: Lynne Rienner, 1988), pp. 141–78.

2. The party was called the Union Progressiste Sénégalaise (Senegalese Progressive Union, UPS) until 1976, when President Léopold Sédar Senghor changed its name.

3. Babacar Kanté, "Senegal's Empty Elections," *Journal of Democracy*, vol. 5, no. 1 (January 1994), pp. 96–108.

4. For a brief biography, see the entry on Senghor in Harvey Glickman, ed., *Political Leaders of Africa South of the Sahara: A Biographical Dictionary* (Westport, Conn.: Greenwood Press, 1992), pp. 259–65.

5. On the Senghor period, see Francois Zuccarelli, *La Vie Politique Sénégalaise* (Paris: CHEAM, 1987); Irving L. Markowitz, *Léopold Sédar Senghor and the Politics of Negritude* (New York: Atheneum, 1969); Donal Cruise O'Brien, "Senegal," in John Dunn, ed., *West African States: Failure and Promise. A Study in Comparative Politics* (Cambridge, England: Cambridge University Press, 1978), pp. 847–53; and Robert Fatton, *The Making of a Liberal Democracy: Senegal's Passive Revolution, 1975–1985* (Boulder, Colo.: Lynne Rienner, 1987).

6. On the Diouf presidency, see Momar Coumba Diop and Mamadou Diouf, *Le Sénégal sous Abdou Diouf: État et Société* (Paris: Editions Karthala, 1990); and

Abdou Latif Coulibaly, *Le Sénégal à l'Épreuve de la Démocratie* (Paris: L'Harmattan, 1999).

7. Joan Nelson, *Access to Power: Politics and the Poor in Developing Nations* (Princeton, N.J.: Princeton University Press, 1979).

8. See Donal Cruise O' Brien, *The Mourides of Senegal: The Political and Economic Organization of an Islamic Brotherhood* (Oxford, England: Clarendon Press, 1971); Christian Coulon, *Le Marabout et le Prince: Islam et Pouvoir au Sénégal* (Paris: A. Pedone, 1981); Leonardo A. Villalòn, *Islamic Society and State Power in Senegal: Disciples and Citizens in Fatick* (Cambridge, England: Cambridge University Press, 1995); and Robert Fatton, "Clientelism and Patronage in Senegal," *African Studies Review*, vol. 29, no. 4 (December 1986), pp. 61–78.

9. On the more recent period, see Leonardo A. Villalòn and Ousmane Kane, "Senegal: The Crisis of Democracy and the Emergence of an Islamic Opposition," in Leonardo A. Villalòn and Phillip A. Huxtable, eds., *The African State at a Critical Juncture: Between Disintegration and Reconfiguration* (Boulder, Colo.: Lynne Rienner, 1998), pp. 143–66; and Linda J. Beck, "Reining In the Marabouts? Democratization and Local Governance in Senegal," *African Affairs*, vol. 100, no. 401 (October 2001), pp. 601–21.

10. For an analysis of the elections, see Franziska Oppmann, "The Myth of Democracy?" *Africa Report*, vol. 33, no. 3 (May–June 1988), pp. 50–52.

11. National Democratic Institute for International Affairs, *An Assessment of the Senegalese Electoral Code*, March 1991.

12. On the 1993 elections, see Kanté, "Senegal's Empty Elections"; Peter Da Costa, "Diouf's Tarnished Victory," *Africa Report*, vol. 38, no. 3 (May–June 1993), pp. 49–51; and Peter Da Costa, "All the President's Men," *Africa Report*, vol. 38, no. 5 (September–October 1993), pp. 64–66.

13. Personal communications between the author and members of these groups, Dakar, May 14–22, 2001.

14. Maomar Coumba Diop and Moussa Paye, "The Army and Political Power in Senegal," in Eboe Hutchful and Abdoulaye Bathily, eds., *The Military and Militarism in Africa* (Dakar, Senegal: CODESRIA, 1998), pp. 315–53.

15. For a sympathetic view of Senegalese civil society and its role in democratization, see Penda Mbow, "La Société Civile Sénégalaise: Identification et Rôle dans le Processus Démocratique," *Revue Sénégalaise de Sociologie*, nos. 2–3 (January 1998–99), pp. 207–29.

16. Analyses of the alternance are found in Hacène Belmessous, "Sénégal: L'Inévitable Alternance," *Politique Internationale*, no. 87 (Spring 2000), pp. 131–44; Richard Vengroff and Michael Magdala, "Democratic Reform, Transformation and Consolidation: Evidence from Senegal 2000 Presidential Elections," *Journal of Modern African Studies*, vol. 39, no. 1 (March 2001), pp. 129–62; and Momar Coumba Diop, Mamadou Diouf, and Aminata Diaw, "Le Baobab a été Déraciné: L'alternance au Sénégal," *Politique Africaine*, no. 78 (June 2000), pp. 157–79.

17. Personal communications with Senegalese officials, Dakar, May 2001.

18. There is a similarity between Wade's idea of democracy and the concept of delegative democracy discussed by Guillermo O'Donnell. See "Delegative Democracy," *Journal of Democracy*, vol. 5, no. 1 (January 1994), pp. 53–69.

19. The two institutes are CODESRIA (Council for the Development of Social Science Research in Africa) and the Gorée Institute. They are among the most im-

portant research institutions dealing with political issues in Africa, but they do not focus on Senegal and are certainly not a force, or even players, in Senegalese politics.

Notes to Chapter Five

1. Report on the April and May 1990 Elections in the Yugoslav Republics of Slovenia and Croatia, Commission on Security and Cooperation in Europe, May 31, 1990, p. 45.
2. Marcus Tanner, *Croatia: A Nation Forged in War* (New Haven, Conn.: Yale University Press, 1997), p. 278.
3. On the HDZ, see Vesna Pusić, "Croatia at the Crossroads," *Journal of Democracy*, vol. 9, no. 1 (January 1998), p. 113; Ian Kearns, "Croatian Politics: The New Authoritarianism," *Political Quarterly*, vol. 67, no. 1 (January–March 1996), p. 29; and Christopher Cviic, "Croatia's Violent Birth," *Current History*, vol. 92, no. 577 (November 1993), p. 374.
4. On election manipulation, see *The April 1997 Parliamentary, County and Municipal Elections in Croatia*, April 13, 1997, Commission on Security and Cooperation in Europe, June 1997, available at <http://www.house.gov/csce/croat.htm>; Parliamentary Elections in Croatia—1995, Commission on Security and Cooperation in Europe, February 1996, available at <http://www.house.gov/csce/croatia 95.htm>; Mirjana Kasapović, "1995 Parliamentary Elections in Croatia," *Electoral Studies*, vol. 15, no. 2 (1996), p. 269; Nenad Zakosek, "The Croatian Parliament during the Period of Democratic Transition: Constitutional and Policy Aspects," in Attila Ágh, ed., *The Emergence of East Central European Parliaments: The First Steps* (Budapest: Hungarian Centre of Democracy Studies, 1994), p. 89; and Human Rights Watch, *Croatia's Democracy Deficit: A Pre-Electoral Assessment* (December 1999), available at <http://www.hrw.org/hrw/reports/1999/croatia2/Electweb-03.htm>.
5. Roman Frydman, Kenneth Murphy, and Andrezj Rapaczynski, *Calling Croatia's Bluff*, Project Syndicate, 1996. Available at <http://www.project-syndicate.cz/surveys/calling_croa.php4>.
6. On the judiciary, see Leonard J. Cohen, "Embattled Democracy: Postcommunist Croatia in Transition," in Karen Dawisha and Bruce Parrott, eds., *Politics, Power, and the Struggle for Democracy* (Cambridge, England: Cambridge University Press, 1997), pp. 87, 88, 112; and Dijana Pleština, "Democracy and Nationalism in Croatia: The First Three Years," in Sabrina Petra Ramet and Ljubiša S. Adamovich, eds., *Beyond Yugoslavia: Politics, Economics, and Culture in a Shattered Community* (Boulder, Colo.: Westview Press, 1995), p. 149.
7. Human Rights Watch, *Croatia's Democracy Deficit*.
8. For more on the military, see Ozren Zunec, "Democracy in the 'Fog of War': Civil-Military Relations in Croatia," in Constantine P. Danopoulos and Daniel Zirker, eds., *Civil-Military Relations in the Soviet and Yugoslav Successor States* (Boulder, Colo.: Westview Press, 1996), pp. 213–30.
9. Drago Hedl, "Living in the Past: Franjo Tudjman's Croatia," *Current History*, vol.

99, no. 635 (March 2000), p. 108. On the privatization, see Vojmir Franičević, "Privatization in Croatia: Legacies and Context," *Eastern European Economics*, vol. 37, no. 2 (March–April 1999), pp. 5–54; Frydman et al., *Calling Croatia's Bluff*; Janez Prasnikar and Jan Svejnar, "Workers' Participation in Management vs. Social Ownership and Government Policies: Yugoslav Lessons for Transforming Socialist Economies," *Comparative Economic Studies*, vol. 33, no. 4 (Winter 1991), p. 31; Cohen, "Embattled Democracy," p. 90; Kearns, "Croatian Politics," p. 3; and *Current Situation in Croatia*, Commission on Security and Cooperation in Europe, March 21, 1997, available at <http://www.house.gov/csce/0321.htm>.

10. On the news media, see Kearns, "Croatian Politics," p. 31; Cohen, "Embattled Democracy," p. 90; *Current Situation in Croatia* (downloaded from <http://www. house.gov/csce/0321.htm>) and *Report on the Media in Croatia*, Organization for Security and Cooperation in Europe, 1999; Human Rights Watch, *Croatia's Democracy Deficit*; Vesna Alaburic, "Legislation and Practice," *Current Situation in Croatia*, Commission on Security and Cooperation in Europe, March 21, 1997, p. 43, available at <http://www.house.gov/csce/0321.htm>; and Stephen C. Markovich, "Democracy in Croatia: Views from the Opposition," *East European Quarterly*, vol. 32, no. 1 (March 1998), p. 89.

11. Ivan Grdešić, "The Politics of Privatization in Croatia: Transition in Times of War," in Mihály Simai, ed., *The Democratic Process and the Market: Challenges of the Transition* (Tokyo: United Nations University Press, 1997), p. 121; Ian Kearns, "Croatia: The Politics behind the War," *World Today*, vol. 49, no. 4 (April 1993), p. 62; Cohen, "Embattled Democracy," p. 110; and Gordana Uzelak, "Franjo Tudjman's Nationalist Ideology," *East European Quarterly*, vol. 31, no. 4 (January 1998), p. 461.

12. Additionally, 1 percent were in favor of army rule, 6 percent were in favor of a return to communism, and 88 percent rejected all three of the nondemocratic alternatives offered in the poll—military, Communist, or strongman rule. Richard Rose and Christian Haerpfer, "Croatia," in *New Democracies Barometer IV: A Ten-Nation Survey* (Glasgow: Centre for the Study of Public Policy, University of Strathclyde, 1996), p. 48.

13. Vesna Pusić, "Dictatorships with Democratic Legitimacy: Democracy versus Nation," *East European Politics and Societies*, vol. 8, no. 3 (Fall 1994), p. 390. See also Cohen, "Embattled Democracy"; Ines Sabalić, "Authoritarianism in Croatia and Prospects for Change," *New Politics*, vol. 5, no. 1 (Summer 1994); Janusz Bugajski, *Ethnic Politics in Eastern Europe: A Guide to Nationality Policies, Organizations, and Politics* (Armonk, N.Y.: M. E. Sharpe, 1994), p. 59; and Kasapović, "1995 Parliamentary Elections," pp. 269–74.

14. Misha Glenny, *The Fall of Yugoslavia* (New York: Penguin, 1996), pp. 12–14, 77; Kasapović, "1995 Parliamentary Elections," p. 270; Human Rights Watch, *Croatia's Democracy Deficit*.

14. Human Rights Watch, *Croatia's Democracy Deficit*.

15. The coalition of the two major parties—the Social Democratic Party (SDP) and the Croatian Social-Liberal Party (HSLS)—won seventy-one seats; the coalition of four minor parties—the Croatian Peasant Party (Hrvatska Seljačka Stranka, HSS), the Croatian People's Party (Hrvatska Narodna Stranka, HNS), the Liberal Party (Liberalna Stranka, LS), and the Istrian Democratic Assembly (Istarski

Demokratski Sabor/Dieta Democratica Istriana, IDS)—won twenty-four seats.

16. Pusić, "Croatia at the Crossroads," p. 116.

17. See *Economic Vulnerability and Welfare Study*, June 2000, and *Croatia: A Policy Agenda for Reform and Growth*, vol. 1, February 2000 (Washington, D.C.: World Bank); "Croatia," *CIA World Factbook*, available at <http://www.odci.gov/cia/publications/factbook/>; and Bronimit Kristofic, "Who Is Running Croatian Enterprises?" *Post-Communist Economies*, vol. 11, no. 4 (December 1999), pp. 503–17.

18. Grdešić, "The Politics of Privatization," p. 121; "Croatia: Political Scene," in *Economic Intelligence Report 2000* prepared by Economist Intelligence Unit (February 15, 2000); *Croatia's Parliamentary Elections*, Commission on Security and Cooperation in Europe, January 3, 2000, p. 4, available from http://www.house.gov/csce.

19. *Republic of Croatia: Parliamentary Elections (House of Representatives) 2–3 January 2000—Final Report*, Organization for Security and Cooperation in Europe, April 25, 2000, downloaded from <http://www.osce.org/odihr/documents/reports/election_reports/hr/cr000-1-final.pdf>.

20. *Parliamentary Elections in Croatia—1995*. Commission on Security and Cooperation in Europe (Washington, D.C.: February 1996). Downloaded from <http://www.house.gov/csce/croatia95.htm>.

21. Personal communication with Glas members, Zagreb, October 3, 2000.

22. David Rieff, "Go West, Young Country," *New Republic*, vol. 222, no. 3 (January 17, 2000), pp. 15–17; Hedl, "Living in the Past," p. 104; Commission on Security and Cooperation in Europe, *Croatia's Parliamentary Elections*.

23. "The Sixty Most Powerful People in Croatia," *Nacional*, February 22, 2001.

24. World Bank, *Croatia: A Policy Agenda for Reform and Growth*, p. 6.

25. All figures based on conversations with Croatian and foreign analysts, Zagreb, October 2–10, 2000.

Note to Introduction to Part II

1. President Robert Mugabe in Zimbabwe offered a textbook example of this resistance in the 2002 elections there.

Notes to Chapter Six

1. Joseph Schumpeter, *Capitalism, Socialism and Democracy* (New York: Harper and Row, 1942).

2. On the techniques of electoral manipulation, see Andreas Schedler, "The Nested Game of Democratization by Elections," *International Political Science Review*, vol. 23, no. 1 (January 2002), pp. 103–22.

3. This conclusion is based on a perusal of many observers' reports from organizations such as the National Democratic Institute for International Affairs and the

Organization for Security and Cooperation in Europe, as well as numerous personal communications with experienced observers.

4. On domestic monitoring, see National Democratic Institute for International Affairs, *How Domestic Organizations Monitor Elections: An A to Z Guide* (Washington, D.C.: National Democratic Institute, 1995).

5. See, for example, pp. 21–22 in Enrique A. Baloyra, "El Salvador: From Despotism to Partidocracia," in Krishna Kumar, ed., *Post-Conflict Elections, Democratization and International Assistance* (Boulder, Colo.: Lynne Rienner, 1998), pp. 15–38.

6. After the 2002 elections in Zimbabwe, the government periodically withheld the sale of a staple food product, corn meal, to areas where the opposition had gained many votes. It even targeted feeding programs for children run by domestic and international humanitarian relief organizations accused of siding with the opposition. The government also accused the opposition of deliberately creating food shortages to embarrass it. See, for example, "Zimbabwe: War Vets Force Feeding Centre Closed" *IRINNEWS*, June 12, 2002; and "Zimbabwe: Opposition Accused of Creating Food Crisis," *IRINNEWS*, July 5, 2002, both published by *IRINNEWS*, a service of the Integrated Regional Information Network, which is part of the United Nations Office for Coordination of Humanitarian Affairs. Its reports are posted at www.irinnews.org.

7. Nevertheless, even authoritarian and totalitarian regimes have been shown to engage in efforts to win support and above all to establish and maintain their legitimacy. See, for example, Juan Linz, "Totalitarian and Authoritarian Regimes," in Nelson W. Polsby and Fred I. Greenstein, eds., *Macropolitical Theory* (Reading, Mass.: Addison-Wesley, 1975), pp. 175–410.

8. For a recent discussion of the relation between charismatic appeal and democracy, see Michael Bernhard, "Charismatic Leadership and Democratizations: A Weberian Perspective," CIAO (Columbia International Affairs Online) working paper (Minda de Gunzburg Center for European Studies at Harvard University), January 1998.

9. J. Michael Turner, Sue Nelson, and Kimberly Mahling-Clark, "Mozambique's Vote for Democratic Governance," in Krishna Kumar, ed., *Post-Conflict Elections, Democratization and International Assistance* (Boulder, Colo.: Lynne Rienner, 1998), pp. 133–52.

10. See Thomas Carothers, "Ousting Foreign Strongmen: Lessons from Serbia," policy brief no. 5 (Washington, D.C.: Carnegie Endowment for International Peace), May 2001.

11. On problems related to the outside funding of political parties, see Peter Burnell and Alan Ware, eds., *Funding Democratization* (Manchester, England: Manchester University Press, 1998); and USAID Center for Democracy and Governance, *USAID Political Party Development Assistance* (Washington, D.C.: USAID, 1999).

12. A similar situation developed in Côte d'Ivoire, where Alassane Ouattara, an International Monetary Fund economist who had served as prime minister from 1990 to 1993, was prevented from becoming a presidential candidate in both 1995 and 2000 as the result of manipulation of the citizenship law.

Notes to Chapter Seven

1. See, for example, Samuel Huntington, *The Third Wave: Democratization in the Late Twentieth Century* (Norman, Okla.: University of Oklahoma Press, 1991), especially pp. 59–72.
2. Adam Przeworski et al., "What Makes Democracies Endure?" *Journal of Democracy*, vol. 7, no. 1 (January 1996), pp. 39–55; see also Guillermo O'Donnell, "Illusions about Consolidation," *Journal of Democracy*, vol. 7, no. 2 (April 1996), pp. 34–51.
3. Seymour Martin Lipset, "The Social Requisites of Democracy: Economic Development and Political Legitimacy," *American Political Science Review*, vol. 53, no. 1 (1959), pp. 69–105; see also Huntington, The Third Wave, and Przeworski et al., "What Makes Democracies Endure?"
4. On first-wave countries, see Huntington, *The Third Wave*, pp. 16–18.
5. Foremost in this category of studies are Barrington Moore Jr., *The Social Origins of Dictatorship and Democracy* (Boston: Beacon Press, 1966), and Dietrich Rueschemeyer, Evelyne Huber Stephens, and John D. Stephens, *Capitalist Development and Democracy* (Chicago: University of Chicago Press, 1992).
6. These figures are from United Nations Development Program, *Human Development Report, 2001* (New York: United Nations, 2001).
7. A notable exception is found in Juan J. Linz and Alfred Stepan, *Problems of Democratic Transition and Consolidation* (Baltimore and London: Johns Hopkins University Press, 1996), pp. 16–37.
8. Charles Tilly, "War-Making and State-Making as Organized Crime," in Peter Evans, Dietrich Rueschemeyer, and Theda Skocpol, *Bringing the State Back In* (Cambridge, England: Cambridge University Press, 1985), pp. 169–91. See also Charles Tilly, ed., *The Formation of National States in Western Europe* (Princeton, N.J.: Princeton University Press, 1975).
9. See Benedict Anderson, *Imagined Communities* (London: Verso, 1985); Eric Hobsbawm and Terence Ranger, eds., *The Invention of Tradition* (Cambridge, England: Cambridge University Press, 1983); and Ernest Gellner, *Nations and Nationalism* (Ithaca, N.Y.: Cornell University Press, 1983).
10. See Terrence Lyons, "Peace and Elections in Liberia," in Krishna Kumar, ed., *Post-Conflict Elections, Democratization and International Assistance* (Boulder, Colo.: Lynne Rienner, 1998), pp. 177–94.
11. On the dangers of a strong popular upsurge, see Guillermo O'Donnell and Philippe Schmitter, *Transitions from Authoritarian Rule: Tentative Conclusions about Uncertain Democracies* (Baltimore: Johns Hopkins University Press, 1986) especially, pp. 33–36.
12. Ivan Doherty, "Democracy Out of Balance: Civil Society Cannot Replace Political Parties," *Policy Review*, vol. 106 (April–May 2001), pp. 25–35; and Ronald Shaiko, "Political Party Development Assistance," *Democracy Dialogue*, Technical Notes from USAID's Center for Democracy and Government (December 1999).
13. This is the same problem Samuel Huntington discusses in relation to revolutions in which the old regime collapses before the new leadership has time to organize. See Samuel Huntington, *Political Order in Changing Societies* (New

Haven, Conn.: Yale University Press, 1968), particularly his discussion of "Eastern" and "Western" patterns, pp. 266–68.

14. See Peter Evans, *Embedded Autonomy: States and Industrial Transformation* (Princeton, N.J.: Princeton University Press, 1995).

15. Other studies are beginning to single out this problem in other countries. See, for example, Laurence Whitehead, "Bolivia and the Viability of Democracy," *Journal of Democracy*, vol. 12, no. 2 (April 2001), pp. 6–16. The author discusses the isolation of the political class from the rest of society as a problem Bolivia shares with other countries in the Andean region.

16. For a discussion of most of these issues as seen from the perspective of recipients of democracy promotion assistance in Eastern Europe, see Ivan Krastev, "The Balkans: Democracy without Choices," *Journal of Democracy*, vol. 13, no. 3 (July 2002), pp. 39–53.

17. On the issue of conditionalities and political participation related to antipoverty programs, see ActionAid, "Inclusive Circles Lost in Exclusive Cycles," January 25, 2002. The report by this transnational NGO is based on experiences in Haiti, Kenya, Malawi, Nepal, Rwanda, Uganda, and Vietnam. The paper emphasizes in particular the tendency among donors to interpret participation as consultation with NGOs, rather than with elected institutions.

Notes to Chapter Eight

1. Agency for International Development, "USAID/Cambodia: Results Review and Resource Request," February 1, 1998, p. 1.

2. Christopher Marquis, "U.S. Bankrolling Is under Scrutiny for Ties to Chávez Ouster," *New York Times*, April 25, 2002, p. A6, col. 1.

3. See, for example, the debate on proportional representation in the *Journal of Democracy*, vol. 6, no. 4 (October 1995): Joel Barkan, "Elections in Agrarian Societies," pp. 106–16, and Andrew Reynolds, "The Case for Proportionality," pp. 117–24.

4. See Donald Horowitz, *Ethnic Groups in Conflict?* (Berkeley, Calif.: University of California Press, 1985); Donald Horowitz, *A Democratic South Africa? Constitutional Engineering in a Divided Society* (Berkeley, Calif.: University of California Press, 1991); Ben Reilly and Andrew Reynolds, *Electoral Systems and Conflict in Divided Societies* (Washington, D.C.: National Academy Press, 1999); and Benjamin Reilly, *Democracy in Divided Societies: Electoral Engineering for Conflict Management* (Cambridge, England, and New York: Cambridge University Press, 1999).

5. On consociational democracy, see the work of Arend Lijphart, especially *Democracy in Plural Societies: A Comparative Exploration* (New Haven, Conn.: Yale University Press, 1977) and *Power-Sharing in South Africa* (Berkeley, Calif.: University of California Press, 1985).

6. See Marina Ottaway, "Rebuilding State Institutions in Collapsed States," *Development and Change*, forthcoming November 2002.

7. J. Michael Turner, Sue Nelson, and Kimberley Mahling-Clark, "Mozambique's Vote for Democratic Governance," in Krishna Kumar, ed., *Post-Conflict Elec-*

tions, *Democratization and International Assistance* (Boulder, Colo.: Lynne Rienner, 1998), pp. 153–76.

8. See Thomas Carothers, "Ousting Foreign Strongmen: Lessons from Serbia," policy brief no. 5 (Washington, D.C.: Carnegie Endowment for International Peace), May 2001.

9. See, for example, U.S. Agency for International Development, Center for Development Information and Evaluation, "Constituencies for Reform. Strategic Approaches for Donor-Supported Civic Advocacy Programs," USAID Program and Operations Assessment Report no. 12 (Washington, D.C.: U.S. Agency for International Development), February 1996.

10. See O'Donnell and Schmitter, *Transitions from Authoritarian Rule: Tentative Conclusions about Uncertain Democracies* (Baltimore: Johns Hopkins University Press, 1986). The idea was picked up by scholars in other countries and applied to their particular situations. The necessity for a pacted transition was a recurring theme in works by South African scholars in the early 1990s, for instance; see Marina Ottaway, *South Africa: The Struggle for a New Order* (Washington, D.C.: Brookings Institution, 1993).

11. A USAID view of the impact of civic education is found in "Approaches to Civic Education: Lessons Learned" (Washington, D.C.: USAID, Bureau for Democracy, Conflict and Humanitarian Assistance, Office of Democracy and Governance), June 2002. For other views, see Steve Finkel, Christopher A. Sabatini, and Gwendolyn G. Bevis, "Civic Education, Civil Society, and Political Mistrust in a Developing Democracy: The Case of the Dominican Republic," *World Development*, vol. 28, no. 11 (November 2000), pp. 1851–75; Philip Aiderfer, Georgia Bowser, Michael Bratton, and Joseph Temba, "The Effects of Civic Education on Political Culture: Evidence from Zambia," *World Development*, vol. 27, no. 5 (1999), pp. 807–25.

Note to Chapter Nine

1. The World Bank's internal discussions and documents at the time of this writing reflected growing concern among officials about the need to broaden the process of consultation, particularly with respect to the preparation of the Poverty Reduction Strategy Paper. Consultations with members of parliament was one of the options discussed. To my knowledge, both on the basis of the reading of documents and personal communications, consultation with members of parliament did not mean submitting any agreement to the parliament for approval.

Bibliography

The "Gray Zone"

Brown, Archie. "From Democratization to 'Guided Democracy,'" *Journal of Democracy*, vol. 12, no. 4 (October 2001): 35–41.

Buxton, Julia. "Venezuela: Degenerative Democracy," *Democratization*, vol. 6, no. 1 (Spring 1999): 246–70.

———. "Venezuela: Degenerative Democracy," in *The Resilience of Democracy: Persistent Practice, Durable Idea*, ed. Peter Burnell and Peter Calvert. London and Portland, Ore.: Frank Cass, 1999: 246–70.

Carothers, Thomas. "Democracy without Illusions," *Foreign Affairs*, vol. 76, no. 1 (Jan.–Feb. 1997): 85–89.

———. "The End of the Transition Paradigm," *Journal of Democracy*, vol. 13, no. 1 (January 2002): 5–21.

Case, William. "Malaysia's Resilient Pseudodemocracy," *Journal of Democracy*, vol. 12, no. 1 (January 2001): 43–57.

Casper, Gretchen. *Fragile Democracies: The Legacies of Authoritarian Rule*. Pittsburgh, Pa.: University of Pittsburgh Press, 1995.

Collier, David, and Steven Levitsky. "Democracy with Adjectives: Conceptual Innovation in Comparative Research," *World Politics*, vol. 49, no. 3 (April 1997): 430–51.

Dawisha, Karen. "Electocracies and the Hobbesian Fishbowl of Postcommunist Politics," *East European Politics and Society*, vol. 13, no. 2 (Spring 1999): 256–70.

Diamond, Larry. "Thinking about Hybrid Regimes," *Journal of Democracy*, vol. 13, no. 2 (April 2002): 21–35.

Enkelbrekt, Kjell. "Unfinished Democracy: Political Transformation in Post-Communist Southeastern Europe," *Problems of Post-Communism*, vol. 44, no. 6 (November/December 1997): 3–12.

Fukuyama, Francis. "Asia's Soft-Authoritarian Alternative," *New Perspectives Quarterly*, vol. 9, no. 2 (Spring 1992): 60–61.

Good, Kenneth. "Enduring Elite Democracy in Botswana," in *The Resilience of Democracy: Persistent Practice, Durable Idea*, ed. Peter Burnell and Peter Calvert. London and Portland, Ore.: Frank Cass, 1999: 50–66.

Heder, Steve. "Cambodia's Democratic Transition to Neoauthoritarianism," *Current History*, vol. 94, no. 596 (December 1995): 425–29.

———. "The Menu of Manipulation," *Journal of Democracy*, vol. 13, no. 2 (April 2002): 36–50.

Tamás, G. M. "Victory Defeated," *Journal of Democracy*, vol. 10, no. 1 (January 1999): 63–68.

Walle, Nicholas van de. "Africa's Range of Regimes," *Journal of Democracy*, vol. 13, no. 2 (April 2002): 66–80.

Young, Crawford. "The Third Wave of Democratization in Africa: Ambiguities and Contradictions," in *State Conflict and Democracy in Africa*, ed. Richard A. Joseph. Boulder, Colo.: Lynne Rienner, 1999.

Zakaria, Fareed. "The Rise of Illiberal Democracy," *Foreign Affairs*, vol. 76, no. 6 (November–December 1997): 22–43.

Uncertain Transitions

Ágh, Attila. *Emerging Democracies in East Central Europe and the Balkans*. Northampton, Mass.: Edward Elgar, 1998.

Antoni, Sorin, and Vladimir Tismaneanu, ed. *Between Past and Future: The Revolutions of 1989 and Their Aftermath*. Budapest and New York: Central European University Press, 2000.

Barkan, Joel D. "Protracted Transitions among Africa's New Democracies," *Democratization*, vol. 7, no. 3 (Autumn 2000): 227–43.

Bratton, Michael, and Nicholas van de Walle. *Democratic Experiments in Africa: Regime Transitions in Comparative Perspective*. New York: Cambridge University Press, 1997.

Casper, Gretchen. "The Benefits of Difficult Transitions," *Democratization*, vol. 7, no. 3 (Autumn 2000): 46–64.

———, and Michelle M. Taylor. *Negotiating Democratic Transitions from Authoritarian Rule*. Pittsburgh, Penn.: University of Pittsburgh Press, 1996.

Dawisha, Karen, and Bruce Parrott, ed. *The Consolidation of Democracy in East-Central Europe, vol 1*. Cambridge, England: Cambridge University Press, 1997.

———. *Politics, Power and the Struggle for Democracy in South-East Europe, vol 2*. Cambridge, England: Cambridge University Press, 1997.

Diamond, Larry. "Is the Third Wave Over?" *Journal of Democracy*, vol. 7, no. 3 (July 1996): 20–37.

———. *Developing Democracy: Toward Consolidation*. Baltimore: Johns Hopkins University Press, 1999.

———. "Is Pakistan the (Reverse) Wave of the Future?" *Journal of Democracy*, vol. 11, no. 3 (July 2000): 91–106.

———, Yun-Han Chu, and Hung-Mao Tien, ed. *Consolidating the Third Wave Democracies*. Baltimore and London: Johns Hopkins University Press, 1997.

———, and Marc F. Plattner, ed. *Democratization in Africa*. Baltimore: Johns Hopkins University Press, 1999.

Di Palma, Giuseppe. *To Craft Democracies: An Essay on Democratic Transitions*. Berkeley, Calif.: University of California Press, 1990.

Domínguez, Jorge I. *Democratic Politics in Latin America and the Caribbean*. Baltimore: Johns Hopkins University Press, 1998.

———, and Abraham F. Lowenthal. *Constructing Democratic Governance*. Baltimore: Johns Hopkins University Press, 1996.

Eisenstadt, Todd. "Eddies in the Third Wave: Protracted Transitions and Theories of Democratization," *Democratization*, vol. 7, no. 3 (Autumn 2000): 3–24.

Elkilt, Jørgen. "Electoral Institutional Change and Democratization: You Can Lead a Horse to Water, But You Can't Make It Drink," *Democratization*, vol. 6, no. 4 (Winter 1999): 28–51.

Fairbanks, Charles H. Jr. "Disillusionment in the Caucasus and Central Asia," *Journal of Democracy*, vol. 12, no. 4 (October 2001): 49–56.

Gill, Graeme. *The Dynamics of Democratization: Elites, Civil Society, and the Transition Process*. Basingstoke, England: Palgrave, 2000.

Gros, Jean-German, ed. *Democratization in Late Twentieth-Century Africa: Coping With Uncertainty*. Westport, Conn.: Greenwood Press, 1998.

Kaldor, Mary, and Ivan Vejvoda. "Democratization in Central and East European Countries," *International Affairs*, vol. 73, no. 1 (January 1997): 59–82.

Karl, Terry Lynn. "Dilemmas of Democratization in Latin America," *Comparative Politics*, vol. 23, no. 1 (1990): 1–22.

Lewis, Paul G., ed. *Party Development and Democratic Change in Post-Communist Europe: The First Decade*. London and Portland, Ore: Frank Cass, 2001.

Linz, Juan J., and Alfred Stepan. *Problems of Democratic Transition and Consolidation: Southern Europe, South America, and Post-Communist Europe*. Baltimore: Johns Hopkins University Press, 1996.

———. "Toward Consolidated Democracies," *Journal of Democracy*, vol. 7, no. 2 (April 1996): 14–33.

Mainwaring, Scott, Guillermo O'Donnell, and J. Samuel Valenzuela, ed. *Issues in Democratic Consolidation: The New South American Democracies in Comparative Perspective*. Notre Dame, Ind.: University of Notre Dame Press, 1992.

Matveeva, Anna. "Democratization, Legitimacy and Political Change in Central Asia," *International Affairs*, vol. 75, no. 1 (January 1999): 23–44.

Munck, Gerardo L. "The Regime Question: Theory Building in Democracy Studies," *World Politics*, vol. 54, no. 1 (October 2001): 119–44.

Nodia, Ghia. "How Different Are Postcommunist Transitions?" *Journal of Democracy*, vol. 7, no. 4 (October 1996): 15–29.

O'Donnell, Guillermo. "Illusions about Consolidation," *Journal of Democracy*, vol. 7, no. 2 (April 1996): 34–51.

———, and Philippe C. Schmitter. *Transitions from Authoritarian Rule: Tentative Conclusions about Uncertain Democracies*. Baltimore: Johns Hopkins University Press, 1986.

Rose, Richard, William Mishler, and Christian Haerpfer. *Democracy and Its Alternatives: Understanding Post-Communist Societies*. Baltimore: Johns Hopkins University Press, 1999.

Smith, Julie, and Elizabeth Teague, ed. *Democracy in the New Europe: The Politics of Post-Communism*. London: Greycoat Press, 1999.

Tulchin, Joseph S., and Bernice Romero, ed. *The Consolidation of Democracy in Latin America*. Boulder, Colo.: Lynne Rienner for the Woodrow Wilson Center, 1995.

Wiseman, John A. *The Struggle for Democracy in Africa*. Aldershot, England: Avebury, 1996.

Hermet, Guy, Alain Rouquié, and Juan J. Linz. *Elections without Choice*. New York: John Wiley, 1978.

Hewison, Kevin. "Political Space in Southeast Asia: 'Asian-Style' and Other Democracies," in *The Resilience of Democracy: Persistent Practice, Durable Idea*, ed. Peter Burnell and Peter Calvert. London and Portland, Ore.: Frank Cass, 1999: 224–45.

Joseph, Richard A. "Africa, 1990–1997: From *Abertura* to Closure," *Journal of Democracy*, vol. 9, no. 2 (April 1998): 3–17.

——. "The Reconfiguration of Power in Late Twentieth-Century Africa," in *State, Conflict, and Democracy in Africa*, ed. Richard A. Joseph. Boulder, Colo., and London: Lynne Rienner, 1999: 57–80.

Kangas, Roger D. "Uzbekistan: Evolving Authoritarianism," *Current History*, vol. 93, no. 582 (April 1994): 178–82.

Kubicek, Paul. "Delegative Democracy in Russia and Ukraine," *Communist and Post-Communist Studies*, vol. 27, no. 4 (1994): 443–61.

——. "The Limits of Electoral Democracy in Ukraine," *Democratization*, vol. 8, no. 2 (Summer 2000): 117–39.

Karl, Terry Lynn. "The Hybrid Regimes of Central America," *Journal of Democracy*, vol. 6, no. 3 (July 1995): 72–87.

Levitsky, Steven, and Lucan A. Way. "The Rise of Competitive Authoritarianism," *Journal of Democracy*, vol. 13, no. 2 (April 2002): 51–65.

Linz, Juan J., and Arturo Valenzuela, ed. *The Failure of Presidential Democracy*. Baltimore: Johns Hopkins University Press, 1994.

Lloyd, Robert. "Zimbabwe: The Making of an Autocratic Democracy," *Current History*, vol. 101, no. 655 (May 2002): 219–24.

Means, Gordon P. "Soft Authoritarianism in Malaysia and Singapore," *Journal of Democracy*, vol. 7, no. 4 (October 1996): 103–17.

Melvin, Neil J. *Uzbekistan: Transition to Authoritarianism on the Silk Road*. Amsterdam: Harwood Academic Publishers, 2000.

Mkandawire, Thandika. "Crisis Management and the Making of 'Choiceless Democracies,'" in *State, Conflict, and Democracy in Africa*, ed. Richard A. Joseph. Boulder, Colo., and London: Lynne Rienner, 1999: 119–36.

Monga, Célestin. "Eight Problems with African Politics," *Journal of Democracy*, vol. 8, no. 3 (July 1997): 156–70.

O'Donnell, Guillermo. "Delegative Democracy," *Journal of Democracy*, vol. 5, no. 1 (January 1994): 55–69.

Ottaway, Marina. *Africa's New Leaders: Democracy or State Reconstruction?* Washington, D.C.: Carnegie Endowment for International Peace, 1999.

Pridham, Geoffrey, and Tom Gallagher, ed. *Experimenting with Democracy: Regime Change in the Balkans*. London and New York: Routledge, 2000.

Putzel, James. "Survival of an Imperfect Democracy in the Philippines," in *The Resilience of Democracy: Persistent Practice, Durable Idea*, ed. Peter Burnell and Peter Calvert. London and Portland, Ore.: Frank Cass, 1999: 198–223.

Roy, Dennis. "Singapore, China, and the 'Soft Authoritarian' Challenge," *Asian Survey*, vol. 34, no. 3 (March 1994): 231–42.

Sandbrook, Richard. "Transitions without Consolidation: Democratization in Six African Cases," *Third World Quarterly*, vol. 17, no. 1 (1996): 69–87.

Schedler, Andreas. "The Nested Game of Democratization by Elections," *International Political Science Review*, vol. 23, no. 1 (January 2002), pp. 103–22.

Index

About the Author

MARINA OTTAWAY, a specialist in democracy and global policy issues, is a senior associate in the Carnegie Endowment's Democracy and Rule of Law Project, a research endeavor that analyzes the state of democracy around the world and the efforts by the United States and other countries to promote democracy. She is also a lecturer in African Studies at the Nitze School for Advanced International Studies at Johns Hopkins University.

Ms. Ottaway previously carried out research in Africa and in the Middle East and has taught at the University of Addis Ababa, the University of Zambia, the American University in Cairo, and the University of the Witwatersrand in South Africa.

She is the author of numerous books, including *Africa's New Leaders: Democracy or State Reconstruction?* (Carnegie Endowment, 1999) and *Funding Virtue: Civil Society Aid and Democracy Promotion*, edited with Thomas Carothers (Carnegie Endowment, 2000). Ms. Ottaway holds a Ph.D. from Columbia University.

Carnegie Endowment for International Peace

THE CARNEGIE ENDOWMENT is a private, nonprofit organization dedicated to advancing cooperation between nations and promoting active international engagement by the United States. Founded in 1910, its work is nonpartisan and dedicated to achieving practical results.

Through research, publishing, convening, and, on occasion, creating new institutions and international networks, Endowment associates shape fresh policy approaches. Their interests span geographic regions and the relations between governments, business, international organizations, and civil society, focusing on the economic, political, and technological forces driving global change. Through its Carnegie Moscow Center, the Endowment helps to develop a tradition of public policy analysis in the states of the former Soviet Union and to improve relations between Russia and the United States. The Endowment publishes *Foreign Policy*, one of the world's leading magazines of international politics and economics, which reaches readers in more than 120 countries and in several languages.